UNDERSTANDING
HUNTER S. THOMPSON

UNDERSTANDING CONTEMPORARY AMERICAN LITERATURE
Matthew J. Bruccoli, Founding Editor
Linda Wagner-Martin, Series Editor

Also of Interest

Understanding Barbara Kingsolver, Ian Tan
Understanding David Foster Wallace, Marshall Boswell
Understanding James Baldwin, Marc Dudley
Understanding John Edgar Wideman, D. Quentin Miller
Understanding John Rechy, María DeGuzmán
Understanding John Updike, Frederic Svoboda
Understanding Philip Roth, Matthew A. Shipe
Understanding Susan Sontag, Carl Rollyson
Understanding Truman Capote, Thomas Fahy
Understanding William S. Burroughs, Gerald Alva Miller, Jr.

UNDERSTANDING
HUNTER S. THOMPSON

Kevin J. Hayes

© 2025 University of South Carolina

Published by the University of South Carolina Press
Columbia, South Carolina 29208

uscpress.com

Printed in the United States of America

Library of Congress Cataloging-in-Publication Data
can be found at https://lccn.loc.gov/2024054573

ISBN: 978-1-64336-538-1 (hardcover)
ISBN: 978-1-64336-570-1 (paperback)
ISBN: 978-1-64336-571-8 (ebook)

To Neal and Rita Carter

CONTENTS

Series Editor's Preface   ix

Chapter 1
An Introduction to Hunter S. Thompson   1

Chapter 2
Foreign Correspondent   15

Chapter 3
Literary Critic   29

Chapter 4
New Journalist   42

Chapter 5
Gonzo Journalist   57

Chapter 6
Campaign Trailblazer   74

Chapter 7
Anthologist   88

Chapter 8
Letter Writer   101

Chapter 9
Novelist   113

Conclusion   125

Notes   133
Bibliography   151
Index   153

SERIES EDITOR'S PREFACE

The Understanding Contemporary American Literature series was founded by the estimable Matthew J. Bruccoli (1931–2008), who envisioned these volumes as guides or companions for students as well as good nonacademic readers, a legacy that will continue as new volumes are developed to fill in gaps among the nearly one hundred series volumes published to date and to embrace a host of new writers only now making their marks on our literature.

As Professor Bruccoli explained in his preface to the volumes he edited, because much influential contemporary literature makes special demands, "the word *understanding* in the titles was chosen deliberately. Many willing readers lack an adequate understanding of how contemporary literature works; that is, of what the author is attempting to express and the means by which it is conveyed." Aimed at fostering this understanding of good literature and good writers, the criticism and analysis in the series provide instruction in how to read certain contemporary writers—explicating their material, language, structures, themes, and perspectives—and facilitate a more profitable experience of the works under discussion.

In the twenty-first century Professor Bruccoli's prescience gives us an avenue to publish expert critiques of significant contemporary American writing. The series continues to map the literary landscape and to provide both instruction and enjoyment. Future volumes will seek to introduce new voices alongside canonized favorites, to chronicle the changing literature of our times, and to remain, as Professor Bruccoli conceived, contemporary in the best sense of the word.

Linda Wagner-Martin, Series Editor

CHAPTER 1

An Introduction to Hunter S. Thompson

Like bourbon, Hunter S. Thompson was born in Kentucky. The first son of Jack Robert Thompson, an insurance agent, and Virginia Ray Thompson, he was born on July 18, 1937, in Louisville, home of the Kentucky Derby, Muhammad Ali, and Daisy Buchanan. His name connects him to his ancestry. Hunter is Grandma Ray's maiden name, and the initial stands for Stockton, a branch of his mother's family with roots in colonial Virginia. The Thompsons lived in the Cherokee Triangle, a middle-class neighborhood in eastern Louisville, but Virginia impressed upon Hunter and his two younger brothers the traditions of Southern gentility.

By seven Hunter had started to rebel. One day Grandma Ray pulled down Gelett Burgess's *Goops and How to Be Them* to correct his behavior. The Goops were three mischievous creatures with bulbous heads and scrunched-up features. The book's illustrated poems taught children to behave by showing them how not to behave. In one a mother enters a room strewn with scraps and crumbs and half-eaten apples. With a facial expression quite severe, she says, "It looks to me / As if the Goops were here." Shaming him for being a Goop, Grandma Ray gave Hunter a sense of rules.[1]

Having a sense of rules does not necessarily mean obeying them. Hunter, a real-life Dennis the Menace, often violated the rules of conduct to gain attention. Next-door neighbor Joanie Henning remembered him playing with firecrackers in the backyard. One winter she saw smoke billowing from a basement window: Hunter had received a chemistry set for Christmas. He befriended Joanie's father, and they enjoyed long talks on the steps of the Henning home. Hunter's intelligence impressed her father; Joanie could not see the genius behind the mischief.[2]

Hunter had the charisma to coax grade school friends to join his pranks. "He almost had demonic power," one said. Jack Thompson kept him in check with a razor strop to the backside, but he died when Hunter was fourteen. His death stunted Hunter's emotional growth. In terms of his irresponsibility, carelessness with money, lack of impulse control, desire for instant gratification, fondness for practical jokes, and belligerence toward authority, Hunter would forever be a fourteen-year-old boy. To support the family Virginia became a librarian for the Louisville Public Library. The full-time position prevented Virginia from giving her wayward son the attention he craved, and Hunter grew more unruly.[3]

While attending Louisville Male High School, he was inducted into the prestigious Athenaeum Literary Association. His friend Paul Semonin, the scion of a Louisville real estate mogul, recalled its Saturday night suit-and-tie gatherings. In theory a literary club, in practice it was "an initiation into the world of drinking under age." Lacking the family connections of other members, Thompson felt like "the 'black sheep' of the Athenaeum." Another member used an alternate animal for comparison, calling him "a skunk of a different stripe." Regardless, Thompson held his own during their weekly literary discussions.[4]

He excelled his peers in one respect. At fifteen, Achilles's age when the Greeks went to Troy, Hunter realized he could write better than all his friends.[5] Two of Hunter's contributions to *Spectator*, the Athenaeum's annual, treat the theme of middle-class conformity. Both "Security" and "Open Letter to the Youth of Our Nation" challenge young readers to avoid the tedious existence that comes with a steady job, a savings account, a thirty-year mortgage, and a lawnmower. Instead, people should have the gumption to forego safety and security and follow ambition and adventure.

Besides articulating his nascent personal philosophy, these two essays gave Thompson a lesson in literary style. A formal theme written by a restless teenager looking at the future and wondering if he must conform to society's expectations, "Security" is heavy-handed. He wrote "Open Letter to the Youth of Our Nation" using a humorous pen name, John J. Righteous-Hypocrite, which echoes the children's song "John Jacob Jingleheimer Schmidt." The fictional persona let Thompson deliver a facetious message.

Mr. Righteous-Hypocrite tells readers to mend their frivolous ways. Instead of running around all night, he devoted himself to hard work and virtuous behavior to become a paragon of society. Thompson's fictional persona let readers draw their own conclusions. Not until he discovered how to unify the two seemingly contradictory narrative positions—to turn his personal voice into a persona—would Thompson establish his place in American literature.

The month before graduation he and two classmates robbed some couples necking in Cherokee Park. The three were arrested and charged with armed robbery. At sentencing a tearful Virginia Thompson pleaded against jail time for her son; Judge Louis Jull—the antetype of *Caddyshack* villain Judge Elihu Smails—responded with sarcasm: "What do you want me to do, give him a medal?" The other boys received no jail time, but Jull sentenced Thompson, a repeat offender, to sixty days in Jefferson County Jail. When he got out early for good behavior, he feared the slightest transgression would send him back to jail.[6]

To escape Louisville, Thompson joined the US Air Force. After training as a radio engineer, he was posted to Eglin Air Force Base in Florida in July 1956. He befriended Larry Callen, editor of *Command Courier*, and finagled a position as its sports editor. He also moonlighted on the Fort Walton Beach *Playground News*. Sometimes he used the penname "Cuubly Cohn," a pseudonym combining references to Samuel Coleridge's "Kubla Khan" and Robert Cohn, the character from *The Sun Also Rises*. Reinforcing his passion for Coleridge, Thompson discovered an old, abandoned beach house, which he named Xanadu.

The *Command Courier* provided a rare measure of freedom for a military base. In spare moments Thompson taught himself American literary modernism. John Dos Passos gave him a sense of style. H. L. Mencken helped develop his caustic wit. William Faulkner showed him how to create a little world all his own. Ernest Hemingway taught him verbal economy. And F. Scott Fitzgerald demonstrated plot and character development. Thompson would type large chunks of text from Hemingway and Fitzgerald to learn the cadence of their prose as he dreamed of writing a great novel of his own.

Honorably discharged on November 8, 1957, Thompson placed a "Situation Wanted" advertisement in *Editor and Publisher* and received an offer from Robert J. Evans, editor of the *Jersey Shore Herald*. An old railroad town, Jersey Shore, Pennsylvania, was so called because two brothers from New Jersey had established a settlement on the western shore of West Branch Susquehanna River. Thompson read Sherwood Anderson's *Winesburg, Ohio* while living in Jersey Shore: the resemblance was uncanny.[7]

Arriving in late November, he rented a dilapidated apartment above Regan's Taproom and went to work. With wry understatement Evans recalled his reaction: "He didn't seem too impressed with Jersey Shore when he arrived." But Thompson's journalistic passion was apparent. Evans could sense his excitement. Thompson wanted to feature professional football and other national sports news. Evans reminded him their readers cared more about high school football.[8]

The *Herald* staff resembled the staff of any small-town newspaper. Charles L. Farley, a fun-loving employee with a flattop haircut, worked in the composing room. Paul I. Overdorf, a former high school English teacher, wrote feature stories about famous buildings. Topped by a great shock of white hair, Joseph Cox dominated the newsroom. The previous decade Cox had begun "Shore Lines," a column combining local history with current events, which he would continue after the *Herald* merged with the Lock Haven *Express*.[9]

Thompson retells his Jersey Shore experience in *Songs of the Doomed*, but his version of events is largely fictional. Overdorf is the unnamed and hitherto unidentified feature writer who befriends Thompson and introduces him to his daughter Carol, but Thompson invented the rest of the story. Its fictional nature illustrates the danger of accepting Thompson's autobiographical self-mythologizing as biographical fact.

His position as sports editor ended after two weeks, but it was long enough for him to enter local history. When *Hell's Angels*, his first book, appeared in 1967 to great acclaim, Cox noticed it in "Shore Lines": "Only two weeks on a modern West Branch Valley newspaper can start a young writer on his way to success." Cox remembered Thompson from the newsroom, but, eager for more information, he consulted Evans, whose written reply came complete with dialogue.[10]

Thompson's departure concerned editorial differences. After Charley Farley bowled a 300 at the YMCA bowling alley, Evans asked Thompson to run a story about his perfect game, a major feat for Jersey Shore, which did have broader ramifications: similar stories were fueling a nationwide bowling craze. Afterward, Farley had a letterman-style jacket specially embroidered with the number 300 on its back. Unimpressed, Thompson put the story at the end of the sports section. In his absence Evans remade the section, leading with Farley's perfect game. Infuriated, Thompson told Evans to keep his mitts off the sports page.

"I am the sports editor!" Thompson exclaimed.

"Not any more," Evans replied. "You're fired."

Thompson left Jersey Shore for New York, a city he called "an education, an initiation, and a stimulant." He enjoyed reading the latest authors, especially Jack Kerouac. As Thompson told Susan Haselden, a Louisville girlfriend who had discovered Kerouac for herself, he had read *On the Road*, *The Dharma Bums*, and *The Subterraneans*. Thompson denied Kerouac's greatness, however: "The man is an ass, a mystic boob with intellectual myopia." His relationship to Kerouac was more complex than this curt dismissal indicates. Such animosity is symptomatic of the anxiety of influence. Pay no attention to the man behind the curtain, Thompson essentially says, masking the profound impact Kerouac's writings had on him. Even after calling him a shortsighted mystic, Thompson kept reading Kerouac. He soon acquired a copy of *Maggie Cassidy*.[11]

In February 1958 Thompson started working at *Time* magazine as a copyboy. The position makes him sound like Jimmy Olsen from *Superman*, but it was fairly prestigious. Publisher Henry Luce liked copyboys with college degrees, but without literary ambitions. Lacking the first but loaded with the second, Thompson was an odd fit. His situation followed that of another literary model, Stephen Crane, who, Thompson quipped, could not get a job as a copyboy today.[12]

The position at *Time* offered some appealing benefits. Thompson had access to a vast file of clippings, which he used to broaden his knowledge of writers and writing. One day he examined the Kingsley Amis file and found a clipping from the London *Times* in which Somerset Maugham recommends *Lucky Jim* as a book of the year for 1955. Amis's eponymous hero would shape Thompson's literary persona, which often sounds very like Lucky Jim.[13]

The William Faulkner file also caught his attention. Eugene McGarr, a friend and fellow copyboy, said Thompson was enthralled with *The Sound and the Fury*. Reading an interview clipped from the *Richmond Times-Dispatch*, Thompson noticed something that Faulkner told the interviewer: "When a writer passes through the wall of oblivion, he will even then stop long enough to write something on the wall like 'Kilroy was here.'" Faulkner's words show how writers imprint themselves on the world. Thompson reflected, "Just as some people turn to religion to find meaning, the writer turns to his craft and tries to impose meaning, or to sift the meaning out of the chaos and put it in order."[14]

Thompson and McGarr enjoyed another benefit. Henry Luce supplied employees with a Sunday night buffet complete with liquor to help them meet their weekly deadline. Thompson took advantage of the spread to get "blind scowling, blabbering drunk every Sunday night." A dozen years later he wrote McGarr to reminisce: "We have come a long way from those Sunday nights at Time Inc. when everything seemed possible."[15]

McGarr loved reminiscing about their time in New York, a time of art galleries, off-Broadway theater, secondhand bookstores, poetry readings, and jazz quartets. McGarr recalled the night he and Thompson heard Gregory Corso and Frank O'Hara read poetry at the Living Theatre. Having filled their rucksacks with cans of beer, they rolled their empties toward the stage and heckled Corso, who got so upset he stormed offstage. Kerouac, who was in the audience, saved the night, rushing onstage to read from *Doctor Sax*.[16]

Given its numerous contrasting stories, that evening manifests the Rashomon effect. The *New York Post* drama critic said that after two Beat writers began arguing over a woman, one demonstrated something sexual onstage, and a riot ensued. A theater historian said Corso heckled O'Hara, sending him offstage in tears, whereupon O'Hara's friend, the abstract expressionist painter Willem de Kooning, heckled Corso. Kerouac, who had come with Allen Ginsberg, later apologized for heckling O'Hara. McGarr's version is not necessarily inconsistent with the others—by all accounts there was a whole lot of heckling going on—but when the event took place, March 2, 1959, Thompson had already been fired from *Time* for insubordination and taken a job seventy miles upstate, a long drive for a poetry reading. Like Thompson, McGarr was a good storyteller and a marvelous liar, so this episode must remain an anecdote with an asterisk.[17]

Thompson's new job was with the *Middletown Daily Record*, an experimental newspaper. The first US daily printed by the offset method, the *Record* had such high-quality typography and photography that its founders sought young, smart reporters to suit. Bob Bone, for one, had recently graduated from Bowling Green State University with a degree in photojournalism. Thompson found him "one of the most decent people I've ever come across."[18]

Bone noticed his new friend's intolerance for hack journalism. One time Thompson telephoned James Reston, the Washington bureau chief for the *New York Times*, at his home after midnight to complain about a story. Bone recalled: "Reston actually talked to him under these outlandish circumstances. They discussed the situation for at least fifteen minutes and then hung up amicably. With his Kentucky accent and Southern gentleman turns of phrase, Hunter could be a charmer when he wanted—even on the phone—even when he was supposedly outraged."[19]

Thompson left the *Middletown Daily Record* two months after arriving. Carol Black, who worked in the production department, remembered the dramatic incident that precipitated his departure. Thompson was standing behind her at the office candy machine as she obtained a candy bar. Walking away, she heard the machine click, but no candy dropped: "Then the real noise began. There was punching, kicking, shouting. . . . He was having a tantrum, and I shrunk into the corner."[20]

Managing editor Al Romm fired Thompson the following day. Although he could be cantankerous, Romm offered some thoughtful parting words. He recognized Thompson's talent but knew he needed time to mature. "You have got more than your share of idiosyncrasies," Romm told him. "Other writers have earned their right to be idiosyncratic—you are being idiosyncratic without any backup. Go earn the right to be flaky!"[21]

In March 1959 Thompson found a cabin in the woods near Cuddebackville to concentrate on his fiction. Cuddebackville was only ten miles from Port Jervis, the inspiration for Whilomville, the fictional setting for several Stephen Crane tales, including *The Monster*. Thompson found his combination of journalism and fiction appealing. Crane's first novel, *Maggie: A Girl of the Streets*, Thompson called a "brutally truthful piece of American journalism." In his Cuddebackville cabin Thompson wrote some short stories and drafted *Prince Jellyfish*, an autobiographical novel.[22]

Poor, bored, and unable to sell his short fiction or finish his novel, Thompson scoured the want ads in *Editor and Publisher*. Bone had taken a job in Puerto Rico on the *San Juan Star*, an English-language daily managed by William J. Kennedy, another would-be novelist, whose motivation applies to Thompson: "I heard good things about Puerto Rico, and it was an expatriate life—Hemingway and Fitzgerald go to Paris, go to Spain, go someplace." Thompson applied for a job with the *Star*, but Bill Kennedy rejected his application. His snide rejection triggered an angry response from Thompson. Strangely, their shared vituperation led to a lifelong friendship. They would often trade letters expressing their frustration with the publishing process and recommending books to read. After reading Faulkner's novella *The Bear* at least twice, Thompson urged Kennedy to read it.[23]

An advertisement for a position with a new magazine caught Thompson's eye. Patterned on *Sports Illustrated* and based in San Juan, *Sportivo: The Monthly Sport Magazine of the Caribbean* would be launched in early 1960. According to its publicity materials, it would be a Spanish/English monthly with feature stories, pictures, and results from many different sports. Editor and publisher Philip Kramer interviewed Thompson in New York and soon hired him.[24]

Much confusion surrounds *Sportivo*, mainly because previous studies have ignored Gonzalo Velázquez, director of library services at Puerto Rico's Department of Public Education. Velázquez recorded the basic details of this short-lived magazine. Kramer, who initially planned a bowling magazine, registered his publishing company as Puerto Rico Bowling News. Between registering the company and producing his publicity materials, Kramer got ambitious. Instead of a bowling magazine, he now planned a general sports magazine, *Sportivo*. Reaching Puerto Rico the first week of January 1960, Thompson was pleased with the position initially. Kramer would assign him one feature per week and give him the freedom to research and write it.[25]

Kramer assigned Thompson one story about Puerto Rico's casinos, for which he interviewed the gambling commissioner. While researching this story, Thompson ordered a copy of *The Gambler*, the Dostoevsky novella dramatizing the psychology of compulsive gambling. Clearly, Thompson was putting Puerto Rican casinos into a much broader context, situating them within the worldwide gambling culture. He also researched and wrote a feature about cockfighting.[26]

In-depth features could not sell magazines in Puerto Rico, Kramer quickly learned. Bowling news might. Nowhere was safe from the bowling craze. Even Hawaii had its own bowling magazine, *50th State Bowler*. Kramer had Thompson make regular rounds of San Juan's bowling alleys and write about local bowlers. It was Charley Farley all over again; Puerto Rico was Jersey Shore with a tan. Thompson did not haunt the bowling alleys for long. The April issue of *Sportivo*, which appeared in late March, was its last.[27]

Thompson's time in Puerto Rico did give him an idea for a novel, *The Rum Diary*, but he could not concentrate on it. In need of ready cash he turned to freelancing and wrote some articles for the Louisville *Courier-Journal*. Having coaxed Semonin to San Juan, Thompson profiled him for their hometown newspaper's Sunday magazine.

"A Louisvillian in Voodoo Country" marks an advance in Thompson's literary style. It conveys some of the same ideas as "Security," but instead of expressing them himself, Thompson turned the article into a game of Semonin Says. After graduating from Yale, Semonin ignored his degree for the life of an artist and beach bum. Although proud of his choices, he disliked playing Charlie McCarthy to Thompson's Edgar Bergen. Thompson's narrative ventriloquism challenged middle-class conformity in a more convincing and entertaining way than "Security." He was learning how to assume an alternate voice to convey his most heartfelt ideas.

Sandy Conklin, who began dating Thompson in New York, joined him in Puerto Rico. She moved into the bungalow that he and Semonin shared in Loiza Aldea, a coastal village outside San Juan. Bone explained the situation: "It seemed a depressing place—or it was, anyway, until Sandy Conklin showed up to take care of Hunter. She brightened the place considerably, and I found myself rather envious of his casual, beachside lifestyle with a beautiful, sarong-clad woman at his side."[28]

After a brief trip to Bermuda, Thompson, Conklin, and Semonin returned to New York. Thompson and Semonin soon crossed the continent to deliver a car in Seattle and hitchhiked from there to San Francisco. Between rides on September 26 they stopped at an Oregon roadhouse to catch the first Kennedy–Nixon debate on television. Thompson would date his political awakening to this moment. Watching the debate, he felt certain the Republican panjandrum could be defeated.[29]

Unable to find steady newspaper work in San Francisco, Thompson moved south to Big Sur to concentrate on his fiction. Conklin joined him. He became the caretaker of Slate's Hot Springs. Located on a rugged oceanside bluff, the property was owned by Vinnie Murphy, whose grandson Michael Murphy would turn it into the Esalen Institute, a touchy-feely retreat designed to help people maximize their innate potential. While visiting the Esalen Institute, novelist Leo Litwak was astonished to see so many people hugging each other all over the place.[30]

Conklin did most of the caretaking while Thompson wrote. An ideal spot for nightly sunset watching, Big Sur was their kingdom by the sea. Thompson developed a small circle of writer friends, including Michael Murphy's younger brother—the novelist Dennis Murphy—and Lionel Olay, another novelist. Thompson kept circulating his short fiction, now hoary with rejection slips, and polished *The Rum Diary*, which was gaining its share of rejections. Thompson told Bill Kennedy about one agent who rejected the manuscript because he found its characters uninteresting: "There's no dealing with that kind of criticism—it's about the last thing I expected. 'A perfectly acceptable novel," he added, but . . .' And so we beat on, boats against the current."[31]

Frustrated with his fiction, Thompson pitched some travel pieces to newspapers and magazines. The *Chicago Tribune* accepted one about Mexico and another about Big Sur. Privately, Thompson called the Baja peninsula "the coccyx bone of the universe." His Mexico piece, "Baja California Has Honky Tonks, Solitude," though fairly positive, is not without sarcasm: "If you want to see what Baja California is like—without really seeing what it is like—Ensenada is the place to do it."[32] The second-person voice indicates that Thompson still lacked the ability or the confidence to make himself the center of the story. In this case he would not have wanted to reveal any personal details. He came to Mexico with Conklin so she could get an abortion, one of two she would have there.

Rogue accepted "Big Sur: The Tropic of Henry Miller," making it Thompson's first article in a national publication. A gentleman's magazine, *Rogue*, gave Thompson more leeway than did the *Chicago Tribune*. The article begins boldly: "If half the stories about Big Sur were true the vibrations of all the orgies would have collapsed the entire Santa Lucia mountain range, making the destruction of Sodom and Gomorrah seem like the work of a piker."[33]

This opening reflects Thompson's fondness for hyperbole, situating him within the American tradition of tall talk and tall tales, which depend on wild exaggeration for their comedic power. Thompson's hyperbole makes his writing function similarly to the way the tall tale functions in the oral culture: both serve as rites of initiation. By understanding the humorous nature of his exaggerations, accepting them, and going along with whatever lies he tells no matter how outrageous, readers can feel like insiders, like members of Thompson's circle of intimates.

An appreciation of Henry Miller fills a third of the essay. When the author of *Tropic of Cancer* settled in Big Sur, he enhanced its reputation as a mecca for sex maniacs. While smashing his readers' preconceptions, Thompson reinforced Big Sur's appeal. To supplement his tall talk he used a rhetorical device that had been part of American literature since Captain John Smith came to Jamestown, the negative catalogue: "Compared to the rest of California, Big Sur seems brutally primitive. No subdivisions mar these rugged hills, no supermarkets, no billboards, no crowded commercial wharfs jutting into the sea."[34]

The *Rogue* article named many Big Sur residents, who were none too pleased with the publicity. Most upset was Thompson's landlord Vinnie Murphy, who booted her caretaker and his girlfriend off the premises. Conklin retreated to New York, taking a job that would let her support Thompson, who went home to Louisville to continue *The Rum Diary*.

While in Kentucky, Thompson wrote a travel piece relating his visit to Renfro Valley. Describing the music lovers who gather on Saturday nights, he turned Kentucky geography into found art: "They come down from Berea and Crab Orchard, and Preachersville, and from places like Egypt and Shoulderblade across the mountains." So, too, the names of singing groups: he chose for example the Coon Creek Girls, a band featuring Lily May Ledford, who came from Pinch 'Em Tight Holler.

The article's title, "Traveler Hears Mountain Music Where It's Sung," uses the local term for the music performed in Renfro Valley. "Bluegrass" is an outsider's term. In addition, the title contrasts where trendy people hear bluegrass—Gerdes Folk City in Greenwich Village, the hungry i in San Francisco—with where it began. The title also assigns Thompson an identity: traveler.

Louisville was not the same when Thompson came home for Christmas in 1961. Grandma Ray had died earlier that year, so she was no longer around to celebrate the holidays. A bequest let her grandson return to journalism on his own terms. Confident he could succeed as a freelance travel writer, he planned an extended overseas trip and bought some pricey camera equipment.

Inspired by John F. Kennedy's Alliance for Progress, a program for North and South American economic and political cooperation, Thompson contacted Clifford Ridley, features editor of the *National Observer* and proposed a series of travel pieces from South America. Before Ridley gave him the green light, Thompson left the United States for South America, where he stayed until May

1963, sending numerous pieces to the *National Observer*, which its editors and readers greatly enjoyed.

Upon coming home, Thompson continued writing for the *National Observer*. Venturing west, he and Conklin reached Louisville in May. They crossed the Ohio River to Jeffersonville, Indiana, and got married on May 20, 1963, in "a marriage parlor with a neon sign by a justice of the peace who talked like Elmer Fudd."[35] The newlyweds detoured to Florida, where her mother lived. She gave them a wedding present, a 1959 Nash Rambler that would take them to California. On the way they spent months in Woody Creek, Colorado, the Aspen suburb they would eventually make their home.

In February 1964 Hunter and Sandy moved to Glen Ellen, California, Jack London's old stomping ground. Following in London's footsteps, Thompson showed that literary ancestry meant more to him than family history. While living in Glen Ellen, Sandy gave birth to their son. Breaking his family's tradition of naming children after their ancestors, Hunter named their son Juan Fitzgerald Thompson, commemorating John Fitzgerald Kennedy and paying homage to the author of *The Great Gatsby*.

Thompson wrote many book reviews for the *National Observer*, but travel writing shaped his contributions to the weekly more than anything else. He filed one report from Butte, Montana: "Whither the Old Copper Capital of the West?" His main source for this piece has previously gone unnoticed, but he cribbed it from a story about Butte in an obscure trade journal.[36]

Butte had a familiar feel. Thompson wrote: "Any long traveler who has seen the coal-dust poverty of Weirton, W. Va., or the silent railyards in Jersey Shore, Pa., will quickly put Butte in the same sorry league."[37] Cox noticed Thompson's derogatory remark in "Shore Lines." The editor of the *Montana Standard-Post* also noticed Thompson's piece and critiqued his bar stool vantage point.[38]

Mike Mansfield, who represented Montana in the US Senate, criticized the article, as well. On June 10, 1964, Mansfield defended his home from the Senate floor. After extolling the wonders of Butte, he refuted Thompson's aspersions: "The writer, who obviously gave the situation a rather limited view, talked of the city's drab appearance. These statements are deeply resented by the citizens of Butte and by me, and I wish to join with them in refuting these inaccurate and confused observations."[39]

The editor of the *Montana Standard-Post* had one final comment about Thompson's Butte piece: "We have often wished, and still do, that the big-time by-liners who appear hereabouts from time to time to 'do' Butte or Montana would veer away from the notion that reporting in depth means scraping the sump." Thompson would get the last laugh. In *Hell's Angels* he depicts the motorcycle outlaws splashing around Bass Lake in jockey shorts, their matted beards making their skin seem pale and moldy: "It looked like the annual picnic for the graveyard shift at the Never Sweat copper mine in Butte, Montana."[10]

Despite what the Montana editor said, Thompson did not feel like a big-time byliner. With his journalism stagnant, he moved his young family to San Francisco. They found an apartment near a hilltop in Haight-Ashbury, 318 Parnassus Avenue, which gave them a view of the Golden Gate Bridge. Their street name commemorates the mountain near Delphi with twin peaks, one consecrated to Apollo and the muses, the other to Bacchus, the god of wine. According to Greek tradition, whoever slept atop Parnassus would either become a great writer or go insane.

Across the bay in Berkeley, students were challenging the restrictions the University of California administration placed on free speech. Their protests became known as the Free Speech Movement (FSM). Folklorist Richard Dorson, then a visiting professor at Berkeley, noticed how this grassroots political movement dramatized the emergence of the counterculture.[41] Thompson also recognized its importance. He pitched an article on the movement to Ridley, who turned it down. Ridley's reluctance to cover the student protests contributed to Thompson's disaffection with the *National Observer*.

Thompson read the *San Francisco Examiner* regularly. On December 3, 1964, Charles Denton, its leading columnist, offered his thoughts on the protesters. He compared them to "self-appointed guerillas who prowl our streets attacking adults, not for their money, but simply because they are adults."[42] A mother of two Berkeley students wrote to challenge Denton's insensitive remarks.

Denton printed her letter but broke it up to insert some snide comments. She criticized how he equated the FSM students with skull-cracking guerillas and warned him not to label them hoodlums, beatniks, or Communists; they were serious students. He quipped, "I'm sure they are. But then, so were Loeb and Leopold. Or have you forgotten that one?!"[43] She was upset when he compared her sons to marauding thugs. He now compared them with murderers!

Denton's snarky answer to this loving mother's impassioned defense was more than Thompson could stand. He wrote a letter to Denton, who excerpted it in his December 15 column:

> I want to help you, old sport, and the best way I can see to do it is to get you off this FSM kick. Your reply to the mother's letter was so inane, oily

and maliciously ignorant that for a moment I couldn't quite believe it. As a matter of fact, your whole point of view is so laden with that same priggish, shallow righteousness that you could probably get away with calling it satire. Is that what you had in mind? I suspect you'll get other help in discovering that your pompous, nutshell interpretation is factually incorrect. Do you have even the vaguest idea what went on over there?

Calling Denton "old sport," Thompson speaks like Jay Gatsby. To Thompson's ear Denton sounded like John J. Righteous-Hypocrite. His self-righteous message was so absurd it resembled satire. Sadly, it was not.[44]

Politics aside, Thompson's hitherto neglected letter to Denton marks an important step in his development as a writer. Thompson is known to posterity for placing himself in the middle of his reportage. Before 1965 he had largely maintained a narrative distance in his public writings. In terms of literary sophistication, his private correspondence had progressed more rapidly than his public writings. His letters from 1964 read like his journalism from 1971. Years later Bone remembered the letters Thompson sent him in the sixties: "I still have many of those letters, whose acerbic terminology presaged those of his later public persona."[45]

Though written as a letter, what he told Denton belongs with Thompson's public writings. He naturally assumed Denton would publish it, as he had published the mother's letter. Although highly critical, Thompson's letter was too entertaining to ignore. With his letter to Denton, Thompson foresaw the possibility of making his private voice public.

Denton linked the protesters with another group of outcasts, "the mechanized irregulars who storm up and down our highways on motorcycles and in hot-rods, terrorizing whole towns and putting even policemen to flight."[46] Thompson's curiosity about motorcycle gangs paralleled his interest in other marginalized social groups and coincided with the rise of New Journalism, which let reporters immerse themselves within the stories they reported. Thompson befriended the motorcycle outlaws to get the story for *Hell's Angels*, an instant classic of New Journalism.

Having established his reputation with *Hell's Angels*, Thompson knew he could take his writing further. He had yet to develop his voice fully, to bring the freewheeling craziness of his private letters into his public writings, but he struggled for years before he could put another book together. With *Fear and Loathing in Las Vegas* and *Fear and Loathing on the Campaign Trail*, Thompson defined and developed gonzo journalism, his unique brand of idiosyncratic and highly subjective reporting, which let him say whatever he wished regardless of truth, buzz, or consequences.

Thompson created his most enduring work once he discovered how to blend person and persona. His drug-addled public persona was so successful that he faced a new problem. The real person had to match the fictional persona: an impossible situation. The demand to live up to the monster he had created made it impossible for Thompson to sustain his thought and write at the level he achieved during the early seventies.

CHAPTER 2

Foreign Correspondent

An original photograph accompanies "Nobody Is Neutral under Aruba's Hot Sun," the first dispatch Thompson sent the *National Observer* as foreign correspondent. Its caption begins: "A tourist relaxes on the eight-mile beach of the island of Aruba."[1] The so-called tourist is Thompson doubling as his model. With a full head of hair, a bare chest, a slim waist, and muscular legs extending from his tight-fitting madras swim trunks, the twenty-four-year-old Thompson looks great.

The part about relaxing in disingenuous. His left hand holds a drink to his lips, but his right holds a pen. A notebook rests on his lap. Thompson portrayed himself striking a favorite pose, and he worked hard to get it right, taking multiple shots to perfect the image. He kept the different versions and, years later, supplied one to Simon and Schuster for the cover of *The Rum Diary*.

Dow Jones had launched the *National Observer* in February 1962. Patterned on the London *Observer*, it was a weekly that supplemented the *Wall Street Journal*. Best known as a financial daily, the *Journal* also had a reputation for detailed feature stories. The *National Observer* would be filled with in-depth, *Journal*-like articles, attempting to do in newspaper form what *Time* and *Newsweek* did in magazine form. Thompson's dispatches would contribute much to the paper's literary quality.

The first story from his South American odyssey in the *National Observer* is "'Leery Optimism' at Home for Kennedy Visitor," which discusses Colombia's president-elect, Guillermo León Valencia. This article appeared before "Nobody Is Neutral" because it was time sensitive. John F. Kennedy would host a luncheon for Valencia on Monday, June 25, so the *National Observer* ran "Leery Optimism" the preceding day. It begins: "At noon Monday a small man with a brush mustache will sit down to lunch at the White House with President Kennedy."[2] This opening sentence sparks our curiosity. Withholding Valencia's name until the second paragraph, Thompson leaves us wondering who this mustache man is. His description evokes images of good and evil: Charlie Chaplin and Adolf Hitler. Even after the second paragraph mentions Valencia, we are still left wondering. Why would any world leader wear the same mustache as Hitler?

"Leery Optimism" is not Thompson's first political piece. That distinction goes to "Munoz Skilfully Keeps Foes Off-Balance," the profile of Puerto Rico's powerful governor, Luis Muñoz Marin, he wrote two years earlier. He called Muñoz "a rip-roaring throwback to those days before the blood of the Western world turned pale."[3] These words sound a note that would reverberate throughout Thompson's work. He often expresses nostalgia for bygone days when men were tougher and life was simpler.

Like the Muñoz article, "Leery Optimism" synthesizes politics and personality. After conveying some uncertainty about Valencia, Thompson asks the logical question, "How, with all these reservations about Dr. Valencia, was he ever elected president?" He takes four paragraphs to answer the question, concluding, "He was picked, they say, because he was 'the only Conservative the Liberals could trust.'"[4]

"Nobody Is Neutral" verifies Thompson's ability to craft evocative openings: "The Trocadero Bar on the Caribbean island of Aruba is spacious, sunny, and breezy, with slated doors and a long white porch that faces the sea. It's the kind of place where you might discover Somerset Maugham, or the ghost of Humphrey Bogart, eyeing you sullenly from the other end of the black marble counter."[5] Combining literary and film references, Thompson recalls Bogart's *Casablanca* and Maugham's Tahiti, places where people escape to only to escape from, where long-bladed ceiling fans and free-flowing liquor help them endure the otherwise unendurable heat.

Thompson continued writing powerful introductions for his South American dispatches. "Democracy Dies in Peru, But Few Seem to Mourn Its Passing," which chronicles the military takeover of the Peruvian government, begins with an epic simile: "The 'death of democracy' has not left much of a vacuum in Peru. It was more like the death of somebody's old uncle, whose name had been familiar in the household for years, but he died where he had always lived, in some far-off town the family never quite got around to visiting —although they had always meant to, or at least that's what they said."[6]

The old uncle gives Thompson's simile a familiar, comfortable feel that levels its epic quality, making a nation's plight resemble a family's. The simile helps American readers understand the predicament Peru faced. Thompson's personal experience inspired a subsequent simile. Later in the article he says Lima "differs from the rest of Peru as Manhattan differs from the mountains of eastern Kentucky." This contrast lets readers understand Peru by imagining somewhere closer to home with a similar geography. Virginia, for example, encompasses Tidewater cities and the peaks and hollers of the Piedmont. The editor of the *Richmond Times-Dispatch* enjoyed "Democracy Dies in Peru" and reprinted the article. Regardless of its setting, Thompson's article is fearsome in implications, showing how easily people could let democracy die.[7]

"Latin Close-Up: Why Ecuador Is Seeking US Aid" is Thompson's first front-page story. It begins on Malecón, the riverside drive in Guayaquil and "one of the filthiest streets in Christendom": "The gutters are full of rotting orange peels, and the sidewalks are littered with fish heads. During the day it crawls with beggars, fruit vendors, drunks, sellers of contraband, and half-naked stevedores loading cargo from riverboats to the army of ancient trucks that jam the piers. At night it crawls with rats."[8] A rhetorical device characteristic of gonzo journalism, the catalog was already a tool in Thompson's writerly toolbox. Since this article concerns Ecuador's financial woes—its easy acceptance of debt and its reliance on Washington for a regular influx of cash to keep it afloat—the introduction's graphic imagery symbolizes the rot that afflicts Ecuador's economy.

Thompson used different techniques to distinguish each introduction. "Operation Triangular," which surveys the Bolivian mining industry, begins somberly: "Near each tin mine in the arid, poverty-ridden nation of Bolivia, where the 12,000-foot altitude makes breathing difficult, stands a large, bleak, and fully visible graveyard." The title of a subsequent article, "A Never-Never Land High Above the Sea," alludes to *Peter Pan*, but the opening sentence uses a much darker literary quotation: "If Bolivia were half as bad as it looks on paper, the government would send a crew to all the country's points of entry to post signs saying 'Abandon all hope, ye who enter here.'" Later in this article he calls Bolivia "a land of excesses, exaggerations, quirks, contradictions, and every manner of oddity and abuse." This catalog illustrates Thompson's perceptive analysis of the nation. His words are remarkably similar to what US Ambassador Ben Stephansky said about Bolivia.[9]

In the introduction to "Uruguay Goes to Polls, with Economy Sagging" Thompson captures a prominent aspect of everyday culture, the deceptively appetizing Uruguayan sandwich. He spreads the sandwich over the first three paragraphs, a lengthy setup for the ensuing simile: "The story would not be worth the telling if not for the fact that Uruguay's economy is very much like one of these niggardly sandwiches: It looks pretty healthy at a glance, but once past the façade there is plenty missing."[10]

Thompson experimented with narrative point of view in his foreign correspondence. He typically used the first person but sometimes wrote in the second or third. "Nobody is Neutral" recreates a conversation among four men seated around a table on the porch of the Trocadero Bar. It introduces two local men—Boeboe and Makaku—in one paragraph, two outsiders in the next: "The third was a Dutchman, Jos Van Kuijk, Aruba editor for the *Amigoe di Curacao.* [. . .] And the fourth was an American—me."[11]

After this first-person pronoun Thompson shrinks from it, subsequently referring to himself in the third person as "the American." To bring the conversation alive, he includes their oddly pronounced words and friendly gestures. "I tink id is time for a cool beer," Van Kuijk says to chill Makaku's heated words. Boeboe's physical and facial gestures work similarly: "Boeboe nudged the American. 'Don't pay any attention to this fanatic,' he said with a smile." Thompson's formal use of "the American" clashes with the casual conversation, but he defended the article, calling it "a good and valid look at island politics, personalities, etc."[12]

"How Democracy Is Nudged Ahead in Ecuador" takes a similar narrative approach. Thompson describes meeting Fred Shaffer, chief of the United States Information Service (USIS) in Guayaquil, but casts himself as "the visitor." After the visitor sees a man hurrying away, Shaffer says: "He owns a radio station that used to broadcast so much anti-American stuff that we nicknamed it the Voice of Moscow." The man has accused Shaffer of forcing him out of business. Shaffer feigns indignation at the accusation, but he really did run the man out of business. The opening section ends with a wry wink: "The visitor detected a note of irony."[13]

Like the Aruba piece, "How Democracy Is Nudged Ahead in Ecuador" incorporates much dialogue, but Thompson excludes himself from the conversation, making the visitor a surrogate for the reader. We experience the chaotic USIS office as he does. We, too, wonder how Shaffer drove the Voice of Moscow out of business. Thompson delays explanation for more drama. The dialogue contributes to the hectic atmosphere, making it resemble the overlapping snatches of newsroom banter between Cary Grant and Rosalind Russell in *His Girl Friday*. When the press officer enters to mention some women waiting outside, Shaffer telephones "Guillermo." Thompson leaves this story hanging, too. Next, the cultural affairs officer announces that they won the election. What election? Thompson again forestalls explanation, driving our curiosity higher.

Thompson's cut from the interior of the USIS office to the exterior street scene reinforces the article's cinematic quality: "Out in the hot sun, the cabs rolled back and forth like animals looking for meat, honking their horns incessantly at every walking prospect."[14] Thompson's figurative use of predatory animals anticipates his animal imagery in *Fear and Loathing in Las Vegas*. The shot of the menacing taxis contrasts with the office interior. Although seemingly chaotic, the office remains under the protection of the US government. Outside nothing can protect people from the predators. After this cutaway the article shifts from drama to exposition. One by one it uncovers the mysteries.

While broadcasting anti-American content, the radio station relied on American companies for advertising revenue. Once Shaffer informed the companies they were supporting pro-Soviet propaganda, they yanked their advertising. Guillermo was supposed to meet the waiting women to develop a USIS-sponsored community center. And the election was for the presidency of the Guayaquil chapter of Ecuador's national association of university students. The USIS had aggressively supported the pro-democracy candidate, who trounced his leftist opponent.

"How Democracy Is Nudged Ahead in Ecuador," which appeared in the *National Observer* on September 17, 1962, caught the attention of Senator Gale W. McGee. The next day McGee spoke on the Senate floor to defend expenditures for the USIS. To illustrate the organization's effectiveness, he pointed to Thompson's article: "This story shows how efficient and dedicated Americans, operating on limited budgets, can advance the cause of freedom." McGee asked fellow senators for unanimous consent to reprint Thompson's article in the *Congressional Record*. With no objections, "How Democracy Is Nudged Ahead in Ecuador" became the second of Thompson's articles in the *Congressional Record*. The previous month it had reprinted "Latin Close-Up."[15]

Thompson came to South America with no high opinion of the Peace Corps, but after meeting some volunteers and viewing their projects, he changed his mind, privately calling the Peace Corps "the only serious and decent effort the US is making in Latin America." He told a friend to join and considered joining himself, or so he said: "I would if I weren't such a reprobate, but then I can be twice as effective for the same idea by writing as I could by joining."[16]

One recent commentator has questioned Thompson's claim that he could accomplish more to advance the Peace Corps as a writer than a volunteer.[17] But Senator McGee's attention to his South American dispatches verifies the claim. McGee was not the only legislator who read the *National Observer*. Thompson's articles influenced the policy makers who held the Peace Corps' purse strings. McGee served on several legislative committees pertaining to foreign policy, and he would later become US Ambassador to the Organization of American States.

The third-person point of view let Thompson distance himself from what he was reporting, giving him a sense of detachment and objectivity. Other times the first-person point of view puts him in the heart of the action and creates a sense of intimacy with readers. He wrote two articles from Colombia in the first person: "A Footloose American in a Smugglers' Den" and "Beer Boat Blues."

Sending "Footloose American" to Ridley, Thompson called it "a sort of offbeat travel piece that might interest you." He spoke modestly; it is his finest article from South America. Eric Newby, the author of *A Short Walk in the Hindu Kush*, would include "Footloose American" in his anthology of great travel writing. It traces Thompson's journey from Aruba to Guajira, a peninsula that shoots from Colombia's shoulder like a left cross. Puerto Estrella, located at the tip of the peninsula, was the entry point for a vast smuggling operation run by the native Wayuu *contrabandistas*. Thompson identifies himself as the first tourist in the history of Puerto Estrella, an aspect of the essay Newby emphasizes. The first-person voice suits the region's first tourist.[18]

The Arubans have warned Thompson about the Wayuu, mentioning their fierce nature and scanty loincloths, "nothing but neckties, knotted just below the navel." Walking from where a fishing boat has landed him to Puerto Estrella, Thompson wonders how he will react when he encounters them: "At the first sign of unpleasantness I would begin handing out neckties like Santa Claus—three fine paisleys to the most menacing of the bunch, then start ripping up shirts."[19]

Traveling with paisley neckties in his kit, Thompson is prepared to meet diplomats and cultural attachés, not naked whisky smugglers. Clothing would remain an important motif in his subsequent writings, especially *Hell's Angels*. Besides devoting considerable attention to what the Angels wear, he discusses his own clothing by way of contrast. When he first meets some Angels at a bar, he arrives wearing a Palm Beach sports coat, which he quickly strips off to fit in. In both "Footloose American" and *Hell's Angels*, Thompson conveys his willingness to sacrifice articles of clothing—emblems of identity—to survive in a strange new world. Once he begins riding with the Angels, however, Thompson adapts a new costume, deliberating wearing a tan sheepherder's jacket to differentiate himself from them.

His description of his first contact with the Wayuu echoes Herman Melville's first contact in *Typee*. Thompson explains, "As I came over the brink of the cliff, a few children laughed, an old hag began screeching, and the men just stared. Here was a white man with 12 Yankee dollars in his pocket and more than $500 worth of camera gear slung over his shoulders, hauling a typewriter, grinning, sweating, no hope of speaking the language, no place to stay—and somehow they were going to have to deal with me."[20] Thompson endears himself to the Wayuu, partly through his gargantuan drinking capacity and partly because he convinces them that he knows Jackie Kennedy, "whom they regard as some sort of goddess." Paralleling primitive worship and modern celebrity culture, Thompson sardonically shows how little they differ.

After days of drinking in Puerto Estrella, he begins wondering how to escape: "Trying to leave can turn a man's hair white. You are simply stuck until one of the Indians has to run some contraband down the peninsula to Maicao."[21] Thompson's temporary shift to the second-person voice facilitates the use of symbolism. So far in his reporting career, Thompson hesitated to make his fictionalizing too obvious. He did not want to say, "It took less than a single day to change these hairs from a jetty black to white," as the fisherman says in Poe's "Descent into the Maelström." But he could imply the possibility. The fisherman's hair turns white from the trauma he experiences inside the maelstrom. Thompson's momentary shift to the second person lets him use this traditional motif, implying that his frustration in Puerto Estrella was sufficient to turn his hair white.

Finally, the *contrabandistas* must go to Maicao, so Thompson hitches a ride in a "Power Wagon." He was talking about a Dodge Power Wagon, a four-wheel drive pickup based on a World War II design. Omitting the brand name, Thompson minimizes the *contrabandistas'* dependence on American-made vehicles packed with Detroit muscle. Instead, the Power Wagon is a general symbol for technology, which establishes another contrast between primitive and modern. The Wayuu may wear skimpy loincloths, but their smuggling operation requires piston-powered trucks.

Years later Thompson would imagine returning to Guajira. In *Fear and Loathing in Las Vegas*, Raoul Duke, his fictional alter ego, wonders how to escape the countless felony charges he faces. He will flee to Guajira, "where the official language of jurisprudence is an obscure dialect known as 'Guajiro.'"[22] The prosecuting attorney will take months to establish jurisdiction and learn the language, by which time Duke will escape into the impenetrable South American jungle. Thompson's time in Latin America supplied vivid memories and motifs for his later writing.

Toward the end of "Footloose American" Thompson awaits a flight to Barranquilla. He tells people about his trip to Guajira; no one believes him. His experience recalls "Nam-Bok the Unveracious," the Jack London story. Having ventured beyond the limits of his native region—the first to do so—Nam-Bok returns home after traveling the globe. When he tells others about what he saw, they do not believe him. Seeing is believing, the proverb goes, but convincing others to believe what you have seen is another matter entirely.

In Barranquilla, Thompson visited the USIS Institute, where he met David Hamilton, a recent college graduate who was teaching there. Hamilton would recall Thompson's personal appearance: "I remember chinos and walking shoes, sleeves rolled up, a shirt with brick in its color, a camera around his neck and another on his shoulder." Hamilton offered him a couch in the apartment he shared with two other teachers. Thompson accepted, setting up his typewriter on a card table, where he wrote "Footloose American." Together they enjoyed drinking beer and talking books. Hamilton got a good sense of where Thompson was in his life: "He thought of writers as actors shaping events of consequence around them. He was insistent on getting into the world, being part of the game, not just savoring but enlivening its strange corners."[23]

Thompson would travel from Barranquilla up the Magdalena River toward Bogotá, an eight-day journey by boat. He had arranged a free ride aboard a tugboat in exchange for taking some promotional photos. A bus would have been faster, but Thompson found the boat ride irresistible. It would give him an experience reminiscent of Marlow's journey in *Heart of Darkness*. Thompson made this motivation explicit in the letter to Semonin he wrote aboard the tug: "There is a definite sense of the Congo here."[24] Venturing upriver into the unknown, Thompson hoped to gather material for his writing. The result was less dramatic.

The tug was pushing seven barges of beer up the river, seven barges of beer! It was hot, muggy, and buggy. The only relief was to swim from the tug to the nearest barge and sneak some bottles of warm beer. "Beer Boat Blues" tells the story of Thompson's river journey. Instead of placing it with the *National Observer*, he published it in the travel section of the Sunday Louisville *Courier-Journal*.[25]

The article identifies its author as a Louisvillian, which makes his first-person voice and casual manner appropriate. Those who live on the Ohio River are naturally curious about life on other rivers around the globe. Thompson shows his neighbors what river travel through Colombia was like. "Beer Boat Blues" is pleasant enough, but it lacks the excitement and cultural significance of "Footloose American." Sneaking beers from a barge is not much of a story. Thompson's letter to Semonin, which portrays the journey as a battle of the bugs, is more entertaining. Seated at his typewriter, he must endure a cavalcade of creepy crawlers.[26]

Thompson also experimented with literary tone in his Latin American pieces. Before Aruba he had stopped in Puerto Rico and written several dispatches for other American newspapers, apparently using a lighthearted, breezy tone. Few saw publication. Another letter to Semonin explains why: "I have been accused, in fact, of submitting articles that read 'like letters and essays,' which of course they were. Needless to say, they have not seen print. And I have not seen money."[27] These remarks suggest that Thompson had been loosening up his prose, unsuccessfully trying to give his dispatches the feel of personal letters. His remarks help explain the formal tone of his *National Observer* articles. He got the impression that the reading public did not want newspaper articles that read like letters.

The personal letters Thompson wrote during the trip reveal his annoyance with South American travel. From what he says to Semonin, he worked hard to keep his "mounting hysteria" from his journalism.[28] He could grouch and grumble all he wanted to friends, but Thompson restrained himself when he spoke publicly as a foreign correspondent for a national newspaper. Restraining himself became increasingly difficult as his South American journey progressed. His personal letters let him vent his frustration, which he largely excluded from his dispatches.

Ridley's mixed signals made Thompson feel like he was playing a game of Red Light, Green Light. Although he enjoyed Thompson's political analysis, Ridley encouraged him to write more articles like "Footloose American." Thompson hoped to do some hunting, which would let him write something similar, but he had been concentrating on politics since Colombia because every country he visited was afflicted with some sort of political turmoil. Thompson now questioned whether writing stories about South American politics was really more important than capturing the everyday lives of its people.

The tone of Thompson's cover letters differs from his dispatches. When Ridley read them aloud at the office, other editors encouraged him to publish a selection from them. Thompson was astonished to receive for proofreading a montage of excerpts from his cover letters. The *National Observer* even paid him $150 for the privilege of publishing them. Although he had been working hard to omit personal feelings from his journalism, the newspaper now wanted to publish them. The montage appeared on New Year's Eve as "Chatty Letters During a Journey from Aruba to Rio." A headnote explains: "There's another side to reporting that seldom shows up in formal dispatches—the personal experiences of the digging, inquisitive newsman."[29]

One selection in "Chatty Letters" comes from a letter Thompson wrote from Bogotá. He promised the Valencia piece would be in the mail the next day, assuming Bogotá's bellringers would stop their incessant clanging: "Between the dysentery, the bells, and the unceasing loudspeakers in the street I am half-mad (Ah here go the bells again.) Ten minutes of it now; a lunatic in the belfry and worms in the stomach. What a town!"[30]

An excerpt from a Guayaquil letter contains a clever plea for additional funds. Explaining the interconnected South American banking system,

Thompson turned a literary reference into a simile: "The moneyed community on this continent, which is what you have to deal with when you want to cash checks, is like Melville's circle of Genius—which 'all over the world stands hand in hand, and one shock of recognition runs the whole circle round.' Which means, in my case, that if I bounce a check in Cali my reputation as a crook will precede me to Buenos Aires. So I have to be careful."[31] Thompson's quotation comes from Melville's essay "Hawthorne and His Mosses." It concerns the spiritual connections great authors share. To acknowledge the genius of one is to acknowledge the genius of all. In its positive sense Melville's phrase connotes a feeling of accomplishment and a sense of belonging. In its negative sense, as Thompson uses it here, the phrase expresses the inability to escape the connections that link individuals to the larger entities that control them.

Jay Leyda had included "Hawthorne and His Mosses" in *The Portable Melville*. Thompson loved the Viking Portables. While working for *Time*, he stole Henry Luce's copy of *The Portable Sherwood Anderson*, and he brought *The Portable F. Scott Fitzgerald* and *The Portable D. H. Lawrence* with him when he went to Puerto Rico.[32] Dave Hirsh carries a set of Viking Portables in his duffel bag in James Jones's *Some Came Running*; it is fun to imagine Thompson traveling the length of South America with *The Portable Melville* in his rucksack. More likely, he borrowed this quotation from a secondary source.

Edmund Wilson's *Shock of Recognition* is an obvious possibility. A likelier and more recent source is *America*, the Catholic weekly. With an excellent worldwide distribution network, the magazine could be found throughout Latin America. Father Gardiner, its literary editor, had recently published "The Recognition of Shock." More homily than literary criticism, Gardiner's article discusses the vulgarity of recent fiction—"unbridled sexuality, desperate squalor, intellectual and moral whoredom, despair nursed in alcoholism"—complaining that such decadence scarcely shocks readers anymore.[33]

To explain his title Gardiner quotes the same Melville passage Thompson would quote, arguing that Melville's words still rang true: "This tingling sense of awareness of kinship still runs like an electric current among the truly eminent of our creative writers." As Thompson would, Gardiner applied the phenomenon more broadly: "Not only genius, but our common fallen human nature stands, in Melville's phrase, 'hand in hand all over the world.'"[34] Regardless of where Thompson encountered Melville's words, they became a personal touchstone. The Guayaquil letter is his earliest known usage of Melville's "shock of recognition," but the phrase would echo across Thompson's oeuvre.

Gonzo journalism may be the biggest impediment to critical studies of Thompson's early work. Since he created his unique and defining style in the early seventies, his previous writings have been measured by the gonzo standard. His South American dispatches, the thinking goes, are important only insofar as they anticipate his gonzo style. To read his foreign correspondence from the perspective of Thompson's later style is to do his early journalism a disservice.

"Chatty Letters" is often cited as a proto-gonzo work. In a letter he wrote from Cusco, Peru, Thompson remarks, "Some S½&?& has been throwing rocks at my window all night and if I hadn't sold my pistol I'd whip up the blinds and crank off a few rounds at his feet." Biographer William McKeen calls this sentence "the earliest species of gonzo journalism."[35] But the sentence is not journalism, gonzo or otherwise. It is an excerpt from a private letter. Other critics have similarly ignored the distinction between Thompson's private and public writings. Thompson would eventually challenge the distinction himself—but not yet. So far, he wrote one way for friends, another way for the newspaper-reading public.

Thompson's personal letters had been filled with outrageous humor since he was a teenager. His South American dispatches, on the other hand, are analytical, informative, insightful, and serious: all qualities of good journalism. After railing against the hacks, Thompson used the *National Observer* to demonstrate what he could do, to show readers what good journalism really was. His South American dispatches demonstrate his knowledge of the subject and his technical proficiency as a journalist. Considering Thompson's literary career as a whole, Bob Bone said that some of his best writing appeared in the *National Observer*.[36]

By printing excerpts from his letters, the *National Observer* essentially told Thompson to incorporate more humorous, lighthearted personal detail in his dispatches, but he still hesitated. Perhaps the word "chatty" irked him. He was constructing an identity as a serious, even cerebral foreign correspondent, not a chatterbox. He did not want to cheapen his dispatches with distracting frivolity.

In September 1962 Thompson reached Rio de Janeiro, which became his base of operations. Bone had taken a position as editor in chief of *Brazilian Business*, a weekly magazine published jointly by the American Chambers of Commerce for Brazil. Thompson also befriended Charles Kuralt, who lived in Rio while serving as Latin American bureau chief for CBS News. Sandy Conklin flew down to Rio, as well. Thompson and friends would gather at one Copacabana bar or another and talk late into the night about books and politics, dreams and ambitions. He continued writing for the *National Observer* and also became a reporter for *Brazil Herald*, Rio's English-language daily. Editor Bill Williamson called Thompson "the best reporter we had."[37]

"Brazilshooting" relates how Brazilian soldiers attacked a nightclub in retaliation for a beating one soldier had received there. This essay assembles all the literary techniques Thompson had been using so far: an eye-catching introduction; the third-person point of view; snappy dialogue; a conversational, yet authoritative tone; and poignant figures of speech. Although written in the third person, "Brazilshooting" dramatizes the news-gathering process. Thompson was disappointed when Ridley edited his original essay and retitled it "Brazilian Soldiers Stage a Raid in Revenge." When Thompson anthologized the article in *The Great Shark Hunt*, he identified the *National Observer* as his source but presented his original text, not the edited newspaper version.[38]

In the second paragraph of "Brazilshooting" a friend telephones "an American journalist" at 4:30 in the morning and urges him to get down to the Domino as fast as possible. He yells: "The Army is all over the streets with machine guns! They've blown the Domino all to pieces and they're killing people right outside the bar where I'm sitting." Given the urgency, the journalist rushes headlong into the street: "He walked quickly, but very casually, toward the Domino Club, with his camera and flashgun cradled in one arm like a football."[39] Thompson's simile turns the journalist into an action hero, comparing him with a running back charging downfield toward the end zone.

Ridley cut the whole section. Where he retained Thompson's prose, he changed his third person to first. Ridley also cut the part where the journalist, blocked from entering the cordoned-off front door, sneaks around back and finds a way inside the Domino. As Thompson had told the story, no police barrier could stop the intrepid journalist from getting his scoop.

Thompson also included another version of himself in "Brazilshooting." Much as he made himself a tourist in the photo accompanying "Nobody Is Neutral," he made himself a bystander in "Brazilshooting." Assessing the crowd's reaction, the journalist interviews several bystanders, including one from Kentucky: "An American wondered what the reaction would be if soldiers from Ft. Knox, Kentucky, shot up a bar in Louisville where a soldier had been cheated, beaten or even killed some weeks before. 'I can't even conceive of it,' he said, 'but if it ever happened I bet they'd all hang.'"[40] Ridley cut the crowd reaction altogether.

"Why Anti-Gringo Winds Often Blow South of the Border" is generally considered one of Thompson's best Latin American pieces, second only to "Footloose American." Written after he returned to the United States, "Anti-Gringo Winds" forms a coda to his South American sojourn. Although it begins with an incident from early in his itinerary, it reflects his experience as a whole. His introduction illustrates the attitude of Anglo-American businessmen in Latin America: "One of my most vivid memories of South America is that of a man with a golf club—a five-iron, if memory serves—driving golf balls off a penthouse terrace in Cali, Colombia. He was a tall Britisher; and had what the British call 'a stylish pot' instead of a waistline. Beside him on a small patio table was a long gin-and-tonic, which he refilled from time to time at the nearby bar."[41]

Some commentators have questioned the veracity of this episode. Ridley found it "a little *too* perfect." Thompson had used an anonymous Britisher to start another South American article, "Recession, Political Upheaval Takes the Fun Out of Life in Argentina": "In the words of one nostalgic Britisher, Buenos Aires used to be 'one of the finest cities in the world, a really splendid place to live.'" Both Britishers resemble protagonists from Graham Greene's fiction. The term "stylish pot" is another fictional element in "Anti-Gringo Winds." There is no evidence of any previous English usage: Thompson coined the phrase. In *Hell's Angels* he would reuse it without mentioning its supposedly British origins as he compares the slovenly beer gut of the outlaw motorcyclist with the "stylish pot of the desk-bound world."[42]

The five iron seems like a specific detail interjected to reinforce the episode's veracity, but any golf club would have had that effect. The five iron enhances the symbolism. A wood could have suggested a connection to the organic world, but an iron, like the Power Wagon, represents the intrusion of technology. The number five symbolizes man in essence: the four limbs of the body plus the head that controls them. Thompson makes this traditional association ironic. The Britisher's head devotes little thought to what his limbs are doing as they send golf balls raining down into the surrounding slums.

Although the Britisher seems fictional, another anonymous informant in "Anti-Gringo Winds" is real: "One young American put it this way: 'I came down here a real gung-ho liberal. I wanted to get close to these people and help them—but in six months I turned into a hardnose conservative. These people don't know what I'm talking about, they won't help themselves, and all they want is my money. All I want to do now is get out.'"[43]

Hamilton did not read "Anti-Gringo Winds" until after Thompson reprinted it *The Great Shark Hunt*. By the time that book appeared in 1979, Hamilton had left Barranquilla, returned to the United States, earned his doctorate from the University of Virginia, and taken a position at the University of Iowa to teach English and edit the *Iowa Review*, which he turned into one of the nation's finest little magazines. This particular passage stunned Hamilton, who found it "the saddest passage" from all the Latin American articles in *The*

Great Shark Hunt. The reason? Hamilton was the young American, and he remembered making the statement.[44]

In his correspondence Thompson refers to "Anti-Gringo Winds" as "my Culture Shock piece." Using the term "culture shock" late in the article, Thompson defines it as "the malady that appears when a North American, with his heritage of Puritan pragmatism, suddenly finds himself in a world with different traditions and a different outlook on life."[45]

Though he had started with a British example, most of what Thompson says in the essay applies to British and North American businessmen in Latin America. Specifying a condition afflicting the "North American," his definition reflects Thompson's attitude at the end of his journey. His time in South America left him with a newfound curiosity about his own country. After a year of sharpening his reporter's skills, he longed to turn them on the United States. Ridley asked him to continue his foreign correspondence through Central America and Mexico, but it was time for Thompson to come home. Replying to Ridley in April 1963, the month before he returned, he said, "I am boiling with ideas and not many of them concern Latin America. We will have to get together on my return so I can tell you how I'm going to write what America means."[46]

CHAPTER 3

Literary Critic

Thompson's dispatches from South America were a hit among the readers of the *National Observer*, and its editors welcomed him back to the United States. In Washington he discussed his travels before the National Press Club, and Ridley offered him a desk job, which Thompson refused, knowing full well he could never be happy in a newspaper office. Instead, he became West Coast correspondent for the *National Observer*, a nonsalaried position letting him contribute occasional articles.

Though eager to turn his reporter's eye on the United States, Thompson owed the newspaper some articles it had paid for already. He also wanted to resume his fiction. He had still published only one short story, and *The Rum Diary* had made no headway among agents or publishers in his absence. He considered rewriting *The Rum Diary* but could not devote too much time to fiction. He needed journalism to generate a subsistence income. Book reviews could help supplement his feature writing.

Thompson considered writing a book about Latin America, but new publications bedeviled him. In 1964 the *National Observer* launched its Newsbook series. Published as large format paperbacks, the Newsbook was a cross between a magazine and a book. Releasing Edwin A. Roberts's *Latin America* in 1964, the *National Observer* scooped Thompson. He was not intimidated. Speaking of the Newsbooks, he told Semonin, "None of the hipsters read that shit, not even me." Despite their uneven quality, other Latin American books were more intimidating.[1]

Irving P. Pflaum's *Arena of Decision: Latin America in Crisis* also appeared in 1964. Pflaum was a Chicago journalist who taught history at Inter-American University in Puerto Rico, but neither his experience as a reporter nor his tenure as a professor qualified him to write *Arena of Decision*. In "Dr. Pflaum

Looks at the Latins But His View Is Tired and Foggy," Thompson observes, "The table of contents is a masterpiece, but from there on the book gets steadily worse." His observation sounds flippant, but he backs it up, identifying Pflaum's numerous mistakes, misconceptions, and misguided generalizations.[2]

Fiction provided an alternate view of Latin America. Set in 1811 during Venezuela's War of Independence, Arturo Uslar Pietri's 1931 novel, *The Red Lances*, was not translated into English until 1963. Reviewing the translation, Thompson brought together his South American expertise and knowledge of modernist fiction. His review appeared as "One of the Darkest Documents Ever Put Down Is *The Red Lances*."

Thompson identified the book's protagonist as a *caudillo*, a familiar Latin American type, "an unprincipled thug who rises to power by violence, duplicity, and sheer animal energy." The book manifests what Thompson called an ugly thesis, the inevitability of *caudillismo*. The violence in *The Red Lances* is unrelenting: "It's hard to recall a book in which the characters meet worse fates than they do in this one. Most of them die violent, futile deaths—'for no good reason at all,' as Hemingway phrased it." Thompson was quoting Hemingway from memory, but he had in mind "Notes on the Next War," in which Hemingway says that in future wars, soldiers will die for neither country nor principles: "You will die like a dog for no good reason."[3]

Although written three decades earlier, *The Red Lances* had a lesson to teach Latin America in the sixties. Thompson's time in South America let him foresee the resurgence of the brutality that Uslar Pietri chronicles. He found *The Red Lances* "a terrifying preview of what's to come if—as a lot of people are saying—Latin America is on the verge of a great revolution."[4]

After *The Red Lances* Thompson reviewed another violent Latin American work, Miguel Angel Asturias's dictator novel, *El señor presidente*. The title of Thompson's review reflects Asturias's status in world literature: "The 'Faulkner of Latin America': First Look at an Old, Old Book." The review itself shows Thompson's limitations as a critic. Since he measured every novel by how closely it approached *The Great Gatsby*, he had difficulty accepting *El señor presidente*, a novel that trades plot and character for a totalizing vision, displaying the phantasmagoric grotesquerie of life under a dictator.

A phenomenal work, *El señor presidente* is one of the finest Latin American novels of the twentieth century. Thompson's inability to appreciate it shows what a big blind spot *The Great Gatsby* created for him. The rich imagery, touching pathos, and hellish brutality of *El señor presidente* were lost on Thompson, who saw Asturias's masterpiece as a bad first novel, worse than *Soldier's Pay*, William Faulkner's first novel. To contrast the glowing review in the *New York Times*, Thompson's critical notice was reprinted in *Hispania*, a journal that went to Spanish teachers across the United States. Toward the end of his essay, he characterizes both *The Red Lances* and *El señor presidente* as books by young Latin authors who were now old men. He wanted more recent Latin American novelists or newer works by the old guard.[5]

He got his wish when Ridley sent him Jorge Amado's *Home Is the Sailor: The Whole Truth Concerning the Redoubtful Adventures of Captain Vasco Moscoso de Aragão, Master Mariner*. This novel let Thompson look on the brighter side of the Latin soul. Amado had established his reputation as a leading Brazilian novelist with a series of hard-hitting political novels celebrating the proletariat, but he entered a new phase in 1958 with *Gabriela, Clove and Cinnamon*, the first of several humorous, yet increasingly complex novels. Thompson's review of *Home Is the Sailor* appeared under the title, "Brazilian's Fable of a Phony Carries the Touch of Mark Twain." Like Holden Caulfield, Thompson enjoyed pointing out phonies, so he was predisposed to enjoy this new novel. Calling Amado "a Brazilian Mark Twain," he found *Home Is the Sailor* one of the funniest books since *Huckleberry Finn*.[6]

Unwilling to limit himself to Latin America, Thompson persuaded Ridley to give him more leeway in the choice of books. The July 1963 issue of *Esquire* made a good starting point. The brainchild of fiction editor Rust Hills, the issue was devoted to the American literary scene. Thompson had sent *Esquire* two short stories, "The Cotton Candy Heart" and "The Almost Working Artist." Terry Southern, whose novel *The Magic Christian* was a Thompson favorite, once substituted for Hills, revealing afterward that *Esquire* divided short story submissions according to the submitter: agent or author. Thompson's went into "the shit-pile," as *Esquire* insiders called the set of author submissions. Hills rejected both.[7]

Since Thompson turned twenty-six the same month the special issue was published, it let him compare where he was in his career with where his predecessors were at that age. Gay Talese's epigraph to "Looking for Hemingway" quotes something Gertrude Stein says in *The Autobiography of Alice B. Toklas*: "I remember very well the impression I had of Hemingway that first afternoon. He was an extraordinarily good-looking young man, twenty-three years old. It was not long after that that everybody was twenty-six. It became the period of being twenty-six. During the next two or three years all the young men were twenty-six years old. It was the right age apparently for that time and place."

Talese discusses the next generation of American writers who walked in Hemingway's shadow: George Plimpton and the other young Americans in Paris who established the *Paris Review*. Directly after the epigraph, Talese presents his parallel: "Early in the Fifties another young generation of

American expatriates in Paris became twenty-six years old, but they were not Sad Young Men, nor were they Lost."[8]

"Norman Mailer Versus Nine Writers," which comes after "Looking for Hemingway," also affected Thompson's attitude. Mailer reminds readers that William Styron was twenty-six when he published his first novel, *Lie Down in Darkness*, which Thompson then considered the finest book written in the United States since World War II. Mailer incidentally observes that Harry "Rabbit" Angstrom is twenty-six in John Updike's *Rabbit, Run*. Despite his success as a foreign correspondent, the twenty-six-year-old Thompson could see that, with two unpublished novels and a sheaf of unpublished short stories, he was well behind his literary predecessors.

In "Where Are the Writing Talents of Yesteryear?" Thompson characterizes this special issue of *Esquire* as "a sort of *Burke's Peerage* of American writers." Asserting that *Esquire* did a pretty good job outlining the present state of American literature, he nonetheless calls the issue depressing. The rest of his article explains why.[9]

The comparison with *Burke's Peerage* best suits "The Structure of the American Literary Establishment," the piece Hills contributed. This article consists of a one-page introduction and a two-page chart, a "shaded heraldic tree," according to the issue's table of contents. Hills's color-coded chart lists agents, authors, critics, periodicals, publishers, and writing schools. The "Cool World" appears to the left as an amorphous blob shaded a dirty lavender color. The "Hot Center" is red, "Squaresville" green. The majority of names appear in the untitled yellow section. Hills's chart gave currency to the phrase "hot center." Several contemporary writers began using it, including Thompson.

The list of little magazines starts in the Hot Center with *Partisan Review*, which Thompson would contact the following month on behalf of Bill Kennedy, who had submitted a short story without hearing back from the journal. When Thompson telephoned, the *Partisan Review* left him cold. He informed Kennedy that "some lazy-sounding girl answered the phone and said she'd think about it. . . . Sounds like a shitty outfit and damned if they'll get anything of mine."[10]

After the *Paris Review* the list of little magazines exits the Hot Center and enters the yellow. Some of the best appear under the writing schools sponsoring them. The *Sewanee Review*, for example, is listed under the University of the South. Mainstream publications like the *New York Times Book Review* are in Squaresville. Jean Seberg had made the *New York Herald-Tribune* hip with the release of Jean-Luc Godard's *Breathless*, but it had since receded into Squaresville.

Individual authors appear in several categories. As a client of the James

Brown Agency, Leo Litwak reaches the Hot Center. Some names appear multiple times. Albert J. Guerard is listed under three headings. With renowned journalist A. J. Liebling, Guerard appears among Macmillan's authors. He is also listed as a faculty member of the Stanford Writing Center and as an academic critic. There are some notable omissions. James Salter had published his second novel in 1961, but he is unlisted. Harper, Salter's publisher, appears in Squaresville with the following note: "Harper is now without a literary writer except for John Cheever."[11]

Some prominent authors objected to Hills's classification scheme. Novelist James Gould Cozzens considered his placement demeaning. His is the last name listed in the section devoted to publishers and their authors. It appears in yellow but comes dangerously close to Squaresville. Cozzens wrote Hills to complain: "Granted I'm not really out; but still this is outrageous."[12]

Other authors objected that the chart unduly stressed literary commercialism. Burton Raffel, best known for his translation of *Beowulf*, felt shame when he saw his name on the list, shame followed by anger. A writer friend of Raffel's who made the Hot Center felt slimy. Mark Harris, the author of *Bang the Drum Slowly*, complained that by placing agents in the Hot Center, *Esquire* ingratiated itself to them at their authors' expense. Harris's complaint reiterates Southern's insight into *Esquire*'s editorial process.[13]

Thompson knew several of the listed agents. The McIntosh, McKee, and Dodds Agency appears in the Hot Center with Styron its first listed author. Thompson had no qualms about seeking advice from established writers. He had already contacted Styron to ask how he published *Lie Down in Darkness*. Styron graciously recommended his own agent, Elizabeth McKee. Thompson approached her with the partly finished *Prince Jellyfish*, which he claimed was better than the first novels of more renowned novelists, better than *Soldier's Pay*, *This Side of Paradise*, and *The Torrents of Spring*. His bluster did not faze McKee, who took him on as a client. Submitting his short stories to several magazines, she bypassed the shit-pile—to no avail.[14]

Sterling Lord, another agent Thompson had contacted, also appears in the Hot Center. His clientele included Jack Kerouac, Ken Kesey, and Donald Barthelme. Lionel Olay was another client, although he was too obscure to appear in the Hot Center or, for that matter, anywhere on the chart. Regardless, Olay considered Lord "the Jay Gould of agentry," meaning he could sell whatever he touched.[15] Lord would not touch Thompson's short stories, which he rejected outright.

Always unable to take rejection, Thompson remitted Lord's return postage, telling him, "I don't want to feel that I owe you anything, because when I see you I intend to cave in your face and scatter your teeth all over Fifth

Avenue."[16] With this threat Thompson depicts himself as a brawler: a fictional pose, as Sonny Barger, a leader of the Hell's Angels, would realize. Barger recalled an argument between the Angels and some local men at Bass Lake: "We were going to fight, and Hunter jumped in the trunk of his car [. . .]. When it was settled, he came out. He didn't write about that part in the book."[17]

Thompson's letter to Sterling Lord also reflects his obsession with teeth, an obsession sufficient to rival the narrator of Poe's "Berenice." Threatening to knock out Lord's teeth, Thompson repeated a traditional motif: knocking out a sorcerer's teeth takes away his magic. He often expressed a desire to defang his enemies, to extract their teeth one by one or en masse, to render them powerless, to make his bark worse than their bite.

Russell and Volkening was the third agency in the Hot Center that Thompson had contacted. He sent the firm an unfinished version of *The Rum Diary*. His manuscript reached the desk of Candida Donadio, who had established her reputation with Joseph Heller's *Catch-22*. She read enough of *The Rum Diary* to determine that its characters were "hard and bitter," but she did not reject it unequivocally. Thompson got the impression that she would be willing to reread *The Rum Diary* once it was finished.[18]

Hills scattered publishers across his chart. Doubleday is in Squaresville. Located in the Hot Center, Random House could boast such authors as Truman Capote, Philip Roth, Terry Southern, and William Styron. Only one publisher appears in the Cool World: Barney Rosset's Grove Press. The era's most avant-garde publisher, Grove had issued the work of leading European novelists and playwrights, Britain's Angry Young Men, and the Beats.

Thompson found Grove a little shady. It had rejected *Prince Jellyfish* with nothing more than a mimeographed form letter that apologized for not responding personally. The rejection infuriated him. The work had cost him so much mental, physical, and emotional stress that Grove's heartless response was almost more than he could stand. Surely, it was not too much to expect that a rejection would come with some constructive feedback.

"Works in Progress, 1963," another section of the special issue, presents a set of excerpts from unfinished novels by several leading American authors. Thompson says nothing about these excerpts, but he does discuss the introductory page: "After reading that page it's hard to argue with the rumor that fiction is becoming passé, that the novel is dead as an art form, and that the short story is on its last legs."[19] He would later join the New Journalists who challenged the novel's place at the top of the literary pyramid, but when Thompson wrote "Where Are the Writing Talents of Yesteryear?" he still accepted the novel's superiority to other literary genres.

Thompson disliked the sound of Nelson Algren's current project. Algren was working on *Notes from a Sea Diary: Hemingway All the Way*, which would combine travel writing and literary criticism. Before finishing the book, Algren would incorporate a facetious allusion to *Esquire* in his opening paragraph: "Everyone else was acting so compulsively I had to do something compulsive too or I wouldn't get invited to any more parties. How is a writer to make The Hot Center unless he mills around where The Center is simmering?" Using Mailer-inspired boxing lingo, Thompson closes his discussion of Algren with a good-bye: "So long, Nelson. You may have been the last of the heavyweights."[20]

"Works in Progress" mentions that Truman Capote had turned from novels to nonfiction with his current project, which would become the explosive bestseller *In Cold Blood* upon its release three years later. The brief description in *Esquire* left Thompson unimpressed. Having always considered Capote a lightweight, he could not imagine him muscling in on the police beat of the *Kansas City Star*, Hemingway's old paper.

Personal experience showed Thompson how hard it was to get a novel published. Most of the authors named in "Works in Progress" had already published at least one. The hardest part was over for them. They had a foot in the door, but now they were denying opportunity and turning their backs on this consummate literary form. Continuing his Capote paragraph, Thompson remarked, "Though there's an old adage about 'every young reporter having a half-finished novel in his desk drawer,' now we get the reverse."[21]

In "Norman Mailer Versus Nine Writers," Mailer says his competitive nature motivated his writing. As the author of *The Naked and the Dead*, he considered himself the greatest living American writer. He need not write anything more unless and until another novelist dislodged him. Mailer was relieved that the quality of James Jones's *Some Came Running* fell short of its length. Had it turned out to be the greatest, instead of the longest, postwar American novel to date, Mailer would have had to write something better.[22]

Mailer's comments about Jones's waning abilities are not unique. Hills put Mailer in the Cool World among such luminaries as Kenneth Rexroth, the godfather of the Beats, and Paul Krassner, the founder and editor of *The Realist*, a sociopolitical-satirical magazine that represents a milestone in the countercultural press. But Hills placed Jones with one foot in Squaresville, which is tantamount to having one foot in the grave. Mailer's attitude toward Styron follows his stance on Jones. Because Styron's second full-length novel, *Set This House on Fire*, was a disappointment, Mailer was again saved from the task of returning to his typewriter. In his self-centered view *The Naked and the Dead* still held the championship belt.

Thompson called Mailer's competitive approach to literary greatness "a small-minded struggle for position in a hierarchy that doesn't mean a thing to anybody except those who are trapped in it." Wanting to be tougher than Hemingway, more glamorous than Fitzgerald, and a better writer than them both, today's writer has failed on all counts: "Scott Fitzgerald's book about Gatsby puts every current American writer in very deep shade."[23]

Elevating Hemingway and Fitzgerald above the American writers who emerged after World War II was a reactionary gesture. Recently, James Baldwin had argued that it was time to stop treating Hemingway, Fitzgerald, and Faulkner as sacrosanct. Using *The Great Gatsby* as an example, he observed, "It is the sorrow of Gatsby, who searches for the green light, which continually recedes before him; and he never understands that the green light is there precisely in order to recede." Baldwin continued, "The curtain has come down forever on Gatsby's career: there will be no more Gatsbys."[24]

Thompson read Baldwin's essay soon after it appeared in early 1962. He gave it much thought and discussed it with Bill Kennedy but found its argument unconvincing. He considered the complex symbolism of *The Great Gatsby* timeless. He told Semonin that Gatsby's green light symbolized "a hell of a lot more than a slack rich girl from Louisville." Thompson refused to accept Baldwin's view that there would be no more Gatsbys. Kennedy explained, "He thought of *himself* as Gatsby, and he reveled in that kind of fate—that green light always receding, boats against the current, borne back into the past, and so on."[25]

By no means was Thompson a systematic literary critic. He cared nothing for academic criticism and paid little heed to theory. He attacks the academics in *Hell's Angels*. Refuting the argument that motorcycle outlaws were repressed homosexuals, Thompson uses two prominent American authors for comparison: "There are literary critics who insist that Ernest Hemingway was a tortured queer and that Mark Twain was haunted to the end of his days by a penchant for interracial buggery. It is a good way to stir up a tempest in the academic quarterlies, but it won't change a word of what either man wrote, nor alter the impact of their work on the world they were writing about."[26]

During the 1963–64 period, when Thompson wrote nearly all his literary criticism, his outlook evolved from one review to another. Although he never formulated a critical theory, a distinctive theory of literary quality is implicit in his reviews. Let's call it Hunter S. Thompson's Two-Book Theory of Literary Greatness.

In a 1962 letter to Donadio, Thompson suggests this theory but hesitates to accept it or apply it to himself. Writing to thank her for reading the incomplete manuscript of *The Rum Diary*, he developed a comparison between a builder constructing a house and an author building an oeuvre. At this point in his career Thompson was not looking beyond *The Rum Diary*, which he foresaw as a great first novel. Even if he never wrote another, *The Rum Diary*, he believed, would be something later authors could build on, much as he constructed his novel atop *The Great Gatsby* and *The Sun Also Rises*.

Toward the end of his letter, Thompson takes Styron for example. Though a great novel, *Lie Down in Darkness* did not necessarily provide a good foundation: "When Styron tried to build a house, it didn't ring true."[27] Thompson was referring to *Set This House on Fire*. In the letter to Donadio he accepts *Lie Down in Darkness* for itself, implying that Styron need not write another novel to secure a lasting literary reputation.

Thompson's discussion of Styron in "Where Are the Writing Talents of Yesteryear?" is more critical. He reiterates his lofty opinion of *Lie Down in Darkness* but criticizes Styron's second full-length novel, comparing its author to a washed-up heavyweight champ: "Styron's performance in *Set This House on Fire* was an awful disappointment, and he is beginning to look more and more like Ingemar Johannson: too fat to fight."[28]

During the year and a half between the letter to Donadio and the summer of 1963, Thompson developed his Two-Book Theory of Literary Greatness, which his discussion of Algren clarifies. He praises Algren because he wrote both *A Walk on the Wild Side* and *The Man with the Golden Arm*. Thompson's theory surfaces elsewhere. In his review of Jorge Amado, he says that after *Gabriela, Clove and Cinnamon*, Amado went one better with *Home Is the Sailor*. And in an appreciation of Ken Kesey, Thompson observes that few American authors have written two books as good as *One Flew over the Cuckoo's Nest* and *Sometimes a Great Notion*.[29]

The Ginger Man, J. P. Donleavy's first novel, was another Thompson favorite. He told the *Washington Post* how it affected him when he first read it as a teenager: "That book made up my mind that I had to be a writer." Donleavy's overall talent so far remained unknown because he had yet to publish a second novel. According to "Works in Progress," he had just finished *A Singular Man*. Thompson hoped it would match *The Ginger Man*: "If Donleavy can buck the trend and pull off another hell-for-leather book like his first one, it will be a blow scored for all of us."[30]

Whereas Mailer saw himself pummeling his novel-writing opponents, Thompson took a brotherly stance. He considered one novelist's success a triumph for all novelists. Without mentioning Melville, Thompson was again applying his shock-of-recognition concept: Donleavy's success would reverberate the whole circle round.

A Singular Man verified Thompson's Two-Book Theory, as the title of his review suggests: "Donleavy Proves His Lunatic Humor Is Original." Thompson enjoyed how different the two books were: "Reading Mr. Donleavy is no longer like being dragged into a beer-brawl in some violent Irish pub—but more like sitting down to an evening of good whisky and mad laughter in a rare conversation somewhere on the edge of reality."[31]

His positive view of *A Singular Man* was a minority opinion. Other reviewers disliked Donleavy's second novel. Some readers of the *National Observer* who accepted Thompson's opinion hated *A Singular Man* and wrote to say so. Florida retirees were especially vocal. Thompson privately remarked: "People keep writing from places like St. Petersburg, saying I gave them a bum steer on books like J. P. Donleavy's *Singular Man*, to mention the worst offender to date. The senior citizens didn't dig that one at all."[32]

Thompson's Two-Book Theory also shaped his review of *The Spire*, William Golding's latest novel: "Golding Tries *Lord of the Flies* Formula Again, But It Falls Short." *The Spire* tells the story of a man obsessed with erecting a forty-story tower atop his church. Thompson found it too similar to *Lord of the Flies*, critiquing their author for not making the two books more divergent. Much as the island of children is an allegory of our society, so, too, is the teetering tower, which is constructed by frauds, fakers, and fanatics.[33]

The key word in Thompson's review of *The Spire* is "formula." *The Spire* had a different setting and set of characters from *Lord of the Flies*, but both books followed the same basic pattern; they presented an unusual place to tell an allegory of modern, Western society. To achieve literary greatness an author must write two books as distinct as possible.

When Thompson talked about putting two great books together, he meant two novels, but Vance Bourjaily's new work forced him to rethink the relationship between fiction and nonfiction. By 1963 Bourjaily had a solid reputation as a novelist. Hills listed him three times. As a faculty member of the Iowa Writers' Workshop, he is on the edge of the Hot Center, but he enters it as a client of Russell and Volkening and a Dial Press author.

Living in Iowa, Bourjaily enjoyed crow hunting, which he describes in *The Unnatural Enemy*. Since few writers hunt, Thompson was pleased to find a fellow writer who was also a hunter. His Bourjaily review, "The Crow, a Novelist, and a Hunt: Man in Search of His Primitive Self," is quite positive: "He can make the chase of a single bird in an Iowa cornfield far more exciting and meaningful than most stories about close combat with grizzlies." Thompson found *The Unnatural Enemy* better than its author's fiction. Bourjaily was a novelist who did not excel as a writer until he switched to nonfiction.[34]

Thompson finished his Bourjaily review the first week of November 1963. Two weeks later the whole world changed. The assassination of John F. Kennedy on November 22 devastated Thompson. That day he wrote Bill Kennedy from Woody Creek: "There is no human being within 500 miles to whom I can communicate anything—much less the fear and loathing that is on me after today's murder."[35]

This sentence contains Thompson's earliest known usage of his signature phrase. Much has been made of its possible sources, but "fear and loathing" was an English idiom that had been in circulation for centuries. This conjoined word pair has a biblical feel. Although it does not occur in the King James Bible, similar phrases do. Paul tells the Philippians: "Wherefore, my beloved, as ye have always obeyed, not as in my presence only, but now much more in my absence, work out your own salvation with fear and trembling." The earliest recorded usage of the phrase "fear and loathing" occurs in *Divine Considerations*, the 1646 English translation of a treatise by sixteenth-century Spanish humanist Juan de Valdés, who "oft-times heard speak of the agony, of the fear and loathing, and sorrowfulnesse, which Jesus Christ our Lord felt at his passion and death."[36]

With each passing century, the phrase occurs more and more frequently. It was a favorite of early nineteenth-century English poet and essayist Robert Southey, who used it in both his verse and his prose. Critiquing the graphic newspaper reports of recent murders, Southey observed, "Publication of them can do no good. Right minds shudder at the recital; tender ones turn from it with fear and loathing." In the twentieth century Thompson could have encountered this idiomatic phrase practically anywhere. In *Lord of the Flies*, for example, Ralph confronts a mysterious, but potentially lethal creature: "He bound himself together with his will, fused his fear and loathing into a hatred, and stood up."[37]

The assassination also affected Thompson's attitude toward writing. Though Bill Kennedy had been emphasizing the literary value of little magazines, they hardly seemed important in the face of John F. Kennedy's murder. As a literary critic, Thompson had so far emphasized the novel's superiority over reportage, but the presidential assassination reinforced his commitment to journalism: "Fiction is dead. Mailer is an antique curiosity. The stakes are now too high and the time too short."[38]

His tirade against fiction the day Kennedy died was a knee-jerk reaction. The following year he returned to fiction but faced the same problem as before. He still could not afford to forego journalism and devote six penniless months rewriting *The Rum Diary*. He wanted a grant to pay living expenses while he rewrote his novel, but this desire ignores Faulkner's advice in the *Paris Review*: "The good writer never applies to a foundation. He's too busy writing something. If he isn't first rate he fools himself by saying he hasn't got time or economic freedom."[39]

The grant idea occurred to Thompson early one morning after he had been up all night drinking—a nightly habit throughout his adult life. He knew exactly whom to ask. Donadio's reputation as an agent had grown since they communicated two years earlier. Mario Puzo, a hungry writer before publishing *The Godfather*, applauded her ability to pull slick magazine assignments out of her sleeve. To get her help on a grant Thompson telephoned Donadio, never mind how drunk he was or what time it was. He related the encounter to Bill Kennedy: "I called Candida Donadio at four in the morning and finished myself there; I was seeking a grant to go back into fiction, but she snapped like a bull-dyke dealing with a subway masher."[40]

Slowly, Thompson developed a new hybrid form of writing, part journalism and part fiction. Describing "When the Beatniks Were Social Lions," a piece he wrote for the *National Observer* in early 1964, he told Gene McGarr, "I have discovered the secret of writing fiction, calling it impressionistic journalism, and selling it to people who want 'something fresh.'" A few weeks later Thompson used an alternate label for this new hybrid form of writing: personal journalism. He told Semonin, "Personal Journalism is the Wave of the Future. Art is passé, and so is *The New York Times*. Now we mix it all up and come on strong."[41]

Pondering the relationship between fiction and nonfiction, he fell back on Hemingway. Of all the critical pieces Thompson wrote during the 1963–64 period, the finest is "What Lured Hemingway to Ketchum?" Combining critical appreciation with travel writing, this essay relates Thompson's visit to Ketchum, Idaho, to see Hemingway's last home and reflect upon his work. Thompson quotes the comment from *Green Hills of Africa* about the United States making its authors into something strange before destroying them altogether. He then turns Hemingway's words against him. Thompson argues that Hemingway never saw how he was being destroyed and thus never understood how to avoid destruction. The fast-paced modern world no longer resembled the one he knew. At the end of his life Hemingway struggled to see what he had once seen "clear and as a whole." This phrase reflects Thompson's deep knowledge of Hemingway. It comes from the end of *Death in the Afternoon*, which only the most dedicated Hemingway enthusiasts have finished.[42]

Thompson interviewed some of Hemingway's old friends in Ketchum. Charley Mason, for one, recalled his remarks about what it took to be a writer: "the power of conviction and knowing what to leave out." Thompson had read variations of this statement in Hemingway's writings, but he was unsure if it applied at the end of his life. He saw Hemingway's final psychological state as a crisis of conviction. Hemingway was not alone. Recent authors faced a similar situation: "Today we have Mailer, Jones and Styron, three potentially great writers bogged down in what seems to be a crisis of convictions brought on, like Hemingway's, by the mean nature of a world that will not stand still long enough for them to see it clear as a whole."[43]

Hemingway was never far from Thompson's thoughts, but the trip to Ketchum let him reconsider his words and works. In his introduction to *Men at War*, Hemingway eloquently expresses the novelist's responsibility to the truth: "A writer's job is to tell the truth. His standard of fidelity to the truth should be so high that his invention, out of his experience, should produce a truer account than anything factual can be. For facts can be observed badly; but when a good writer is creating something, he has time and scope to make it of an absolute truth."[44] The greatest novelists have the capacity for writing fiction that captures truth. Hemingway's approach gave Thompson license to incorporate fictional elements in his journalism, provided they would express a truth that transcended mere factuality.

Thompson maintained a casual attitude toward the literary criticism he wrote. He told Olay, "My new gimmick is book reviews—$75 a crack, with my own choice of books. One a week keeps me in beer and bullets."[45] But Thompson's stint as a book reviewer coincided with a crucial period in his life, after establishing himself as a serious journalist but before deciding whether to resume his novel. Reading and reviewing other authors helped him reconcile fact and fiction to develop his concept of impressionistic journalism.

CHAPTER 4

New Journalist

Neither "impressionistic journalism" nor "personal journalism" caught on to describe the fiction-infused style of reporting Thompson developed, but his approach was not unique, at least not yet. Several contemporary journalists followed a similar path, using literary techniques associated with the novel: recurrent motifs, extensive dialogue, well-developed characters, experimental points of view, innovative organizational schemes, and details drawn from the material culture. A name for this general approach would catch on: New Journalism.

Tom Wolfe, New Journalism's leading advocate and practitioner, could not say for sure who coined the phrase or when it was coined. In his introduction to *The New Journalism*, an anthology he coedited, the earliest example Wolfe mentions is Talese's "Joe Louis: The King as a Middle-Aged Man," which appeared in *Esquire* in 1962. Talese would include it in his 1970 collection, *Fame and Obscurity*. Wolfe's first contribution to New Journalism appeared in *Esquire* in 1963. It would become the title essay for his 1965 collection, *The Kandy-Kolored Tangerine Flake Streamline Baby*. Also in 1963 *Esquire* published Terry Southern's "Twirling at Ole Miss," a groundbreaking experiment in subjective journalism. These articles support John Seelye's claim that *Esquire* was New Journalism's prime mover.[1]

New Journalism was not without antecedents. Lillian Ross's *Picture*, a 1952 chronicle of John Huston's struggle to bring *The Red Badge of Courage* to the cinema, is one influential precursor. Terry Southern identified another. An interviewer once asked him, "Hunter Thompson's whole 'gonzo' oeuvre is right there in something like your 'Twirling at Ole Miss' and a few others. Can you discuss how you formulated this 'revolutionary' approach to your journalism?" Southern replied: "There are some Edgar Allan Poe stories—particularly one called *The Narrative of A. Gordon Pym*—where he uses a narrative style which has a strangely authentic documentary quality; I mean, in light of its times, natch. Anyway, I think I first picked it up there, from the great E. Poe."[2]

Wolfe heard the term "New Journalism" in conversation in late 1966. Both he and Thompson would use it privately the following year. One of its earliest published usages occurs in October 1966 in *Women's Wear Daily*, an untapped resource for understanding contemporary American literature. Its literary editor Peter S. Prescott mentions New Journalism in his review of *Paper Lion*, George Plimpton's story of trying out for quarterback with the Detroit Lions: "Plimpton is unique among those who write the New Journalism: he collects experience."[3]

Prescott's observation reflects his blurry comprehension of New Journalism. Identifying Plimpton's process of collecting experience as unique among New Journalists, Prescott revealed that their techniques were not fully codified or understood in 1966. Fascinated, he quickly learned more. Within four months Prescott would understand that collecting experience was not unique to Plimpton: it was essential to this emerging journalistic approach.

In a later article Prescott observes, "Much of what the novel had to offer—social reporting, exotic landscapes, and vivid characterization, all patted into place by the author's controlling hand—has been preempted by the New Journalism and by the Experience Collectors who write it." Prescott devotes five thoughtful paragraphs defining New Journalism. He explains, "Avoiding analysis, objectivity, and self-expression the New Journalism concentrates on the dramatic presentation of an experience."[4]

The New Journalists' literary techniques may resemble the novelists', but their work habits differ. Whereas novelists can use their imaginations to create dialogue, New Journalists must endear themselves to their subjects, spending long periods of time with them and gaining their confidence to such an extent that they would agree to be tape-recorded. To write book-length, novel-like works, journalists must immerse themselves in the milieu of their subjects so thoroughly that their argot and mind-set become second nature. Being a New Journalist requires an open mind, dogged determination, and considerable freedom from other responsibilities.[5]

Although New Journalism is typically participatory journalism, it does not have to be. New Journalists can be arranged along a most-to-least participatory spectrum with Plimpton at one end and Talese at the other. Regardless of where they fit, New Journalists have sought to establish stronger and more distinctive personal voices than traditional journalists. When asked if New Journalism had ever appealed to him, David Hamilton said that a few colleagues at the Iowa Writers' Workshop were into it, but he found New Journalism "a little too show-offy for my taste." He explained, "I distrusted putting that much of me in my essays."[6]

Not until New Journalists have become thoroughly aware of their subjects can they write their stories. Prescott continues:

> When, after a few months or a few years, they scurry off to their typewriters, anxious to drop their carefully nurtured commitments and, like rat finks, eager to expose everything they have learned from milking the confidence of others, they are pregnant with the actuality, the totality, of it all. They can write a new kind of book: Not just the facts, ma'am, but the "truth" of the experience—the smell, the taste and the temperature of it, the nitty-gritty which is not only fact, but a projection of the facts into reasonable invention as well.[7]

Prescott's language suggests connections between New Journalism and popular culture. The term "rat fink" sounds derogatory, but Alan Sherman's hit song "Rat Fink" softened the phrase's sordid connotations, making it lighter and more humorous. "Just the facts, ma'am" is Joe Friday's catchphrase from *Dragnet*, of course. Although New Journalism is more than just the facts, it does share with *Dragnet* a basic approach, starting with true stories but embellishing them to enhance their entertainment value and emphasize their messages.

Despite the attitude toward truth and fiction they share, *Dragnet* and Thompson's journalism are otherwise opposites. When the television series was reprised in 1967, *Dragnet* gained a new opening sequence. It begins with an establishing shot that depicts Los Angeles from a distance. Accompanying this shot, Jack Webb's voice-over intones, "This is the city, Los Angeles." An ensuing montage of increasingly close-up shots brings viewers into the heart of the city. By the end of each episode, Los Angeles is restored to the home of God-fearing, law-abiding citizens. In contrast, *Fear and Loathing in Las Vegas* begins with a high-speed drive away from Los Angeles after a frenzied shopping spree across the city for all sorts of dangerous and highly illegal drugs.

By 1973, the year Wolfe published his anthology, New Journalism was well established. That same year Kurt Vonnegut called it "the literary equivalent of Cubism: all rules are broken; we are shown pictures such as no mature, well-trained artist ever painted before, and in the crazy new pictures we somehow see luminous aspects of beloved old truths." Joe Klein found a musical comparison appropriate. New Journalism was ready "to wash all that Old Journalism out to sea, just as Bob Dylan, Janis Joplin, the Jefferson Airplane and others had overturned the music business and recreated it in their own image."[8]

The impressionistic journalism Thompson wrote for the *National Observer* did little to advance his literary career, which looked grim entering 1965. He and his young family were still living in San Francisco. One day he queried *Nation* editor Carey McWilliams, who recommended improving upon the story of the motorcycle outlaws, which the news magazines had treated superficially. McWilliams could only pay him a hundred dollars, but Thompson liked the idea and said yes. Within a month he had finished "The Motorcycle Gangs: Losers and Outsiders," which appeared in the May 17 issue of *Nation*.

"Motorcycle Gangs" is the great turning point in Thompson's career. Soon after its appearance he received offers for book contracts from four publishers. The article would form the basis for *Hell's Angels*, but Thompson initially had a different book in mind. He hoped to parlay the publishers' interest into a contract for *The Rum Diary*; they preferred a nonfiction work akin to "Motorcycle Gangs." One suggested a book about several fringe groups. Angus Cameron, who had edited *The Catcher in the Rye* for Little, Brown, was now working for Knopf. He suggested a book about other American losers and outsiders.[9]

Thompson signed with Ballantine Books to do *Hell's Angels*. Given Knopf's interest, his choice of Ballantine, a paperback house, seems unusual. Expedience was his primary motivation. Ballantine was willing to take "Motorcycle Gangs" in lieu of a formal book proposal. It offered a $6,000 advance, one-quarter of which Thompson would receive up front. Since Ballantine was affiliated with Random House, Thompson's contract for the paperback would lead to a contract for a hardback edition with Random House. Jim Silberman, a Random House editor, would oversee *Hell's Angels*.

After signing with Ballantine, Thompson still considered *Hell's Angels* a stepping-stone for *The Rum Diary*. Unwilling to lose contact with Cameron, he responded to his offer. Actually, Thompson had sent Cameron *Prince Jellyfish* seven years earlier. Cameron rejected the manuscript but gave Thompson some constructive criticism. Now, while turning down Cameron's losers-and-outsiders idea, Thompson pitched *The Rum Diary* as a replacement, using Hemingway's rhetoric to support his argument: "Fiction is a bridge to truth that journalism can't reach."[10]

Contrasting fiction and nonfiction in the letter to Cameron, Thompson mentioned *The Kandy-Kolored Tangerine Flake Streamline Baby*. He enjoyed Wolfe's title chapter and the one about North Carolina stock car racer Junior Johnson. Thompson explained, "In order to write that kind of punch-out stuff you have to add up the facts in your own fuzzy way, and to hell with the hired swine who use adding machines."[11] To write with power journalists must develop a new attitude toward fact and fiction, to realize that writing well was not just a matter of compiling facts, to understand that a well-placed fiction could give journalism a deeper truth.

The use of fictional elements in purportedly nonfiction prose represents the greatest controversy New Journalism faced. John Seelye, its finest critic, predicted that New Journalism would ultimately amount to nothing more than "a mouldering pile of stylish inconsequentia." Despite his skepticism, Seelye did admire some aspects of New Journalism: it was tough, jazzy, immediate, and, best of all, readable. But Seelye, who also enjoyed pointing out phonies, found something sneaky about New Journalism's willingness "to sacrifice a fact for the Larger Truth."[12]

Researching *Hell's Angels*, Thompson achieved a level of equanimity he had rarely known. Over the July 4 weekend in 1965 he attended his first holiday run with the Angels, which took him to Bass Lake, a mountain resort just south of Yosemite and about two hundred miles east of San Francisco. Bass Lake would provide the setting for his book's most fully dramatized episode. Thompson would not write the Bass Lake story until the following year, but that weekend showed him he was onto something. The day after returning to San Francisco, he conveyed his Eureka moment to Paul Semonin: "It has finally come home to me that I am not going to be either the Fitzgerald or the Hemingway of this generation [. . .]. I am going to be the Thompson of this generation."[13]

Hell's Angels gave Thompson a creative excitement he had previously experienced only while writing fiction. Years later he reflected, "This subject was so strange that for the first time in any kind of journalism, I could have the kind of fun with writing that I had had in the past with fiction. I could bring the same kind of intensity and have the same kind of involvement with what I was writing about, because there were characters so weird that I couldn't even make them up. I had never seen people this strange. In a way it was like having a novel handed to you with the characters already developed."[14] Thompson's sense of fun shows from the opening paragraph of *Hell's Angels*, a roll call of weird characters: "Little Jesus, the Gimp, Chocolate George, Buzzard, Zorro, Hambone, Clean Cut, Tiny, Terry the Tramp, Frenchy, Mouldy Marvin, Mother Miles, Dirty Ed, Chuck the Duck, Fat Freddy, Filthy Phil, Charger Charley the Child Molester, Crazy Cross, Puff, Magoo, Animal and at least a hundred more."[15]

To start writing *Hell's Angels* Thompson assembled his source material: the Lynch report, that is, the scathing document prepared by California attorney general Thomas C. Lynch; the *Time* and *Newsweek* articles, which were derived from the Lynch report; his *Nation* piece; the typescript of an article

Playboy had commissioned him to write but had subsequently rejected; Nelson Algren's *Notes from a Sea Diary*, the source for his epigraph from François Villon; *The Press*, A. J. Liebling's survey of the newspaper business, which Thompson would quote to situate himself within the journalistic tradition; and Burton Stevenson's *Home Book of Quotations*, the hitherto unidentified source for Thompson's sententiae from Thomas Jefferson and Lord Halifax.

Stevenson's *Quotations* was the kind of book Thompson used to make his range of reading seem wider than it was. Generally, readers fall into two categories: extensive and intensive. Extensive readers read many books; intensive ones read the same books many times. Considering the number of literary references in his work, commentators have generally assumed Thompson was an extensive reader.[16] Actually, his reading was more intensive than extensive. He would read a handful of favorites over and over—*The Bear*, *The Catcher in the Rye*, *The Ginger Man*, *The Great Gatsby*, *Heart of Darkness*, *Huckleberry Finn*, *The Magic Christian*, *The Sun Also Rises*. Raised on robbery, Thompson became a literary Autolycus. He would snatch quotations from secondary sources to create the illusion of extensive reading.

Despite his methodical start, Thompson procrastinated like a grad student writing a dissertation. He got Random House to push back his deadline from December 1, 1965, to March 1, 1966. Tuesday, March first loomed large on Thompson's calendar. If he missed that deadline, he feared Random House would cancel the contract and demand its advance, which he had already spent.

The last weekend of February he left Sandy and Juan in San Francisco, packed up the Rambler, and drove south, checking into a motel down in Monterey. He brought only the essentials: typewriter, typing paper, bourbon, and speed. It would be a long weekend, but not, as so many others, a lost weekend. Once he started typing, Thompson stopped only to dash out to McDonald's. Given his nagging poverty and nearing deadline, one can almost hear Hunter S. Thompson echo the words of J. Wellington Wimpy: "I will gladly pay you Tuesday for a hamburger today." After writing for a hundred hours straight without sleep, Thompson, sure enough, finished his manuscript and put it in the mail that Tuesday.[17]

Silberman and his staff spent the next several months helping him polish the manuscript. Thompson resented the editorial intrusion. When the copy editor supplied some additional sentences to clarify his prose, he found them inappropriate, much preferring his own unclarified prose over the insertions of another. After much back-and-forth between author and editors, *Hell's Angels* was in galleys by early December.

Random House sold the magazine rights to *Esquire*, which turned the Bass Lake story into a feature article. Designed to promote the forthcoming book, this article appeared in the January 1967 issue, which was available by mid-December. *Esquire* had rejected Thompson's short stories, but now, with a work of New Journalism, he broke into the magazine. His article appeared as "Life Styles: The Cyclist," which introduced a series of similar articles. The May issue would include "Life Styles: The Boxing Fan," a piece by Robert Christgau, another New Journalist Wolfe would include in his anthology. The following blurb introduces Thompson's piece: "After the Pioneer, the Westerner, the Babbitt, the Drugstore Cowboy and the Suburbanite, there emerges now a figure in a black leather jacket."[18]

Noticing the January issue of *Esquire* in "Shore Lines," Joseph Cox objected to the blurb. The modern types hardly seemed significant when compared with early American pioneers. In a weird instance of one-upmanship, Cox, ever the local historian, mentioned the pioneers who settled Pennsylvania's Wyoming Valley, where they faced a brutal attack from a mixed force of Loyalist soldiers and their Iroquois allies during the Revolutionary War. The attackers slayed hundreds of pioneers. The Wyoming Massacre, Cox observed, makes "tales of the toughness of mad motorcyclists seem like nursery stories."[19]

When *Hell's Angels: A Strange and Terrible Saga* appeared in January 1967, it received a warm reception from many friends and most critics. Cox asked Robert J. Evans, Thompson's old boss in Jersey Shore, what he thought about the book. Evans held no grudge against Thompson. He told Cox, "I am happy to hear of his success. I'm always happy to hear of anyone's success in this very difficult field of journalism." Bob Bone called *Hell's Angels* "a terrific piece of personal reporting." And Charles Kuralt sent his compliments: "The book is good, really good. I read it at a sitting, and read the best parts again. You write damned well, which I guess I knew all along but of course I've never had a chance to read extended Thompson before, and it really pleased me."[20]

The reviewers had never read anything like *Hell's Angels*. To understand it they sought comparisons beyond the world of books. British readers thought of their own motorcycle or motor scooter gangs, but the Mods and the Rockers in no way prepared them for the Hell's Angels. The Bristol *Evening Post* called *Hell's Angels* a "frightening, but thoroughly authentic book."[21]

Reviewing *Hell's Angels* for the London *Times*, Julian Mitchell remembered the two motorcyclists in Jean Cocteau's *Orpheus*, who serve as the messengers of Death. Adorned in identical garb—leather helmets, shaded goggles, gauntleted gloves—these Cocteau twins are quite intimidating. The sound of their noisy engines as they approach signals that someone is about to die, the sight of their speedy departure that someone has died. *Orpheus* appeared three years before *The Wild One*, meaning that Cocteau was the first filmmaker to portray motorcyclists as a menacing force. Connecting *Hell's Angels* to *Orpheus*, Mitchell recognized the lyrical depiction of violence the two works share.[22]

Prescott reviewed *Hell's Angels* positively, finding it "informative, lively and funny," although he preferred John Sack's *M*. Another classic of New Journalism, *M* relates Sack's experience with M Company from Fort Dix to Vietnam. Prescott also discussed Thompson's style: "*Hell's Angels* progresses by free association—subjects and stories are picked up, examined, and dropped unfinished." Progressing by free association would become a hallmark of New Journalism, receiving its ultimate expression two years later in Talese's saga of the *New York Times*, *The Kingdom and the Power*. Peter Worsley, a leading British sociologist, also noticed Thompson's use of free association and connected him with Wolfe, finding in *Hell's Angels* "a candy-coloured, tangerine-flaked prose that leaps about the subject."[23]

Chester Anderson made a similar comparison, albeit with a negative slant, aligning Thompson's writing with lurid, rumormongering sensationalism and calling it "a cardboard blend of Tom Wolfe and the *National Enquirer*." The book's harshest critic, Anderson found Thompson to be "a classical typehead, trapped in a typographical, mechanical reality of unrelated fragments of no whole." Although he does not say so, Anderson cribbed these comments from Marshall McLuhan. His words may sound cryptic to those who know nothing of McLuhan's work, but they stem from a comment in *Understanding Media*. McLuhan argued that the invention of typography fragmented the world and separated humans from nature and from each other.[24]

Leo Litwak wrote what may be the most sensitive review of *Hell's Angels*. Thompson's energetic irony reminded him of H. L. Mencken, and he also heard echoes of Mark Twain, finding Thompson's point of view reminiscent of Huck Finn's: "He'll look at anything; he won't compromise his integrity. Somehow his exuberance and innocence are unaffected by what he sees."[25]

The publication of *Hell's Angels* also marks Thompson's emergence as a cult figure among college students. Teaching folklore at Berkeley in 1968, Richard Dorson had students compile field collections on topics he approved in advance. Their topics had to be both feasible and folkloric. Having read *Hell's Angels*, several students wrote about motorcycle outlaws. Instead of preparing original field collections, however, a few students plagiarized theirs from Thompson without realizing their professor had also read *Hell's Angels*.[26]

After the book's release Thompson received many lucrative offers from the national magazines. Reading a reference to the Texas Rangers in *Hell's Angels*, Peter Collier, editor of *Ramparts*, invited him to write a piece on the subject.

Thompson accepted the assignment, only to become disenchanted with its subject. Alternatively, he proposed a general article about Texas, which would use its iconic lawmen as a leitmotif.[27] Thompson reneged on the Texas article, too, but his alternate proposal offers a way to understand the artistry of *Hell's Angels*.

Beginning in chapter 1 and running throughout the book, Thompson features a prominent motif: the double. The motif pervaded the literature and culture of the sixties. Jean-Luc Godard called the decade the "Age of the Double-Man." Psychedelic drugs encouraged people to experiment with altered states of consciousness, helping reveal the double within. In *Stories of the Double*, a classroom anthology published the same year as *Hell's Angels*, Albert J. Guerard observed that the drug that transforms Dr. Jekyll into Mr. Hyde was akin to LSD. Studs Terkel saw Thompson's book as a mirror image revealing the true identity of the Angels: "They are *us* in grotesque attitude."[28]

Thompson introduces the motif with Terry the Tramp, the book's most prominent Angel. Terry works for General Motors, which seems strange given his odd physical appearance: "Terry at a glance looks hopelessly unemployable, like a cross between Joe Palooka and the Wandering Jew."[29] Thompson's double simile reflects the Angels' dual nature. Joe Palooka is a comic-strip hero, a good-natured prizefighter. Tall, blond, and barrel-chested, he prefers not to fight but always puts up his dukes to defend the little guy.

The Wandering Jew is a mythical figure condemned to roam the earth forever as punishment for blasphemy. Although Thompson owned a copy of *My First Two Thousand Years*, a novel George Sylvester Viereck and Paul Eldridge cowrote as the Wandering Jew's autobiography, he did not get his visual image there.[30] Clean shaven in the novel, the Wandering Jew traditionally has long scraggly hair and a flowing beard, the image that inspired Coleridge's Ancient Mariner. Thompson evokes the traditional image to portray Terry. Synthesizing Joe Palooka and the Wandering Jew, Terry combines several opposites: good and evil, youth and old age, innocence and experience.

Elaborating his character in a subsequent chapter, Thompson describes Terry's appearance as he materializes at his apartment one day:

> He had been up all night and was groggy from pills and wine. It was a cold wet day, and on the way to my place he had stopped at a Salvation Army store and bought the shaggy remains of a fur coat for thirty-nine cents. It looked like something Marlene Dietrich might have worn in the twenties. The ragged hem flapped around his knees, and the sleeves were like trunks of matted hair growing out of the armholes of his Hell's Angel's vest. With the coat wrapped around him, he appeared to weigh about three hundred

pounds . . . something primitive and demented, wearing boots, a beard, and round black glasses like a blind man.[31]

This description develops Terry's personality further. He is resourceful, thrifty, and practical. He cares more about keeping warm than looking good. Thompson's successive similes enhance the passage's complexity. Resembling what Marlene Dietrich might have worn in the twenties, Terry's fur coat reinforces the influence of the movies on the identity on the Angels. It also challenges traditional gender boundaries and gives Terry a campy look.

Although the fur coat may suggest that Terry was unconcerned with appearance, one aspect of his clothing does indicate his concern. It is a tight squeeze, but Terry has managed to pull his colors over the coat. In the argot of the Angels the term "colors" means the sleeveless jeans jacket covered with patches and stained with the mud and the blood and the beer of countless debauches. Terry looks like the Incredible Hulk wearing the tattered remains of David Banner's Oxford shirt. The difference, of course, is that Terry appears more primitive, more animalistic than the smooth-skinned Hulk. Glasses, normally a symbol of the intellect, become a mockery of human intelligence on Terry's hairy face.

Their colors give the Hell's Angels uniformity. This item of clothing emerged from necessity. Angels formerly adorned their black leather jackets with insignia, but they needed something they could remove and stash quickly in case of cops. The induction ceremony when an Angel gets his colors is the Angels' rite of initiation. Thompson's account of an inductee's clothing being doused in urine is apocryphal, but it does reinforce the symbolism of the sleeveless jeans jacket. According to folklore, urine can trigger a magical transformation. The colors give members a sense of belonging. Similarly adorned, the Hell's Angels are a band of brothers. They are doubles for one another. Thompson's conjoined word pairs recall the wedding ceremony: "Each Angel is a mirror in the mutual admiration society. They reflect and reassure each other, in strength and weakness, folly and triumph."[32]

The werewolf is another traditional image that conveys the Angels' dual nature. Buzzard enjoys talking and telling jokes during the day, but at dusk he starts gobbling Seconal, which affects him as a full moon affects a werewolf: "His eyes glaze over, he snarls at the juke box, pops his knuckles and wanders around the premises in a mean funk. By midnight he is a real hazard, a human lightning bolt looking for something to zap."[33]

Later in the book Thompson reinforces the physical resemblance between the bearded, long-haired Angels and the werewolf, but he also identifies a more fundamental similarity, which he calls "the transmogrification factor." Like Dr.

Jekyll and the werewolf, Thompson asserts, the Hell's Angels have the capacity to alter their physical structure. He was being facetious, but the astonishing claims that public officials made about the Angels seemed to Thompson nothing short of supernatural transformation.

Shape-shifting has been part of American literature from its beginnings. Colonial promotion literature encouraged people to come to America to start life anew, to be in the New World the kind of person they could not be in the Old. Changing identities is often associated with the American Dream, which enables people to work hard and get ahead, transforming themselves in the process.

When it comes to the Hell's Angels, the transmogrification factor has little to do with the American Dream, which is beyond the realm of possibility for them. Thompson explains: "They are out of the ballgame and they know it. [. . .] But instead of submitting quietly to their collective fate, they have made it the basis of a full-time social vendetta. They don't expect to win anything, but on the other hand, they have nothing to lose."[34] No weekend seminar at the Esalen Institute will ever help a Hell's Angel realize his human potential. Whatever transformation he undergoes only works in one direction: backward. The Hell's Angel backslides toward the primordial ooze. Like the werewolf, he becomes more animalistic.

Broadening his perspective, Thompson links the Angels to other marginalized groups in American society. A quotation from a San Francisco police officer supplies the epigraph to chapter 14. It begins: "Basically, they're just like Negroes." The chapter itself reinforces this idea. Speaking of the Angel's stance toward authority, Thompson observes, "He knows that somewhere behind the moat, the Main Cop has scrawled his name on a blackboard in the Big Briefing Room—with a notation beside it: 'Get this boy, give him no peace, he's incorrigible, like an egg-sucking dog.'" The word "boy," a racist term for an African American man, reinforces the parallel. Thompson's words echo the bellerophonic letter Ralph Ellison's Invisible Man carries in his briefcase, which implores whoever receives it to keep this boy running.[35]

In one unusual episode Thompson does let Terry elevate himself to a new level. When the Angels visit Ken Kesey and the Merry Pranksters at their compound in La Honda, Terry almost sounds like a keynote speaker at a Kiwanis banquet. Taking advantage of Kesey's high-tech audio equipment, Terry picks up a microphone and addresses the police. He discusses morals and madness, "finishing on a high, white note which the San Mateo sheriff's department will not soon forget."[36]

Characterizing the end of Terry's speech as a "high white note," Thompson paid him a great compliment. He borrowed this phrase from F. Scott Fitzgerald, using it to mean the greatest, most elevated passage of prose in a larger work. David Wills considered this concept so integral to Thompson's work that he titled his critical study *High White Notes*. An author can demonstrate a flash of extraordinary brilliance with one high white note.

The Angels' visit to La Honda would form a major episode in Tom Wolfe's story of Kesey and the Merry Pranksters, *The Electric Kool-Aid Acid Test*, which he released in 1968 the same day he released *The Pump House Gang*, another collection of magazine pieces. Thompson read both. *The Electric Kool-Aid Acid Test* is Wolfe's masterpiece, but Thompson preferred *The Pump House Gang*. His letter of congratulations helps explain what he meant by a high white note. Thompson liked *Pump House* better because its peaks surpassed the best stuff in *Acid Test*: "I value peaks far more than continuity or sustained efforts."[37]

Among Thompson's favorite writers, Joseph Conrad exerted the greatest influence on *Hell's Angels*. Quoting *Heart of Darkness* in his postscript, Thompson makes his literary debt explicit, but Conrad's influence permeates the book. Thompson knew several primary works, but he also read the secondary literature. In a letter to Semonin he brings up "Conrad's contention that 'we live amid romantic ruins pervaded by rats.'" Thompson was quoting from memory, but he had in mind something Conrad told Edward Garnett about his frustration with *The Rescue*. Thompson could have read Conrad's words in any of several biographies. *Lord Jim* was another influential work. Thompson appreciated the novel's "darkly elegant character development," but one prepositional phrase from the book influenced him more. Mixing with a violent gang of outlaw motorcyclists to get his story, Thompson lived out his favorite phrase from *Lord Jim*: "In the destructive element immerse."[38]

Another Conrad work is important to *Hell's Angels*: *The Secret Sharer*. While living in Puerto Rico, Thompson had one Conrad volume with him. His library inventory is detailed enough to identify the precise edition.[39] It was the Signet Classics edition of *Heart of Darkness*, which also contained *The Secret Sharer* and Albert J. Guerard's fine introduction to both works. Guerard discusses their similarities, analyzing them as doppelgänger tales.

The influence of *The Secret Sharer* is most obvious during the Bass Lake episode. As the Angels gather for the July 4 weekend, they discover a stowaway in their midst. Thompson sees him standing by the fire next to another prominent Angel—the ironically nicknamed Tiny—and finds the contrast mind-bending. The stowaway is a clean-cut teenager wearing chinos and a white T-shirt. Huge and hirsute, Tiny wears a motorcycle jacket with a patch that says, "I'm bound to go to heaven because I've already served my time in hell." Thompson concludes his comparison: "Together they looked like figures in some ominous painting, a doomsday portrait of the human animal confronting itself . . . as if a double-yolked egg had hatched both a chicken and a wildebeest."[40]

In *The Secret Sharer* Conrad emphasizes the physical similarities between the nameless captain who narrates the story and Leggatt, the escaped sailor he stows away in his cabin. Contrasting the physical attributes of Tiny and the chino-clad stowaway, Thompson stresses their external differences. Their physical appearance is what distinguishes these Thompson twins. Otherwise, they seem close enough to resemble an individual facing itself.

The paired characters in *Hell's Angels* serve as miniature versions for the story as a whole, which parallels Thompson with the archetypal Hell's Angel. Like Leggatt in *Heart of Darkness*, the Hell's Angel is a less rational, more intuitive, more primitive version of the narrator who tells his story. Throughout *Hell's Angels* Thompson is a Marlow figure descending into the heart of darkness; the archetypal Hell's Angel is a Kurtz figure, a man degenerating into savagery.

Wolfe stressed that New Journalism requires the reporter to develop an intimacy with his subject: a process fraught with danger. Early in the book Thompson fears turning into an outlaw motorcyclist: "By the middle of the summer I had become so involved in the outlaw scene that I was no longer sure whether I was doing research on the Hell's Angels or being slowly absorbed by them."[41] Thompson takes steps to avoid that possibility, purchasing a BSA 650 Lightning, a bike no self-respecting Hell's Angel would ride. The BSA was faster than the stock Harley 74, but no serious biker rides a stock machine. They customize their bikes, which are called choppers because their riders chop them down to the bare essentials to make them as light and fast as possible. Thompson also avoids dressing like the Angels. In addition to his sheepherder's jacket, he wears a white tennis shirt and L. L. Bean wellies.

Even with these precautions, Thompson's identity still seems in danger of being rent in two. At first he shows sympathy for the Angels, but he gradually separates himself from them. Worsley observed, "Thompson's attitudes change as the book unfolds: his tolerance appears to dry up. At first, he seems to be writing an apologia [. . .]. Increasingly, however, the epithets become less equivocal; they are psychotic, illiterate, hairy-fisted, thuggish, sadistic, drug-crazed blood-letters."[42]

As he originally wrote it, *Hell's Angels* culminated in a set piece Thompson would later excerpt and republish as "Midnight on the Coast Highway." Richard Elman, who compared Thompson to Arthur Rimbaud, saw this set piece as a prose poem. Its lyricism is reminiscent of *On the Road*. Kerouac's biographer found "Midnight on the Coast Highway" a "two-page *tour de force*."[43] In one sense it reinforces the parallel between Thompson and the Angels. A *mise en abyme*, Terry's speech at La Honda is a miniature version of Thompson's book. Much as the speech culminates in a high white note, Thompson's book hits a high white note with "Midnight on the Coast Highway."

In a different sense this set piece distinguishes Thompson from the Angels. As it begins, months have passed since his last major encounter with them, but he still owns his BSA Lightning, which he sometimes rides after dark. He explains: "So it was always at night, like a werewolf, that I would take the thing out for an honest run down the coast."[44] Having compared the Hell's Angels to werewolves earlier, Thompson now applies the same comparison to himself. It reveals that he has acquired attributes of the Hell's Angels, although he now separates himself from them as he rides alone. He leaves their world of violence behind but takes with him what they share: a love of the bike and a willingness to push himself to The Edge.

Hell's Angels has given rise to a sociological theory of risk taking known as "edgework." Stephen Lyng, who coined the term and defined the concept, credits Thompson with providing the inspiration. Edgework is a form of boundary negotiation. Risk takers explore "edges," that is, boundaries between a variety of polar opposites: high and straight, sanity and insanity, consciousness and unconsciousness, life and death. The edge Thompson explores in "Midnight on the Coast Highway" is the boundary between life and death.[45]

Whereas Lyng found his concept of the edge in Thompson, Thompson found his in Conrad. "Midnight on the Coast Highway" parallels the conclusions of *The Secret Sharer* and *Heart of Darkness*. In both Conrad takes his narrators near the edge. Giving Leggatt a chance to swim to safety, the captain maneuvers his ship dangerously close to the cliffs overhanging the shore. He approaches "the very edge of a darkness thrown by a towering black mass like the very gateway of Erebus." There are few better epithets to describe the edge between life and death than Conrad's "gateway of Erebus." *Heart of Darkness* also explores the edge between life and death. Toward the end of his narrative, Marlow portrays both Kurtz's situation and his own as a matter of approaching the edge: "True, he had made that last stride, he had stepped over the edge, while I had been permitted to draw back my hesitating foot."[46]

Guerard's analysis of *The Secret Sharer* and *Heart of Darkness* suits *Hell's Angels*. With few revisions it can be applied to Thompson's motorcycling odyssey in *Hell's Angels*. Like Marlow and the nameless captain, Thompson undergoes an initiation into manhood and knowledge. His story is also a dramatized test of personal strength and integrity. Furthermore, it is a psychological study in half-conscious identification. Like Conrad's protagonists, Thompson identifies with outcasts and more primitive beings and lives vicariously through them. Like *The Secret Sharer* and *Heart of Darkness*, *Hell's Angels* exploits the ancient myth of the night journey, a provisional descent into the primitive and unconscious sources of being.⁴⁷

As the conclusion to *Hell's Angels*, "Midnight on the Coast Highway" shows that Thompson comes away from his contact with his darker self a fuller and more integrated person. There is one problem, however. "Midnight on the Coast Highway" is not the conclusion to *Hell's Angels*. It had been Thompson's conclusion, but he joined one final holiday run with the Angels after initially completing his manuscript. During this run, which took place over the Labor Day weekend in 1966, Thompson got "stomped," that is, beat up by some Angels. Reading the galleys afterwards, he added a postscript to tell the story of getting stomped.⁴⁸

Thompson exaggerated his injuries for the book. Eyewitnesses said that he was not beaten up too badly and that it was one Angel, not a whole group of them, who stomped him. In the postscript Thompson drives himself to the emergency room in Santa Rosa before returning home. *Hell's Angels* now ends as follows: "On my way back to San Francisco, I tried to compose a fitting epitaph. I wanted something original, but there was no escaping the echo of Mistah Kurtz' final words from the heart of darkness: "The horror! The horror! . . . Exterminate all the brutes!"⁴⁹

Force-fitting Conrad's words to suit himself, Thompson linked two utterances that Kurtz made separately. "The horror, the horror" are the final words Kurtz utters on his deathbed. They express his awareness of his own horrific behavior. "Exterminate all the brutes" is his postscript to the report he had written for the International Society for the Suppression of Savage Customs, which he added after his mind had gone. Making them the last words of his own work, Thompson puts himself in Kurtz's place and thus undermines his identification with Marlow. In "Midnight on the Coast Highway" Thompson demonstrates that he has matured beyond the dark world into which he had descended, but the postscript puts him back into it, undercutting the maturity and integrity he displays in "Midnight on the Coast Highway."

CHAPTER 5

Gonzo Journalist

Thompson became a freelance journalist partly because he lacked the discipline to function in the structured environment of a newspaper office. The problem is that he also lacked the qualities a good freelancer usually needs. Once he left the *National Observer*, he had trouble coming up with publishable ideas, and he had difficulty motivating himself to write. The success of *Hell's Angels* led to a bonanza of invitations to contribute to national magazines, but Thompson struggled to take advantage of the offers. He agreed to write many articles he would never write. He needed a patient, dedicated editor to motivate him and see his work into print. Thompson's gonzo journalism flourished because he had the good fortune to work with a series of devoted and sensitive editors.

In April 1967 Gerald Walker, the culture editor for the *New York Times Sunday Magazine*, invited Thompson to contribute a feature article. Walker seemed like a kindred spirit. In his spare time he was writing a novel, *Cruising*, a doppelgänger tale that descends into darkness as it tells the story of a police detective who enters the sadomasochistic homosexual underworld to catch a serial killer preying on gay men who resemble him. Walker asked Thompson to write about the hippie culture of Haight-Ashbury—but he needed the article soon. Walker wanted to publish it before San Francisco lured vacationing college students across the continent.

The sense of urgency was just what Thompson needed. The writing process he used for the second half of *Hell's Angels*—a nonstop, bourbon-and-speed-fueled marathon session—would not be a one-off. It became Thompson's typical writing process. He went to San Francisco, interviewed hippies in mid-April, and put the whole article together by month's end. It appeared in the *New York Times Sunday Magazine* on May 14 as "The 'Hashbury' Is the Capital of the Hippies."

In terms of style "Hashbury" comes closer to Thompson's South American journalism than *Hell's Angels*. Unlike his other New Journalism, it shows little fictionalizing. He did invent one interviewee, a young radio engineer named Brent Dangerfield. The man's profession replicates Thompson's training in the Air Force, and his name comes from Sebastian Dangerfield, the protagonist of *The Ginger Man*. Brent Dangerfield's comment—"I'm 22, [. . .] but I used to be much older"—echoes "My Back Pages," the Bob Dylan song The Byrds had recently covered.¹

That Thompson retained fond memories of Haight-Ashbury helped motivate him to write the article, which identifies how the Bay area youth culture differed from when he lived there: "During 1966, the hot center of revolutionary action on the Coast began moving across the bay to San Francisco's Haight-Ashbury district." A change in attitude came with the change in location. Former activists had quit politics for mind-expanding drugs. Thompson also mentions the anticipated onslaught of college students: "The real influx is expected this summer. The city is rife with rumors, reliable and otherwise, that anywhere from 50,000 to 200,000 'indigent young people' will descend on San Francisco as soon as the school year ends."²

Joseph Cox mentioned Thompson's article in "Shore Lines" and quoted his rumors, complimenting him before backtracking: "Young Mr. Thompson is a brilliant writer. He is good at giving fearsome effects that sort of fade away when you look them over."³ Cox compared the San Francisco rumors with those plaguing Jersey Shore and found them baseless. Cox was wrong in this case. Flooding into San Francisco, the students turned the summer of '67 into the Summer of Love.

As Walker intended, "Hashbury" gave readers a primer on the San Francisco counterculture in time for the arriving students. Thompson scooped Joan Didion, a New Journalist whose career-defining essay on the subject, "Slouching Towards Bethlehem," did not appear until late September, after most students had gone back to school. Thompson's "Hashbury" was an anticipation; Didion's "Slouching" was a retrospective. Look at her article's original appearance in the *Saturday Evening Post*.⁴ Adjacent to it appear advertisements for tubes of denture adhesive and Preparation H. (Be careful not to get those two mixed up.) Thompson wrote about hippies for the hippie generation; Didion wrote about hippies for the hemorrhoid generation.

Pleased with "Hashbury," Walker invited Thompson to write a piece about the Nevada state prison system's therapy retreats, which sought to teach guards and inmates to get along. Walker, it turned out, was not Thompson's kind of editor. Despite the edginess of *Cruising*, he was quite conservative in his personal habits. One interviewer called Walker "something of a Prufrock." Thompson's experience bears out this characterization. When Thompson used a challenging literary style for the Nevada piece, Walker—"Do I dare to eat a peach?"—asked him to rearrange his information into chronological order. When Thompson refused, the article went unpublished. The episode would gain Walker an anonymous, yet derogatory cameo in *Fear and Loathing in Las Vegas*, which mentions a "nervous drone behind a grey formica desk in the bowels of a journalistic bureaucracy."[5]

Bill Cardoso, on the other hand, was Thompson's kind of editor. The two met in New Hampshire when both were covering Nixon's 1968 presidential campaign. Cardoso found Thompson "a very graciously distracted hillbilly gent." By year's end Cardoso had advanced from a reporter for the *Boston Globe* to the editor of its Sunday magazine, a promotion that gave the future of journalism hope. Thompson told his agent Lynn Nesbit, "Cardoso is the reality of the New Journalism." His open-mindedness and easy-going manner impressed Thompson: "I talked to him on the phone today and it was astounding to realize that I could actually *talk to an editor* like talking to a person who knew what I was talking about. My normal reaction to editor-calls is a nervous sense that I'm busting the routine in an Old Folks home."[6]

Cardoso invited Thompson to write a piece about Nixon's inauguration, so he did. "Memoirs of a Wretched Weekend in Washington" appeared in the *Boston Globe Magazine* on February 23, 1969. Cardoso took a risk publishing this piece. Although the *Globe* had the reputation of a writer's newspaper, "Memoirs of a Wretched Weekend" disturbed many readers and cost Cardoso some points with the higher-ups.[7]

Best known for coining the term "gonzo" journalism, Cardoso saw "Memoirs of a Wretched Weekend" as an early example of Thompson's defining style. Looking back, he called the piece "a sort of gonzo in embryo." Describing the article at the moment, Thompson stuck with his earlier term, calling it "almost pure impressionistic journalism."[8]

Throughout "Memoirs of a Wretched Weekend" Thompson bears witness to the breakdown of American society. He uses hyperbole to emphasize the horror inherent in a Nixon presidency. Violence will be normalized, a part of everyday life, so common that people will hardly notice it. Constitutional rights will erode, and people will devolve into animals. Thompson is not just an eyewitness he is also an ear witness. He captures the sounds of Nixon's America. In "One Hundred Years from Now," the de facto theme song for Nixon's presidency, The Byrds chant about unknown troubles the nation faces, but the ambient sound of violence nearly drowns out the folk rock. Nixon's

America is filled with noise, noise, noise, noise! Having been beaten to a pulp by militant protesters, a cop yells "like a guinea hen just worked over by a pack of wild dogs."[9]

Drug abuse has become part of his reporter persona, although Thompson insists he will report the Nixon inauguration straight, only smoking one or two joints to mellow his perspective. "Memoirs of a Wretched Weekend" also includes a fictional character that would become essential to gonzo journalism. A visiting dignitary here, Raoul Duke would evolve into his creator's alter ego, saying and doing what Thompson himself hesitated to say or do.

Warren Hinckle was another good editor, although he lacked the stereotypical look of a radical journalist. Having lost an eye in a car accident, he wore an eye patch and, with a passion for fine dining, he often overindulged. In short, Hinckle resembled a pirate with a glandular problem, a vast matey. He took *Ramparts*, a Catholic quarterly with two thousand subscribers, and turned it into a monthly with a circulation of over a quarter million. Wolfe had coined the term "radical chic" to characterize the wealthy dilettantes who rubbed elbows with leftist protesters; *Ramparts*, which combined left-wing politics with high-tone graphics, became known as a "radical slick."

No mere organ of opinion, *Ramparts* contained hard-hitting investigative journalism. It broke the story about the CIA covertly funding leftist American organizations and periodicals, including *Partisan Review*, to shape intellectual opinion during the Cold War. After *Ramparts* folded, Hinckle started another radical slick, *Scanlan's Monthly*.

Playboy had invited Thompson to write a piece on Olympic-skier-turned-corporate-shill Jean-Claude Killy. What had started as a personal profile turned into an exposé of the mercantilism of sports-celebrity endorsements and revealed the inner workings of Chevrolet's promotional campaign. *Playboy* refused the article, mainly because Hugh Hefner had long been courting Chevrolet to secure its advertising for his magazine. Hinckle was happy to publish it. "The Temptations of Jean-Claude Killy" appeared in the premiere issue of *Scanlan's*, March 1970.

The article begins in medias res with Thompson arriving at the Boston airport. Bill Cardoso, who meets him there, serves as his sidekick for the first part of the article. We see Thompson through Cardoso's eyes. His chinos were long gone. Thompson wears a sheepskin vest, wing tips, sunglasses, and a necklace adorned with the insignia of the Condor Legion, a division of the Luftwaffe sent to aid Generalissimo Franco during the Spanish Civil War. They find Killy in a hotel meeting room filled with ski retailers who swill beer and gobble cocktail weenies, whose crass behavior reflects how vulgar the commercial exploitation of an Olympic hero can be. After this introduction Thompson flashes back to Chicago.

The Chicago Auto Show took place at the Stockyard Amphitheater, the same venue that had hosted the 1968 Democratic National Convention, "that rotten slaughterhouse where Mayor Daley had buried the Democratic party." Thompson launches a rebuke to Chicago, which surpasses in eloquence Carl Sandburg's paean to the city. Again, Thompson hits a high white note: "Chicago—this vicious, stinking zoo, this mean-grinning, Mace-smelling boneyard of a city; an elegant rockpile monument to everything cruel and stupid and corrupt in the human spirit."[10]

Thompson follows Killy from Chicago to Squaw Valley and back to New Hampshire, where a honky-tonk guitarist impresses him: "I recognized the weird smile of a man who had found his own rhythm, that rumored echo of a high white sound that most men never hear." The musician parallels Killy, whose world-class skiing had taken him to "that rare high place where only the snow leopards live; and now, 26-years-old with more dollars than he can use or count, there is nothing else to match those peaks he has already beaten."[11]

For his next piece in *Scanlan's* the three vital elements—idea, editor, urgency —came together to let Thompson create a landmark in his literary career. The idea came from James Salter, who had recently befriended him. Salter shared Thompson's belief in the high white note. In *Light Years*, his fourth novel, Salter portrays a woman while reading. When she pauses after a spine-tingling passage, the narrator remarks, "The power to change one's life comes from a paragraph, a lone remark. The lines that penetrate us are slender, like the flukes that live in river water and enter the bodies of swimmers."[12]

The Salters had a winter home in Aspen. One night in late April they invited Hunter and Sandy to dinner. Thompson captured the evening in *Songs of the Doomed*, complete with dialogue. Like other personal anecdotes in *Songs of the Doomed*, this one must be taken *cum grano salis*, but Salter independently verified that evening's conversation.[13]

"My God, what are you doing here?" Salter asked upon learning that Louisville was Thompson's hometown. "You should be back there writing about the Derby."

Although Thompson had attended the event as a boy, he had never considered writing about the Kentucky Derby. It was only a few days away, so he had to act fast. Hinckle loved the idea but insisted Thompson complete the article for the June issue of *Scanlan's*. The Derby would take place on May 2; Hinckle would need the article less than a week later. The tight deadline gave Thompson the urgency he needed.

As editor, Hinckle provided the third essential component. Thompson did not see a good editor as one who tinkered with an author's text to get it into publishable form. Hinckle was a good editor because he facilitated the authorial process. Cardoso agreed. Hinckle had no qualms about spending his investors' money to his authors' benefit. A few years later he would book Cardoso a two-night stay in San Francisco's Claremont Hotel to give him the peace and quiet necessary to write a review of *The Fight*, Norman Mailer's account of the 1974 heavyweight title bout between Muhammad Ali and George Foreman.[14]

Once Salter planted the idea, Thompson saw how to approach it. He told Hinckle, "The story, as I see it, is mainly in the vicious-drunk Southern bourbon horse-shit mentality that surrounds the Derby than in the Derby itself."[15] Thompson understood the place horses, horse racing, and horsemanship played in the culture of the South. His plan to write a piece using the Derby to chronicle the mind of the South is reminiscent of the humorists of the Old Southwest, whose most well-known work was Augustus Baldwin Longstreet's short story "The Horse Swap," which was anthologized in textbooks Thompson could have read in high school. Longstreet used a horse swap not only to document the connivance of men who swap horses, but also to record the behavior of the crowd of gawkers, who get wrapped up in the trade and treat it almost as a spectator sport.

Thompson wanted an illustrator to help realize his grotesque vision. Hinckle recruited Ralph Steadman, a Welsh artist then visiting New York. Don Goddard, the managing editor at *Scanlan's* Manhattan office, brought Steadman home and introduced him to his wife Natalie, a representative for Revlon. Steadman had accidentally left his ink and colors in the back seat of a taxi, so Natalie gave him some eyeliner and lipstick samples, which would give his Derby illustrations their distinctive palette.[16]

Once the Derby ended Thompson flew from Louisville to New York. Hinckle had booked him a room at the Royalton Hotel, just up 44th Street from the magazine's office. The Royalton could boast some distinguished visitors. Jacques Cousteau stayed there when he came to New York. So did Kurt Vonnegut, who put the hotel into *Slaughterhouse-Five*. While visiting New York, Billy Pilgrim takes a room on the top floor of the Royalton.[17]

Goddard rode Thompson hard. Supposedly, he locked him in his hotel room with a typewriter. A copyboy would bring in cigarettes, Heinekens, and Chivas Regal and bring out sheets of paper fresh from Thompson's typewriter. Ultimately, the copyboy started taking sheets ripped from the spiral notebook Thompson had kept in Kentucky.[18]

Before finishing, Thompson walked to the magazine's office, where he and Goddard worked together to isolate the pages about the Derby and put them in order. The New York and San Francisco offices of *Scanlan's* each had an early Xerox telecopier, which Thompson dubbed the "mojo machine." The term stuck. His editors at *Scanlan's* and, later, *Rolling Stone*, used the word "mojo" for both the machine and its faxes. Once Goddard got his mojo working, it took six minutes to transmit each page to San Francisco. Hinckle found reassembling the fragments more Lego than Scrabble.[19] In other words, his editorial work for Thompson was less a matter of recreating an established form than fitting the building blocks together to create something new.

Given its unorthodox compositional process, Thompson thought "The Kentucky Derby Is Decadent and Depraved" would be a disaster, but people loved it. Cardoso read the article with awe. He wrote Thompson, "You've changed everything. It's totally gonzo." Thompson took to the word instantly. Steadman recalled, "He said, 'O.K., that's what I do. Gonzo.'" The phrase "gonzo journalism" is not typically capitalized, but Thompson would capitalize it like a brand name.[20]

Hinckle was the midwife of gonzo journalism. Years later he would say that *Scanlan's* was "the devil's womb which gave breach birth to the gonzo genre." To call gonzo a genre is imprecise. Phil Baker was more on target when he called it a "mutant strain of New Journalism." Many contemporaries could write New Journalism, but only Hunter S. Thompson could write gonzo journalism, and only Ralph Steadman could illustrate it. Taking a cue from guerilla theater—the provocative, spontaneous, street-level counterculture performance art—Fred Bruning suggested an alternate label: "guerilla journalism." Bruning's label did not stick, but his playful definition illustrates how gonzo went beyond New Journalism: "This is when the journalist not only lives the story but wrestles it to the ground and kicks it in the groin and considers the possibility of cutting out its tongue."[21]

"The Kentucky Derby Is Decadent and Depraved" contains many elements that would become associated with gonzo journalism. Describing the end of Derby Day, Thompson finds himself descending into a maelstrom of unspeakable terror: "The rest of the day blurs into madness. The rest of that night too. And all the next day and night. Such horrible things occurred that I can't bring myself even to think about them now, much less put them down in print."[22]

Though Thompson would make the trope of the indescribable a vital element of gonzo journalism, it has a long heritage in American literature, going back to colonial Virginia. Recalling the horror and bloodshed of the Battle of the Monongahela, George Washington wrote, "The shocking scenes which presented themselves in this night's march are not to be described." *Huckleberry Finn* is another precedent. Describing the Grangerford feud, Huck says, "I ain't agoing to tell *all* that happened—it would make me sick again if I was to do that. I wished I hadn't ever come ashore that night, to see such things. I ain't ever going to get shut of them—lots of times I dream about them."[23]

Partway through "The Kentucky Derby Is Decadent and Depraved," Thompson says he and Steadman sought a representative face for the lead illustration: "It was a face I'd seen a thousand times at every Derby I'd ever been to. I saw it, in my head, as the mask of the whiskey gentry—a pretentious mix of booze, failed dreams and a terminal identity crisis." Toward the end of the piece Steadman enters Thompson's room and rouses him from bed: "My eyes had finally opened enough for me to focus on the mirror across the room and I was stunned at the shock of recognition. For a confused instant I thought that Ralph had brought somebody with him—a model for that one special face we'd been looking for. There he was, by God—a puffy, drink-ravaged, disease-ridden caricature . . . like an awful cartoon version of an old snapshot in some once-proud mother's family photo album. It was the face we'd been looking for—and it was, of course, my own."[24] Once again, Thompson uses Melville's phrase "shock of recognition," this time to convey a sense of inevitability. Try as he might to break free from his Kentucky roots, he cannot escape his heritage.

Later that year Wolfe would send Thompson a copy of his new book, *Radical Chic and Mau-Mauing the Flak Catchers*. His presentation inscription begins, "Dear Hunter, I present this book in homage after reading the two funniest stories of all time—J. C. Killy and The Derby." Wolfe would anthologize "The Kentucky Derby Is Decadent and Depraved" in *The New Journalism*. His headnote to the piece explains how Thompson's emotions control the narrative. In lesser hands this approach could be cloying, but Thompson, following Louis-Ferdinand Céline's self-deprecating narrators, portrays himself as a "frantic loser, inept and half-psychotic."[25]

Thompson did not spend all his time in New York that May locked in a room at the Royalton or working the office mojo. One night he met Jim Silberman at the Waldorf-Astoria to discuss his current book project. This dinner was reminiscent of one Thompson had with Silberman at Four Seasons Restaurant almost two and a half years earlier.

Flashback to Wednesday, January 3, 1968. Amid the swanky decor at Four Seasons, Thompson and Silberman discussed possible ideas for a new book. Silberman noticed the nostalgia that ran through his writings.[26]

"You're really writing a lifelong book called 'The Death of the American Dream,'" Silberman observed.

"Anything I write is going to be about the death of the American Dream," Thompson replied.

The idea stuck. They would settle on a two-book deal. Random House agreed to publish *The Rum Diary*—provided Thompson would thoroughly revise the manuscript—and a book tentatively called "The Death of the American Dream." *The Rum Diary* was just a sweetener. Random House really wanted another nonfiction book in the manner of *Hell's Angels*.

Thompson returned to Woody Creek before January 1968 ended and got to work. At the time he and Sandy were renting a house they called Owl Farm from George Stranahan. Born in Toledo, Ohio, an heir to the Champion Spark Plug fortune, Stranahan had spent his summers in Aspen while in graduate school studying theoretical physics. In 1959 he founded the Aspen Center for Physics, which opened three years later. Slowly, Stranahan bought land around Aspen and Woody Creek to protect it from developers. Thompson paid his rent irregularly, partly because of his profound sense of entitlement. Stranahan explained: "He always felt entitled to more than he got—that there was a certain societal abuse of his talent, that society was not giving him enough." Thompson resented paying rent to a multimillionaire from the pittance he made as a freelancer. Stranahan changed their rental agreement to a lease-purchase, which put Thompson at ease. Owl Farm would be his home the rest of his life.[27]

His sense of entitlement affected Thompson's writing, as well. While researching "The Death of the American Dream," he asked Silberman for expense money. Travel, he argued, would provide the necessary narrative structure. Thompson felt Random House owed him for whatever expenses he incurred while researching his book, no matter how extravagant. He would always abuse his publishers' expense accounts, but in this instance his intuition was on target. There are few better ways for a writer to generate ideas than going on the road.

From January 1968 to May 1970 Thompson often wrote Silberman pleading for guidance. "The Death of the American Dream" was too big, too nebulous. Romanticizing the era of Hemingway and Fitzgerald, Thompson imagined having an editor like theirs, but Silberman was no Max Perkins. His talent was understanding how he could turn a profit from an author. Not being an idea man, he could not give Thompson what he needed most: guidance. Before April 1968 ended, Thompson began referring to the project in derogatory terms, calling it "that stinking fat compendium on the American Dream."[28]

Random House did provide him with expense money and press credentials to attend the Democratic National Convention in Chicago, where, on orders from Mayor Richard Daley, the riot police notoriously clubbed protesters. The violence surrounding the convention seemed to sound the death knell of the

American Dream. But Thompson could not bring himself to write about it, and the book languished. After returning to Woody Creek, he told a friend, "Ever since I got back from Chicago I've been a ball of fangs, ready to tackle almost anything except this goddamn long-range never-ending book on the American Dream."[29]

In Chicago, Thompson had befriended Hughes Rudd, a correspondent for CBS News. Rudd's sardonic humor and good-natured cynicism made him an ideal sounding board. Thompson revealed to him the new direction his writing had taken after the convention. Frustrated with the American Dream project, he began to spoof it: "I've decided to write the first Fictional Documentary Novel. To wit: 'Hey Rube! The Memoirs of Raoul Duke . . . or a report on the rape and looting of the American Dream by a gang of Vicious Swine.' My friend, Raoul, has agreed to provide details of his secret life. And I'll provide the journalism."[30]

Describing Raoul Duke's narrative as a "secret life," Thompson put himself within another American literary tradition extending back to colonial Virginia. Remember William Byrd's *Secret History of the Line*, the racy insider's version of his more serious account of the survey of the border between Virginia and North Carolina, *History of the Dividing Line*, both of which had recently been republished.[31] What Thompson purports to write is a secret history of the death of the American Dream.

Although Thompson's letter to Rudd says nothing about *Fear and Loathing in Las Vegas*, which remained a thing of the future, it does show him transforming Raoul Duke from a walk-on character into a full-fledged literary persona. The letter also shows that so far Thompson was unwilling to let his persona supplant his personal voice. Instead, he would use the device of the sidekick, which had worked well in the first part of "The Temptations of Jean-Claude Killy" and throughout "The Kentucky Derby Is Decadent and Depraved." Speaking in his own voice, the voice of a serious journalist, he would play the straight man, a foil for the outrageous Raoul Duke.

By February 1969, over a year into the project, Thompson's "Death of the American Dream" had become Penelope's web. He seemed to tear up what he wrote almost as quickly as he wrote it. On the plus side Thompson was gaining confidence with his experimental combination of journalism and fiction. He checked with Silberman to make sure this new concept would be okay. Silberman gave him the go-ahead, but Thompson hesitated, suggesting an alternate idea. He now said that he could write the whole book in the manner of "Memoirs of a Wretched Weekend."[32]

During the summer of '69, Neil Armstrong landed on the moon and half a million hippies sloshed around in the mud at Yasgur's farm to the sounds of Jimi Hendrix and Jefferson Airplane, but Thompson made little progress on his manuscript. One revealing admission occurs in a late August letter to Silberman: "I'm just finishing a book section telling how me and Raoul Duke delivered a new Pontiac from the Bronx to Seattle in 1960 and then became politicized while hitch-hiking down to San Francisco."[33] This episode suggests that Thompson was choosing pivotal moments from his life and fictionalizing them. It recalls the time he and Paul Semonin watched the first Nixon-Kennedy debate on television. To explain the inspiration for this interim version of Raoul Duke, Thompson could have said, "I think of Dean Moriarity."

Thompson's Two-Book Theory of Literary Greatness contributed to his angst. To establish a reputation as a great writer, he wanted his second book to be better than his first. His published correspondence seldom mentions the status of his ongoing project as his second book, but occasionally it surfaces. At one point he calls his inability to write "The Death of the American Dream" a "sophomore jinx on all fronts." In January 1970, two years after starting, Thompson worried about "producing a 'bomb'—a bad 'second book'—and by 'bad' I mean rotten reviews (or none), wretched sales and a general all-round bummer."[34]

For his second book Thompson wanted something more than a collection of magazine articles in the manner of Wolfe's *Pump House Gang*. Mailer's *Advertisements for Myself* was one possible model. A collection of fugitive pieces, Mailer's book has an elaborate framework for connecting and organizing them, a framework that, let truth be told, has not held up well. Thompson wished to incorporate previously published newspaper and magazine articles, but he wanted a compelling narrative to connect them.

To end this lengthy flashback let's return to the dining room of the Waldorf-Astoria in May 1970. Over two years since their dinner at Four Seasons, Silberman and Thompson again found themselves discussing "The Death of the American Dream" over drinks and dinner. Thompson had since become involved in the Aspen political scene, first as campaign manager for mayoral candidate Joe Edwards and now as candidate for sheriff of Pitkin County. Silberman suggested that he use his political activities to focus the book. There was a key problem with this suggestion. Edwards had come so close to winning the mayoral race that, instead of sounding its death knell, the near victory affirmed that the American Dream was alive and well and living in Colorado.

Thompson's run for sheriff occupied much of his time through the summer. In October he published his bold political vision, "The Battle of Aspen," in *Rolling Stone*. One plank of his platform illustrates his forward-thinking plans. It proposes banning automobile traffic from Aspen. People could either walk or bicycle. Thompson proposed that the local police maintain a fleet of public bicycles for anyone to ride.³⁵ By the time the dust of election day settled, Thompson had won the city vote but lost the rural vote and thus the election.

In an effort to realize Silberman's latest suggestion, Thompson returned to his manuscript after election day. He hoped the Aspen political scene could provide the basis on which to build a superstructure treating American culture and politics. Thompson also told Silberman he wanted to include "The Temptations of Jean-Claude Killy." Irrelevant to the Aspen theme, this proposed inclusion reveals that Thompson still remained unsure where to take the book.

January 3, 1971, marked the three-year anniversary of their dinner at Four Seasons, but Thompson was still nowhere near completing "The Death of the American Dream." Penelope's web had become the bow of Ulysses, an almost impossible task. A new element had entered Thompson's writing process, which broadened his perspective on editors and editing. Being the first article he published in *Rolling Stone*, "The Battle of Aspen" represents the first time he worked with its editor, Jann Wenner, who understood how to deal with Thompson.

Born in New York, Wenner came to California to attend the University of California at Berkeley, where he was active in the Free Speech Movement. Ralph J. Gleason, jazz critic for the *San Francisco Chronicle* and a contributor to *Ramparts*, was Wenner's mentor, and he helped him obtain a position with the monthly magazine's weekly spin-off, *Sunday Ramparts*. Both Gleason and Wenner left *Ramparts* in 1967 and founded *Rolling Stone*.

The success of *Hell's Angels* prompted Wenner to send Thompson an open invitation to contribute to *Rolling Stone*. Initially, Thompson had neither the time nor the desire to write for the magazine. The publication of "The Battle of Aspen" marked the start of their working relationship. Wenner agreed to publish "Strange Rumblings in Aztlan," an account of the murder of *Los Angeles Times* reporter Ruben Salazar, which Thompson wrote on behalf of his friend Oscar Acosta. While working on "Strange Rumblings," he amused himself by drafting the first part of *Fear and Loathing in Las Vegas*. He showed it to Wenner, who recognized its genius, agreed to publish it in *Rolling Stone*, but urged Thompson to finish "Strange Rumblings" first, which he did.

How did Thompson get the idea for *Fear and Loathing in Las Vegas*? Having taken three years to write "The Death of the American Dream" with no luck, he suddenly had an original, and quite brilliant, idea. The road trip to Las Vegas to cover the Mint 400, which he took with Acosta—the model for Dr. Gonzo in the book—provided one inspiration. Las Vegas, their destination, was so weird in itself that it provided another. Thompson's work on "The Death of the American Dream" also affected the new manuscript, a release valve letting him vent his frustration with the never-ending project.

Perhaps most important to *Fear and Loathing in Las Vegas* are the narrative possibilities that "The Kentucky Derby Is Decadent and Depraved" had created. Running with "gonzo journalism," Thompson applied it more forcefully in the new work. When he wrote it, he was still planning to finish the American Dream book, so he hoped to keep them separate. He wanted "The Death of the American Dream" to remain a serious work of journalism; *Fear and Loathing* would be pure gonzo. To distinguish the two he wrote *Fear and Loathing* in the persona of Raoul Duke.

Whereas Thompson had experimented using Duke, a gonzo journalist, as the narrator with himself, a serious journalist, as a sidekick, he removed himself as sidekick in favor of Dr. Gonzo, his three-hundred-pound Samoan attorney. Making the sidekick a man of color, Thompson incorporated another long-standing motif in American culture, which includes such memorable pairs as Natty Bumppo and Chingachgook, Ishmael and Queequeg, Huck and Jim, and Jonny Quest and Hadji. Like his predecessors, Dr. Gonzo dispenses words of wisdom, although his advice is ironic and usually involves some form of drug-fueled craziness. Dr. Gonzo's decadence matches Raoul Duke's. In other words, Thompson eliminated the straight man from the equation, making the sidekick as outrageous as the protagonist. The pharmacological obsession they share is clear from the opening sentence, one of the great opening sentences in American literature: "We were somewhere around Barstow on the edge of the desert when the drugs began to take hold."[36]

Thompson's full title, *Fear and Loathing in Las Vegas: A Savage Journey to the Heart of the American Dream*, echoes "Written with a Pencil," a Robert Burns poem about an excursion through the Scottish Highlands: "O'er many a winding dale and painful steep, / The abode of covey'd grouse and timid sheep, / My savage journey, curious, I pursue."[37] Whereas the unthreatening animals in Burns's poem reinforce the rugged, yet idyllic terrain, the predatory animals Duke sees are drug-induced hallucinations reflecting his paranoia: alligators, iguanas, Gila monsters, and various other walking or creeping or slithering reptiles. Burns's savage journey takes the speaker of the poem through a natural landscape before human hands reshaped it. Thompson's savage journey takes Raoul Duke to Las Vegas, a city whose development has totally effaced the natural landscape. Entropy is boss, and the city—a microcosm of the world—spirals into chaos.

Fear and Loathing in Las Vegas begins where *Hell's Angels* ends. Thompson reused the epigraph from the last chapter of the earlier book as the epigraph for the new one: "He who makes a beast of himself gets rid of the pain of being a man." Samuel Johnson said these words, but Thompson almost surely took them from the first chapter of Allen Tate's collection of essays, *The*

Man of Letters in the Modern World. Thompson had this quotation hanging above his mantelpiece on Parnassus Avenue.[38]

Thematically, the work also picks up where *Hell's Angels* had left off: Thompson has returned to the edge. Raoul Duke and Dr. Gonzo are physically on the edge of the desert, but they consume enough drugs to take them to another edge, the edge between straight and high, in and out of control, reason and madness. Starting on the edge, the book reinforces the American fascination with frontiers, boundaries, and other liminal spaces.[39]

As the author of a psychological study of aberrant behavior, Thompson follows in Poe's footsteps. Late in the work Thompson alludes to "The Murders in the Rue Morgue," having Raoul Duke contact a man about buying a huge pet ape. A different Poe story more deeply influenced Thompson. "The Imp of the Perverse" conveys the innate human impulse to commit acts motivated by self-destruction. He summarized this short story in one letter to Steadman, who could tell how much the tale affected him. The behavior of Raoul Duke and Dr. Gonzo seems motivated by the impulse Poe identified. Manifesting such impulsive perversity, these two characters, according to Declan Lynch, give *Fear and Loathing in Las Vegas* its universal appeal. Writing in 2005, Lynch observed, "A hundred years from now, when everyone has forgotten about LSD, *Fear and Loathing* will yet capture some ungovernable streak in the human spirit, the urge to run amok."[40]

In part 1 Raoul Duke and Dr. Gonzo drive around in a car they call the "Great Red Shark," a Chevrolet Impala convertible. Although the Chevrolet is an ideal vehicle for seeking the American Dream, the object of their quest may have already become a washed-up concept. The year *Fear and Loathing* appeared in *Rolling Stone* Don McLean drove his Chevy to the levee, but the levee was dry. Choosing a Chevy as his pursuit vehicle, Thompson had in mind the automobile company's successful advertising jingle, "See the USA in your Chevrolet." For two decades television commercials had encouraged viewers to travel the nation in their Chevrolets. The journey of Raoul Duke and Dr. Gonzo parodies the modern American family vacation.

Fear and Loathing in Las Vegas has ramifications beyond the boundaries of the United States. Canadian journalist Patrick Hynan associated Raoul Duke's search for the American Dream with other great adventures in literature: Odysseus sailing home to Ithaca after the Trojan War, Theseus threading his way through the labyrinth to slay the Minotaur, Dante descending into the Inferno, and Don Quixote tilting at windmills. Homer, Plutarch, Dante, Cervantes: placing Thompson in such heady company, Hynan reinforced the mythological significance of Raoul Duke's quest. Hynan makes these literary comparisons briefly, almost in passing. His article is a seedbed for future critical interpretation.⁴¹

In part 2 Thompson's intrepid heroes return to Las Vegas to attend an institute concerning narcotics and dangerous drugs sponsored by the National District Attorneys Association. Duke trades the rented Chevrolet for another convertible, a white Cadillac Coup de Ville, which he dubs the "White Whale." Seated in the White Whale, Duke puts himself Jonah-like in the belly of the beast. An obvious reference to *Moby-Dick*, the White Whale is not the book's only Melville reference.

Thompson's nod to *Moby-Dick* reflects the times. Melville is a postmodern cult figure. Rust Hills placed what he called the "Beat Saints" in the Cool World: Henry Miller, Edward Dahlberg, and William Burroughs. Had Hills not restricted himself to living writers, he could have included Melville among the Beat Saints. Hills noted that Grove Press published the leading postmodernist authors in world literature, but Grove's first imprint was a reissue of *The Confidence-Man*. Melville launched Grove Press, and his influence shows in much postmodern literature. Kerouac said *The Confidence-Man* was the best book to read while high. Thompson's allusion to *Moby-Dick* follows Kesey's playful reference in *One Flew over the Cuckoo's Nest*. Decorated with white whales, Randle McMurphy's undershorts were a gift from an Oregon State English major. He tells Chief, "She gave them to me because she said I was a symbol."⁴²

The title of chapter 8 forms another Melville reference, as it repeats his familiar sentence from "Hawthorne and His Mosses": "Genius 'Round the World Stands Hand in Hand, and One Shock of Recognition Runs the Whole Circle 'Round." The use of a literary quotation as a chapter title seems unusual, but it was not unprecedented. In his great autobiography, *Because I Was Flesh*, Dahlberg uses literary quotations for all his chapter titles.

Oddly, Thompson attributes the quotation to popular television host Art Linkletter. The deliberate misattribution is ironic. The chapter celebrates drug use; Linkletter was the nation's foremost antidrug advocate. His advocacy took him to hearings in the US House of Representatives, where Joseph Nellis, special counsel for the Select Committee on Crime, questioned him about many aspects of drug culture, including subliminal messages in recorded music. Responding to Nellis, Linkletter said the darndest things, wildly estimating that half of all current rock-and-roll albums send "a constant secret message to the whole teenage world to drop out, to turn on, to groove with chemicals."⁴³

Thompson told an interviewer that his attribution to Linkletter was a joke: "If I had a wreck on my motorcycle, with a head full of acid, maybe I would have blamed it on [Timothy] Leary. But it would have been a joke, like when I attributed Melville's quotation 'Genius round the world stands hand in hand, and one shock of recognition runs the whole circle round' to Art Linkletter."[44] To understand Thompson's explanation, some further background is necessary. Linkletter had become an antidrug advocate because his daughter Diane, an LSD noviciate, committed suicide. Linkletter blamed her death on the people who manufactured and sold LSD, which Thompson found absurd.

In other words, Thompson's twisted joke stems from Diane Linkletter's tragic death. American writers have often used dark humor to convey personal tragedy. Captain John Smith's account of the Starving Time reinforces gonzo humor's colonial Virginia roots. One colonist was so hungry he murdered his wife; powdered her, that is, sprinkled her with salt as a preservative; and then ate her. Smith quipped, "Whether she was better roasted, boyled or carbanado'd, I know not, but of such a dish as powdered wife I never heard of."[45]

San Francisco's psychedelic drug culture forms the general subject of chapter 8. The shock of recognition pertains to the people who were into that scene in the mid-sixties. They felt a sense of belonging at the time, which carried over once the moment passed. The shock of recognition still represented a shared kinship, a feeling of having belonged to a special moment in American cultural history.

Chapter 8, which differs in tone from the rest of the book, forms the high white note of *Fear and Loathing in Las Vegas*. Those who stood hand in hand and experienced the thrilling possibilities of the moment could feel a "sense of inevitable victory over the forces of Old and Evil." The chapter's closing paragraph is beautiful in its melancholy: "So now, less than five years later, you can go up on a steep hill in Las Vegas and look West, and with the right kind of eyes you can almost *see* the high-water mark—that place where the wave finally broke and rolled back."[46]

The first part of *Fear and Loathing in Las Vegas* appeared in *Rolling Stone* on November 11, 1971, the second two weeks later. Thompson sent both parts to Cardoso, who had left journalism and moved to the Canary Islands, where he co-owned The Half Note, a Las Palmas jazz club. Given Cardoso's career change, Thompson dubbed him "the retired Dean of Gonzo Journalism." Upon reading *Fear and Loathing in Las Vegas*, Cardoso called it a "most wonderful, thigh-slapping breakthrough, deeper, darker, and wider than all that went before."[47]

Random House released the book version of *Fear and Loathing in Las Vegas* in June 1972 to great fanfare. Thompson was never comfortable with the pomp that went with publicity. The following anecdote comes from Kesey by way of Krassner, but it sounds like pure Thompson. Random House hosted a launch party for the book at a New York hotel penthouse, but when it started at nine that evening Thompson was nowhere in sight. An hour later there was still no sign of him. When he arrived about eleven, he saw everyone sipping Chardonnay and nibbling brie. Without a word he walked through the penthouse, entered a bedroom, closed the door, and locked it. A half an hour later he emerged from the bedroom, silently walked back through the penthouse, and left. No one could understand what he had been doing in the bedroom, but minutes later, room service arrived with two hundred ham sandwiches and two hundred bottles of Heineken.[48]

Fear and Loathing in Las Vegas received fewer reviews than *Hell's Angels*, but the ones it did receive were enthusiastic. *Women's Wear Daily* said, "It sizzles, it snaps, it dazzles. It is one whoosh of a book." The *San Francisco Examiner* linked it with the counterculture's how-to guide to modern living, Abbie Hoffman's *Steal This Book*. In the United Kingdom the paperback edition of *Fear and Loathing in Las Vegas* rose to number three on *Bookseller's* monthly bestsellers' list.[49] According to Thompson's Two-Book Theory of Literary Greatness, his second book established his place in American literary history, but no literary theory is necessary to identify its significance. By any standard *Fear and Loathing in Las Vegas* is a masterpiece of American humor.

CHAPTER 6

Campaign Trailblazer

When Paul Krassner invited Thompson to contribute to *The Realist*, he quickly discovered Thompson's irresponsibility, his contempt for deadlines, and his increasingly bellicose attitude toward editors, whom he enjoyed manipulating to gratify his ego. Even after learning about Thompson's self-centered idiosyncrasies, Krassner tolerated them for the sake of presenting his literary talent—with no luck. Thompson accepted his invitation but never wrote the promised article.[1]

Jann Wenner faced a similar, though more formidable problem. Now that Thompson had two excellent books under his belt, Wenner felt that, to apply Al Romm's words, he had earned the right to be flaky. Recruiting Thompson to contribute to *Rolling Stone*, Wenner set a higher goal than Krassner. He hoped to use the gonzo style to establish his magazine's tone. But how could he harness Thompson's literary ability, overcome his immaturity, and turn him into a productive writer?

His solution was ingenious. Wenner gave Thompson a title—national affairs correspondent—paid him a salary, and assigned him to cover the 1972 presidential campaign. The position would require him to leave Owl Farm and move to Washington for the year, but he agreed. The Thompsons left Woody Creek for Rock Creek, settling into a townhouse near the park, where they reestablished their daily routines. Wenner assigned *Rolling Stone* staffer Timothy Crouse to supervise. Crouse often visited the Thompsons' Washington home, where he saw Sandy bring Hunter his late afternoon breakfast: "It was rather like Phileas Fogg being served by Passepartout."[2] Wenner also gave Thompson a mojo machine, which would let him wait until the last moment to submit copy.

Filing a regular column throughout the campaign, Thompson himself faced a challenge, not the challenge of meeting deadlines every two weeks, which was hard enough for him (even as newspaper reporters faced daily deadlines), but the challenge of continuing to develop gonzo journalism while writing a regular column. Thompson had to invent the far-fetched and fanciful episodes his readers expected from him while presenting insightful commentary about candidates and issues. Earlier Thompson had opposed Silberman's plan to include *Fear and Loathing in Las Vegas* as part of "The Death of the American Dream," afraid his uproarious fiction would undermine the book's serious journalism and make him look like a clown.

Thompson now confronted a similar situation. Readers of *Rolling Stone* who enjoyed *Fear and Loathing in Las Vegas* might be put off by too much political discussion; those looking for political analysis might have trouble taking the humor-laden columns seriously. After reading Thompson's reports through much of the campaign, one commentator called him the "Lost in Space journalist": a derogatory epithet suggesting that his flights of fancy obscured his political insight.[3]

Capitalizing on *Fear and Loathing in Las Vegas*, Wenner used the phrase "Fear and Loathing" to title Thompson's reports about the presidential campaign in *Rolling Stone*. Once the election was over in November and Nixon reelected, Wenner had Thompson assemble his columns into a collection. Straight Arrow, the book-publishing arm of *Rolling Stone*, released the collection as *Fear and Loathing on the Campaign Trail '72*, which appeared in 1973. Incorporating the election year as part of the title, Wenner had his eyes on a franchise, hoping for a similar book from Thompson every four years. With the familiar title and the characteristic gonzo prose, Wenner established continuity between *Fear and Loathing in Las Vegas* and *Fear and Loathing on the Campaign Trail*, giving Thompson's literary output the quality of a manufactured product. People could now speak in the plural about his *Fear and Loathing* books.

Its unique prose style is what separates *Fear and Loathing on the Campaign Trail* from other campaign narratives. Before Thompson came along, journalists struck a pose of objectivity, seeing themselves as unbiased. Thompson challenged the concept of objective journalism. In his January chapter he observes, "The only thing I ever saw that came close to Objective Journalism was a close-circuit TV setup that watched shoplifters in the General Store at Woody Creek, Colorado." He adds a few more exceptions before busting the myth of objective journalism: "With the possible exception of things like box scores, race results, and stock market tabulations, there is no such thing as Objective Journalism. The phrase itself is a pompous contradiction in terms."⁴

Reviewers greeted *Fear and Loathing on the Campaign Trail* enthusiastically. Steven d'Arazien, who had served on Democratic candidate George McGovern's staff in New Jersey during the presidential race, reviewed the book for *The Nation*, finding it "the most exciting book written about the 1972 campaign and one of the best about American politics of the last decade." He predicted its future status as "a classic in the genre."⁵

Half a century later d'Arazien's prediction has come true. Topical humor often dates quickly, but *Fear and Loathing on the Campaign Trail* remains quite readable. To appreciate the work as literature, recall Thompson's comment about *The Pump House Gang*, which he valued less as a sustained effort and more for its peaks. *Fear and Loathing on the Campaign Trail* is structured like a saw blade.

Thompson's peaks take many forms. Kurt Vonnegut, who reviewed *Fear and Loathing on the Campaign Trail* for *Harper's*, found it filled with "exciting, moving collages of carefully selected junk."⁶ Vonnegut's observation complements something Thompson told *Women's Wear Daily* during the campaign. "I'm a writer more than a journalist," he said. "Politics bore me, so I have to go off on weird tangents to make it interesting."⁷ *Fear and Loathing on the Campaign Trail* is a collage of weird tangents. They fall into several broad categories.

The Chance Encounter

Thompson's campaign narrative contains numerous chance encounters that let him make new insights into presidential politics. The most startling encounter occurs when he meets Senator McGovern in the men's room of the Exeter Inn. In this Hotel New Hampshire, McGovern appears "leaning into a urinal and staring straight ahead at the grey marble tiles." William Greider, who covered the 1972 presidential campaign for the *Washington Post* and knew Thompson personally, was nonetheless astonished to read this unprecedented episode in *Fear and Loathing on the Campaign Trail*: "Where else could you read about Thompson's interview with Senator George McGovern at the urinal of a New Hampshire men's room?"⁸

Having asked McGovern—"the Willie Loman of the Left"—why Senator Harold Hughes endorsed Senator Edmund Muskie for president, Thompson presents his reply: "He flinched and quickly zipped his pants up, shaking his head and mumbling something about 'a deal for the vice-presidency.'" Continuing the interview from urinal to sink, Thompson asks why Hughes changed allegiances. While washing his hands, McGovern says, "I guess I shouldn't say this, Hunter, but I honestly don't know. I'm surprised, we're *all* surprised."[9]

Other chance encounters occur throughout the book. The first chapter, "December 1971," describes Thompson's drive from Colorado to Washington. The experience recalls Kerouac's *On the Road*, but it also resembles a more recent journalistic effort with the same title. In 1967 Charles Kuralt had begun "On the Road," a long-running segment for CBS News that took him back and forth across the continent, interviewing whomever he met.

Hunter Thompson is the counterculture's Charles Kuralt. In one early episode he meets two long-haired freaky people in the middle of Pennsylvania: "Here I was all alone on the Pennsylvania Turnpike on a fast downhill grade—running easily, for a change—when suddenly out of the darkness in a corner of my right eye I glimpsed what appeared to be a white gorilla running toward the road." Unsure what the white gorilla could be, he stops to check it out, creating a dark, yet funny sense of foreboding: "My instincts were purely humanitarian—but what about that Thing I was going back to look for? You read about these people in the *Reader's Digest*: blood-crazy dope fiends who crouch beside the highway and prey on innocent travelers."[10]

The white gorilla turns out to be a hippie named Jerry. Unable to get anyone to stop, he and his friend Lester had taken drastic measures, using a white blanket to reflect the passing headlights and attract a kindly motorist. Unsure what to expect, Thompson walks to their car carrying his .357 magnum. Relating the episode, he outdoes the scare stories in *Reader's Digest*, conveying the danger Jerry and Lester face by asking for help from a stranger: "For all they knew I was half-mad on PCP and eager to fill my empty Wild Turkey jug with enough fresh blood to make the last leg of the trip into Washington and apply for White House credentials . . . nothing like a big hit of red corpuscles to give a man the right lift for a rush into politics."[11]

A fine example of gonzo humor, the Jerry-and-Lester episode is hardly gratuitous. These two freaks perform an important narrative function: they say what the magazine's readers are thinking. Once Jerry and Lester change their flat with Thompson's help, the three stop at Breezewood to talk. When Thompson says he is moving to Washington to cover the presidential campaign for *Rolling Stone*, Jerry exclaims, "That's weird! The Stone is into politics?" Lester asks, "Why would *anybody* want to get hung up in a pile of shit like Politics?"[12] Introducing these two realistic characters, Thompson welcomes readers to the world of presidential politics.

Driving to New Hampshire for its primary, Thompson has another chance encounter when he picks up a nameless female hitchhiker six months out of

Boston University. With a degree in journalism, the young woman might seem like an ideal staffer for a presidential campaign, but she sees politics as "some kind of game played by old people, like bridge." Thompson sees her as part of "a whole subculture of frightened illiterates with no faith in anything." She is hitchhiking to New Hampshire to join a commune.[13]

With these two chance encounters Thompson makes a case for political involvement. Speaking about Jerry, Lester, and the anonymous Boston hitchhiker, one literary critic observed, "These minor figures are supposed to be Everyhead, or the typical *Rolling Stone* reader. Bringing them into his tales is a measure of how hard Thompson has been trying."[14] Presenting these characters, Thompson shows a keen awareness of his readers, something he would forget in his later and less effective writings.

The Hoax

The put-on had already become a defining component of gonzo journalism. In the opening scene of "The Kentucky Derby Is Decadent and Depraved," Thompson meets a Texan named Jimbo and convinces him that Black Panthers and other left-wing protesters would invade the Derby. Believing what Thompson says, Jimbo grows indignant that protesters would sully such a fine Southern tradition. *Fear and Loathing in Las Vegas* contains a parallel episode. In a hotel bar Raoul Duke and Dr. Gonzo meet a district attorney from small-town Georgia. They convince him that violent drug addicts are invading the hidden corners of rural America.

In a put-on in *Fear and Loathing on the Campaign Trail*, Thompson accidentally finds himself in a roomful of Nixon Youth at the Republican National Convention. He tells them NBC anchor John Chancellor had put acid in his drink during the Democratic National Convention. With Jimboesque gullibility they take what he says at face value and ask what kind of acid, expecting him to say something like "hydrochloric" or "sulfuric." When Thompson says "Sunshine" acid, they have no idea what he means. The Nixon Youth are so square they do not know their acid from a hole in the ground. It takes a series of questions before they realize that, golly, Thompson is talking about LSD.[15]

The hoax is closely related to the put-on. Whereas the put-on is enacted within the text between the narrator-journalist and unwitting dupes, the hoax takes place between the narrator-journalist and the readers, who become dupes as they believe what they read. Thompson had many predecessors who excelled at hoaxes. Warren Hinckle, for one, perpetrated a hoax on the back cover of *Scanlan's*. Reprinting a Lufthansa advertisement, Hinckle retained its format and advertising copy but substituted two illustrations. One displays uniformed Nazis with arms outstretched in the Sieg-Heil salute; the other is a pornographic image of Nazi violence against women.[16]

Hoaxes go much further back than Hinckle's Lufthansa job. Thompson continues an American literary tradition that stretches back to Benjamin Franklin. "The Speech of Miss Polly Baker," Franklin's most renowned hoax, presents the courtroom address of a prostitute who has given birth to five children out of wedlock but speaks so eloquently that the presiding judge marries her. Poe wrote several hoaxes. His most accomplished one is "The Balloon Hoax," which tells the story of a transatlantic balloon flight. What makes this hoax so good is that every detail in it was within the realm of possibility. No one had yet to cross the Atlantic in a balloon, but it was technically feasible in Poe's day.

Besides situating *Fear and Loathing on the Campaign Trail* within a major tradition of American literature, Thompson establishes the hoax as another defining feature of gonzo journalism. The two most memorable hoaxes in the book concern Senator Muskie, who was the front-runner at the start of the 1972 presidential campaign and thus a ripe target for satiric attack.

Thompson asserts that Muskie was taking Ibogaine to cope with his campaign's daily pressures. A derivative of the root bark of the African iboga tree, *Tabernanthe iboga*, Ibogaine is a psychoactive drug with a twofold effect on its users, initially putting them in a visionary state, which transitions into an introspective phase, making them feel as if they are dreaming, but dreaming with complete consciousness and awareness. Thompson sees Muskie's bizarre behavior as symptomatic of Ibogaine abuse: "I immediately recognized The Ibogaine Effect—from Muskie's tearful breakdown on the flatbed truck in New Hampshire, the delusions and altered thinking that characterized his campaign in Florida, and finally the condition of 'total rage' that gripped him in Wisconsin." Thompson continues, "There was no doubt about it. The Man from Maine had turned to massive doses of Ibogaine as a last resort."[17]

Muskie's supposed abuse of Ibogaine seems the only way to explain his bizarre behavior on the caboose platform at the Miami train station: "It is entirely conceivable—given the known effects of Ibogaine—that Muskie's brain was almost paralyzed by hallucinations at the time; that he looked out at that crowd and saw gila monsters instead of people, and that his mind snapped completely when he felt something large and apparently vicious clawing at his legs."[18]

The story of Muskie's Ibogaine dependence, although entertaining, was ineffective as a hoax. It was too outrageous to fool many readers. A parallel story, one that also culminates in Miami at the end of Muskie's whistlestop tour of Florida, fooled almost everyone. As the story goes, Thompson loans his press credentials to a hazy figure named Peter Sheridan, who rides the Muskie train to Miami, getting drunk, attacking the cheerleading Muskie-teers, and making a nuisance of himself. Once the train reaches Miami, its final stop, Sheridan jumps off but stands near the caboose platform, where he heckles Muskie and grabs at his pants legs.

Thompson swears the story is the God's honest truth, and the hoax worked. Readers believed him then, and they believe him now. Histories of the 1972 presidential campaign often repeat Thompson's story of Peter Sheridan. He refers unbelievers to *Women's Wear Daily* to confirm all the salient details. Thompson had in mind Kandy Stroud's report in the February 22, 1972 issue. Far from confirming what Thompson says in *Fear and Loathing on the Campaign Trail*, Stroud puts the lie to his story:

> In Miami, where the mob was less than wildly enthusiastic, Washington-based Peter Sheridan, a friend of Muskie's number two campaign man, Richie Evans, was allowed to stand below the platform and heckle Muskie.
>
> And that was the best media gimmick of the trip. It gave the candidate the opportunity to come across just like he did in 1968—cool, calm, and collected under pressure. Muskie just reached out his preacher-like hands, looked at Sheridan with those clear honest blue eyes and said, "Please, I'll let you make your points if you let me make mine."
>
> And the crowd shouted, "We want Muskie."[19]

Although Thompson's inclusion of characters like Jerry and Lester shows him ingratiating himself with his readers, this hoax laughs at the readers. He tells them to read Stroud's report in *Women's Wear Daily* for confirmation, but few, if any, did. The hoax worked because Thompson's readers have been too lazy to look up Stroud's article. Even as he perpetrates a hoax, Thompson gives his readers the tools to discover the truth, which they have willfully neglected.

The Fantasy Piece

Like its hoaxes, the fantasy pieces in *Fear and Loathing on the Campaign Trail* are fictional episodes set within the larger, ostensibly truthful work. They differ in two key ways: intent and length. Seeking to dupe readers, hoaxes are generally longer than fantasy pieces. To enhance their believability hoaxes require considerable narrative development. Since fantasy pieces make no attempt to dupe the reader, they need not be developed as fully. Thompson typically presents his fantasy pieces in italics to distinguish them from the main text.

One fantasy piece concerns Larry O'Brien. The chair of the National Democratic Party in 1972, O'Brien had encountered Thompson years earlier. Thompson wrote a jokey letter to President Johnson asking to be appointed governor of American Samoa. O'Brien, then working for the Johnson administration, responded seriously and promised to consider Thompson's application. The February chapter of *Fear and Loathing on the Campaign Trail* contains a "Message to O'Brien" in which Thompson claims to have purchased a whole wardrobe of white sharkskin suits to wear as governor of American Samoa. He asserts that O'Brien's inability to secure the governorship for him does not bode well for his role as Democratic chair.

"Message to O'Brien" illustrates how personal details from Thompson's life entered gonzo journalism. Once O'Brien took his humorous letter seriously, Thompson began fantasizing about the governorship of American Samoa. This personal fantasy enters the story of the 1972 presidential campaign because O'Brien had emerged as a major figure in the Democratic Party. O'Brien's rising political importance gave his earlier letter renewed significance, letting Thompson use it, though in a distorted manner, to comment on O'Brien's way of conducting politics. Thompson's personal fantasy becomes a political reality.

Frank Mankiewicz, McGovern's campaign director, is often the butt of Thompson's humor in *Fear and Loathing on the Campaign Trail*. After one perceived slight, Thompson imagines thugs attacking Mankiewicz in an alley near the US Capitol and slicing off both his big toes, a loss making it difficult for him to maintain his balance. Imagining Mankiewicz sans big toes, Thompson launches another fantasy piece that depicts him trying to fulfill his role as campaign director.

Upon hearing a rumor that the Texas delegation to the Democratic National Convention was about to sell out to a coalition between Hubert Humphrey and George Wallace, Mankiewicz lunges from his cubicle, bouncing off his doorjamb and then grabbing the nearby Coke machine to steady himself. He then lunges into an underling's office and asks for dirt on the Texas delegates. He requests a breakdown of their bad debts and deviant sex lives. Trying to catch his breath, Mankiewicz gasps for air before lunging back down the hall to his cubicle. After these specific details, Thompson generalizes, "It is very hard to walk straight with the Big Toes gone; the effect is sort of like taking the keel off a sailboat—it becomes impossibly top-heavy, wallowing crazily in the swells, needing outriggers to hold it upright . . . and the only way a man can walk straight with no Big Toes is to use a very complex tripod mechanism, five or six retractable aluminum rods strapped to each arm, moving around like a spider instead of a person."[20] This bizarre passage, like many in *Fear and Loathing on the Campaign Trail*, has the quality of the Fool's utterances in *King Lear*. Thompson, like Lear's Fool, is "all licensed," that is, he seems to have a privileged status that lets him get away with saying things other reporters dare not say, things that may seem nonsensical on the surface but actually cut to the quick.

It was during the 1972 presidential campaign that the term "opposition research" was coined. Oppo research, as it is now called, involves finding dirt to discredit a political opponent. Portraying Mankiewicz in the process of doing opposition research, Thompson captures a strategy of presidential politics in its genesis. His portrayal of a big-toe-less Mankiewicz searching for dirt on the Texas delegates illustrates how grotesque oppo research is. Fantasizing about Mankiewicz, who must lunge hither and thither before he gets fitted with retractable aluminum rods, Thompson gives readers a memorable image revealing the ugliness of presidential politics.

The Flashback

Thompson's use of flashbacks reflects the influence of film on his writing, an influence that has yet to be fully gauged. Although the term was not coined until the motion picture era, the flashback is as old as *The Iliad*. As he developed gonzo journalism, the flashback became another useful weapon in Thompson's arsenal. The flashbacks in *Fear and Loathing on the Campaign Trail* take two basic forms. Sometimes Thompson flashes back to moments in his life that offer analogies to illustrate new situations. Other times he flashes back to earlier moments during the 1972 campaign, moments he had not elaborated previously but have gathered significance in retrospect.

To illustrate Muskie's appearance in Florida, Thompson flashes back to the Floyd Patterson-Sonny Liston heavyweight championship bout in Las Vegas. Arriving in Florida, Muskie resembles Patterson, whose face belied a "nervous sense of impending doom." Thompson turns his comparison into a personal anecdote. Before the fight begins, he purchases two beers to avoid hassling with vendors during the bout. As Thompson drains one beer, Patterson turns to wax the first time Liston hits him. With a minute to go in the opening round Liston hits him again, and Patterson goes down for the count. The fight is over before Thompson can touch his second beer. The picture of Patterson's defeat gives readers an evocative illustration of Muskie's plight.[21]

Visiting New York for its presidential primary, Thompson flashes back to an earlier trip to the city, which he commemorates with a personal anecdote. As the story goes, Thompson brings to Random House a cardboard box containing his pet snake—a six-foot long eastern indigo, *Drymarchon couperi*—along with a live mouse, *Mus musculus*, as its evening meal. Thompson leaves the box there overnight. Sensing doom, the mouse chews a hole in the box and escapes, and the snake comes slithering after. When the night watchman,

Homo noctus, sees the creature, he uses the metal extension from a vacuum cleaner as a club to make mincemeat out of that snake.

The snake box and the Random House building together form a set of nesting boxes, microcosm and macrocosm. The night watchman is to the snake what the snake is to the mouse. Thompson does not draw any conclusions from this episode, but its presence in a presidential campaign narrative implies an even larger nesting box holding both: Nixon's America. Richard Nixon, *Praeses malus*, is the snake that seeks to destroy the mouse, the American citizen.

The nature of Thompson's campaign narrative gives it a basic chronological order, an organizational scheme he generally disliked. Remember how he balked when Gerald Walker insisted he rearrange his piece on Nevada prisons in chronological order. Flashbacks gave Thompson a way to jazz up his organization, letting him occasionally break from chronology to recall the past.

While reporting from New Hampshire, Thompson had encountered McGovern at a smorgasbord table, but the incident had seemed so minor he did not bother to report it, especially because McGovern was not a major candidate then. Once he emerged as the Democratic front-runner, the earlier episode acquired new significance, so Thompson reported it in flashback.

As he did with the Floyd Patterson flashback, Thompson records the minutiae of the episode in fascinating detail: "The bar was closed, but one of McGovern's advance men had arranged a sort of beer/booze and sandwich meat smorgasbord for the press in a lounge just off the lobby . . . so all six of us climbed out of the bus, which was actually an old three-seater airport limousine, and I went inside to kill time."[22]

At the smorgasbord Thompson bumps into "somebody in a tan gabardine suit who is quietly loading his plate with carrots and salami." Without looking at one another, both mumble apologies. Thompson continues: "The only noise in the room was coming from the *LA Times* corner. Everybody else was either reading or eating, or both. The only person in the room not sitting down was the man in the tan suit at the smorgasbord table. He was still fumbling with the food, keeping his back to the room."[23]

Thompson suddenly realizes the man in gabardine is McGovern. The realization astonishes him: "Where was his entourage? And why hadn't anybody else noticed him? Was he actually *alone*?" Sure enough, McGovern is alone: "There were no aides, no entourage, and nobody else in the room had even noticed his arrival."[24]

Occasionally, Thompson intertwines two flashbacks. Early in *Fear and Loathing on the Campaign Trail*, he flashes back four years to Nixon's campaign tour of New Hampshire, where Thompson spoke privately with him about professional football. Later in *Fear and Loathing on the Campaign Trail*, Thompson recalls Nixon's passion for football, which he hopes to apply to understand his politics. To accomplish this unusual feat, Thomson flashes back to Brazil.

The South American flashback is an invented episode, but it does show how Thompson could take a slight encounter and develop it into a full, albeit fictional episode. He recalls a Brazilian psychiatrist he supposedly met in the Mato Grosso who taught him the concept of "rhythm logic," a method letting a person align his or her thoughts with another's. There is no evidence that Thompson met such a Brazilian psychiatrist, but in Bolivia he spoke with some people at the American embassy, who told him about "Doctor Brainwaves," a Bolivian con man who claimed he could communicate via brain waves, a technique that enabled him to read the minds of Nikita Khrushchev and Jackie Kennedy. There is no evidence that Thompson met Doctor Brainwaves, either. Instead, he took what he learned from his embassy contacts and turned it into a mock autobiographical episode. The flashback format reinforces its veracity.[25]

Thompson now applies rhythm logic to understand the president: "Since Nixon is a known football addict, I decided to get my head totally into the rhythm of this exhibition game between the Rams and Kansas City before attempting the jump into politics."[26] It sounds like a classic procrastinator's rationalization, but, by the end of the first quarter, Thompson is ready to undertake the task: "By means of intense concentration on *every detail* of the football game, I was able to 'derail' my own inner brain waves and re-pattern them temporarily to the inner brain wave rhythms of a serious football fanatic. The next step was to bring my 'borrowed' rhythms into focus on a subject quite different from football—such as presidential politics."[27] Thompson uses his flashbacks to portray himself as someone who can combine the memories of two wildly different experiences to understand and interpret new situations.

Episodes from the Journalist's Life

In gonzo journalism Thompson, the writer himself, becomes part of the action. Ostensibly a narrative of the 1972 presidential campaign, *Fear and Loathing on the Campaign Trail* also relates a year in the life of Hunter S. Thompson. The book's leading character is neither Muskie nor McGovern nor Nixon; it is Thompson. One reviewer commented, "As a character in his own work, Thompson is bizarre as anyone ever invented by Joseph Heller or Terry Southern."[28]

Several episodes portray the author in the process of writing. At a Florida bungalow he sits at his typewriter as it pours outside: "The sound of rain smacking down on my concrete patio about ten feet away from the typewriter, rain beating down on the surface of the big aqua-lighted pool out there across the lawn . . . rain blowing into the porch and whipping the palm fronds around in the warm night air." The scene resembles something from film noir, Thompson's narrative resembling a first-person narrator's voice-over: "Wind, rain, surf. Palm trees leaning in the wind, hard funk/blues on the radio, a flagon of Wild Turkey on the sideboard." Thompson is a master of sound effects. The rain gets so loud it masks other noises, making them difficult to hear distinctly and thus enhancing their mystery: "Are those footsteps outside? High heels running in the rain?"[29]

To get his story the gonzo journalist endures all sorts of weather. In Milwaukee Thompson must negotiate State Street after a spring snowstorm, which has left the pavement icy. His rental car, a purple Mustang, is "one of those Detroit classics apparently assembled by junkies to teach the rest of us a lesson." The accelerator gives him the most trouble: "At some stoplights the car would move out normally, but at others it would try to stall, seeming to want more gas—and then suddenly leap ahead like a mule gone amok from a bee sting." Sometimes, the Mustang would "come thundering off the line at top speed with no traction at all and the rear end fishtailing all over the street about halfway to the next corner."[30]

Thompson's destination is the Milwaukee Inn, McGovern's local headquarters. Perhaps the personal story of his drive down State Street is unnecessary to illuminate the bigger story—McGovern's surprise win in the Wisconsin primary—but it adds to the drama of the moment, stressing the role of the reporter, whose presence is essential to the democratic process. The reporter is the one who informs the public who won the primary and why. Sometimes, as Thompson implies, a vital report depends on the slightest detail, such as the tenuous grip of a muscle car on an icy street.

In his story of the 1972 presidential campaign Thompson's rented Mustang is more than merely a reporter's mode of transportation. It illustrates current problems the nation faces. The faulty accelerator reflects the quality-control issues that plagued American manufacturing that decade. It also indicates the automakers' emphasis on image over practicality. During the early seventies automobile plants were turning out speedy, mean-looking vehicles that ignored real-life road conditions. A rear-wheel-drive muscle car is about the worst possible vehicle for negotiating the ice-covered streets of a Milwaukee winter.

The Tape-Recorded Conversation

In *Fear and Loathing in Las Vegas* Thompson makes memorable use of a tape recorder, thus turning it into another component of gonzo journalism. Late one night Raoul Duke and Dr. Gonzo enter a Las Vegas café to ask the waitress and grill cook what they know about the American Dream. Assuming it was the name of a defunct local nightclub, they speculate where it could have been. The recorded conversation captures a poignant moment in the story, showing how elusive and uncertain the search for the American Dream could be.

Thompson returns to the motif of the tape-recorded conversation in *Fear and Loathing on the Campaign Trail*. One chapter presents a discussion of the backroom machinations at the Democratic National Convention. Thompson had recorded a lengthy conversation between two of McGovern's key strategists, who manipulated parliamentary procedure and the convention's intricate rules of order to prevent opponents from using procedure to undermine McGovern's victory. His strategists applied the technicalities to their advantage, thus assuring McGovern's success. Thompson recognized that, given the technical nature of the proceedings, the tape-recorded conversation would be difficult to paraphrase, so he presented a transcription instead.

Once Nixon was reelected, Thompson lost all motivation to continue reporting. The story was over. Wenner still wanted one large final article summarizing the campaign. He put Thompson up at San Francisco's Seal Rock Inn, brought him a tape recorder, and had him dictate his story. Wenner got his article, but he may have been better off following Thompson's impulse and leaving the last chapter unwritten. The tape recording reads like what it is: a determined editor forcing his star author to fulfill his responsibility.

After the November 1972 election but before the book version of *Fear and Loathing on the Campaign Trail*, McGraw-Hill released Jack Kerouac's *Visions of Cody*, a posthumous work that had been partly published years earlier. The completed work contains a 128-page transcription of a tape-recorded conversation between Kerouac and Neal Cassady. Kerouac changed their names to Jack Duluoz and Cody Pomeroy, but otherwise the book presents their conversation as it took place. Much as Kerouac saw tape-recording as an extension of his spontaneous prose, Thompson saw tape-recording as an extension of gonzo journalism. Reading the monotonous transcription in *Visions of Cody*, Anatole Broyard said that Kerouac confused literature and reality.[31] Broyard's criticism suits Thompson's Seal Rock Inn soliloquy.

The tape-recording may not be an essential component of gonzo journalism, but Thompson often attempted to make his writing style akin to a recording and a close cousin to Kerouac's spontaneous prose. To do "pure gonzo journalism" the reporter must try to complete the story quickly, no second thoughts, no revisions, no chance to change a single word. Much as he supposedly completed "The Kentucky Derby Is Decadent and Depraved" by ripping pages from his notebook and feeding them into the mojo, he attempts a similar task in *Fear and Loathing on the Campaign Trail*. Thompson introduces his account of the Ohio primary with the following explanation: "What follows, then, is one of the most desperate last-minute hamburger jobs in the history of journalism—including the first known experiment with large-scale Gonzo Journalism—which we accomplished, in this case, by tearing my Ohio primary notebook apart and sending about fifty pages of scribbled notes straight into the typesetter."[32]

The best parts of *Fear and Loathing on the Campaign Trail* are not its tape-recordings or its "pure gonzo" notebook-based sections. The best parts are the chance encounters, hoaxes, fantasy pieces, flashbacks, and episodes from the journalist's life. In other words, the best parts form the tallest peaks, those carefully crafted sections that transcend the historical moment and endure as literature.

CHAPTER 7

Anthologist

Joe Klein vividly remembers 1974, the year he became deputy Washington bureau chief for *Rolling Stone*. Early that summer he met Hunter Thompson, whom he continued to encounter. One night the two enjoyed a marathon conversation about books and authors, culminating in Thompson's surprise assessment of his career. He feared becoming a parody of himself but hesitated to disturb the universe, to depart from the literary style that had made his reputation. Klein asked if he ever considered abandoning his drug-fueled gonzo journalism for "a serious, straight-ahead novel." Of course, Thompson responded before qualifying his response.[1]

"Without that," he said, gesturing toward his satchel filled with various mind-altering substances, "I'd have the brain of a second-rate accountant."

Klein caught Thompson in a rare moment, when he dropped his characteristic tough talk and revealed his weakness: Thompson had a self-esteem problem. Far from liberating his thought, drugs had become a crutch. He never needed them to write well. His excellent South American dispatches prove that. Thompson masked his low self-esteem with defensive braggadocio, but it surfaces in other aspects of his life. Cultivating a passion for firearms was one way he compensated for feelings of inadequacy. Calling himself a doctor was another. In 1970 he had purchased a mail-order doctor of divinity, letting him go by "Dr. Hunter S. Thompson." The title suited his hoaxy nature and jibed with his impulse to create a fictional persona, but it also compensated for his low self-esteem. Tom Wolfe, who had earned his doctorate, never went by "Dr. Wolfe."

Within a one-year period *Rolling Stone* would assign Thompson three major stories, and he would blow each one. The summer of '74 he was staying at the Washington Hilton to follow the Watergate hearings. Thursday night,

August 8, Richard Nixon announced he would resign the presidency at noon on Friday. Thompson promised to meet *Rolling Stone* photographer Annie Leibovitz at the White House Rose Garden to chronicle the event.

Well-positioned in the Rose Garden Friday morning, Leibovitz captured Nixon's departure for posterity. Thompson was nowhere in sight. Instead, he was poolside at the Hilton, watching the event on a battery-powered TV. As Nixon's helicopter lifted off for the final time, Leibovitz took a chilling shot of the presidential guard rolling the red carpet—up, not out. Her photographs were supposed to illustrate Thompson's story, which he never wrote. *Rolling Stone* ran her photographs as the story.[2]

That October, again traveling on *Rolling Stone*'s nickel, Thompson flew to Kinshasa, Zaire, to report the heavyweight prize fight between Muhammad Ali and George Foreman. On the plane he sat next to George Plimpton, marking the start of their friendship. Norman Mailer was in Kinshasa, and so was Bill Cardoso, having left the Canary Islands and the nightclub business and returned to journalism. Ralph Steadman came to Kinshasa to illustrate the story for *Rolling Stone*, but Thompson sold their tickets before the bout. Steadman never saw the fight, and Thompson never wrote the story. As Ali successfully challenged Foreman using his innovative rope-a-dope technique, Thompson was lounging around his hotel pool. Mailer got a book from the experience; Thompson got a tan.

With the fall of Saigon imminent Thompson traveled to Vietnam in April 1975 to cover the story for *Rolling Stone*. In Saigon he met Laura Palmer, who had first come to Vietnam in 1972, the year she graduated from Oberlin College. Beyond a job in Washington one summer during college—"the first girl copyboy at NBC News"—Palmer had no journalism experience, but in 1972 she began reporting from Vietnam for ABC radio and freelancing for *Time* and *Rolling Stone*. Her description of Thompson's personal manner resembles that of practically every woman he ever sweet-talked: "Behind the outlaw mask were the contours of a Southern gentleman, a bit courtly and old-fashioned."[3]

Palmer, at twenty-five, was a seasoned war correspondent; Thompson, now thirty-seven, was the greenhorn. She showed him the ropes and helped him get organized. Other reporters feared his recklessness would get them killed. Happily for them, he did not stay in Vietnam long. The last week of April he left "to get his head together." The day Saigon fell Thompson was in Hong Kong. Palmer fled with other evacuees, scrambling up a helicopter tail ramp just as it was closing before takeoff. She was the one who wrote the story of the fall of Saigon for *Rolling Stone*, not Thompson. Her thrilling, yet contemplative piece was one of only two feature-length, first-person accounts of the evacuation.[4]

Taken together, the reminiscences of both Klein and Palmer show Thompson at a crossroads. He told Klein that a new departure would be a considerable risk and feared he lacked "the gumption to jump the gravy train." Although Thompson had cautioned his fellow high school students against a safe and secure existence, he now hesitated to abandon the security his gonzo reputation had brought him. Like Klein, Palmer thought Thompson should drop gonzo journalism: "He's a fine writer and a terrific reporter until he trips over the persona he's created."[5]

Every author who writes a popular book faces a tough decision going forward. Upon establishing a successful formula, the author can assure continued commercial success by writing more books that follow it. But commercial success rarely means artistic success. Authors grow by experimenting with their work, testing out new themes, concepts, structures, settings, characters, everything. Great authors willingly risk their livelihood for their art.

Thompson's next book reveals the decision he reached. It is not so much the book's title—*The Great Shark Hunt: Strange Tales from a Strange Time*—that reveals his decision, but the series title under which it appears: Gonzo Papers, Vol. 1. Thompson had established his reputation with gonzo journalism, and a gonzo journalist he would remain. All his recently blown assignments scarcely mattered to him because he could keep skating on his reputation. Designating his new book as the first volume of Gonzo Papers, Thompson indicated that he would stay the course into the foreseeable future. He would stick with the style he invented, measuring out his life with coke spoons.

Perhaps no one was more disappointed with Hunter Thompson's refusal to advance his writing than Sandy Thompson. When they met, Hunter convinced her he would be the next great American novelist. Sandy admired his talent and ambition so much that she was willing to sacrifice herself for him, to tolerate his verbal and emotional abuse, to subsume her life within his. The blown assignments opened her eyes. Sandy reflected, "I was living for Hunter and his work—for this great person, this great writer, who was so disciplined—and then when he couldn't write anymore, what was I doing? It was sad to see. I was taking care of a drug addict."[6] She left him in 1978.

Although Thompson never did write the American Dream book, the crafty Jim Silberman knew he could still make money from him. Silberman had left Random House for Simon and Schuster, where he received his own imprint, Summit Books, which issued *The Great Shark Hunt* in 1979. Over a fifteen-year period, 1979–1994, four volumes would appear as Gonzo Papers. All are anthologies, that is, collections of newspaper pieces, magazine articles, or excerpts from finished and unfinished books, but each takes a different approach.

Norman Snider, a Canadian journalist and screenwriter, thought Thompson should have organized *The Great Shark Hunt* chronologically. The coauthor of another excellent doppelgänger tale—David Cronenberg's *Dead Ringers*—Snider was a good writer in his own right, but he failed to recognize the logic underlying *The Great Shark Hunt*. Even as he criticizes the book, Snider was not stingy in his praise of its author: "If whoever edited this collection had had the sense to group the articles chronologically instead of in the present haphazard arrangement, the reader would have been able to follow Thompson's evolution from a competent but ordinary journalist to the Brooding Prince of Fear and Loathing, the diabolic master of Gonzo that he eventually became."[7]

Thompson divided *The Great Shark Hunt* into four parts. Two one-page documents from his time in the Air Force precede part 1. Printed with Air Force letterhead, they resemble official documents, but they are not. Rather, they are items Thompson wrote himself and palmed off as official documents. His passion for literary hoaxes obviously began long before *Fear and Loathing on the Campaign Trail*.

Part 1 emphasizes Thompson's characteristic style, presenting the texts that defined gonzo journalism: "The Kentucky Derby Is Decadent and Depraved," "The Temptations of Jean-Claude Killy," and "Memoirs of a Wretched Weekend in Washington." Thompson also included a selection from *Fear and Loathing in Las Vegas* in part 1, which makes sense, given its status as the single greatest work of gonzo journalism. The selection Thompson chose, however, was the book's least gonzoesque. He reprinted the Linkletter/Melville chapter, which forms the high white note of *Fear and Loathing in Las Vegas*.

Directly after his reprint of that chapter comes "Jacket Copy of *Fear and Loathing in Las Vegas*." This piece never appeared on the jacket; *The Great Shark Hunt* represents its first printing. Snider found it the most interesting item in the volume. Whereas Thompson wrote *Fear and Loathing in Las Vegas* in the persona of Raoul Duke, he wrote "Jacket Copy" in his own voice. It is reminiscent of "The Philosophy of Composition," Poe's tongue-in-cheek explanation of how he wrote "The Raven." Regardless of the book's knee-slapping hilarity, Thompson speaks as a serious journalist to explain how he wrote the work.

Presenting the story of Nixon's 1969 inauguration, the last item in part 1, "Memoirs of a Wretched Weekend," forms a segue to part 2, which is devoted to Nixon's 1968 campaign, George McGovern's 1972 campaign, and Nixon's second term in office. Part 2 has the structure of a Tootsie Pop. Nixon's story is the hard outer shell, McGovern's candidacy the sweet chewy center. The literary heritage of the Nixon pieces stretches back to antiquity. Thompson's gleeful attacks on the perfidious, underhanded, double-dealing Nixon are reminiscent of Juvenal's satirical attacks on the cruel, vindictive Emperor Domitian.[8]

Ending with the end of Nixon's presidency, part 2 offers a mystery: where will Thompson go next? Part 3 begins with "Traveler Hears Mountain Music Where It's Sung." In other words, Thompson goes back in time, back thirteen years. But his time warp goes back even further. Set in Kentucky, this piece also goes back to his childhood, and, by presenting the story of Kentucky's traditional music, it essentially goes back eons. The mountain music sung and played in Kentucky is the same kind of music that has been sung and played for centuries. The placement of the piece stresses the nostalgia that runs through Thompson's work. After the horror of Nixon, he reverts to a simpler time, a time when mountain folk played banjos and slide guitar, sang songs of the heart, and cared not a hoot for cretins like Nixon.

The next six pieces all come from Thompson's time in South America. This cluster begins with "A Footloose American in a Smugglers' Den" and ends with "Chatty Letters During a Journey from Aruba to Rio." Thompson was ambivalent about "Chatty Letters" earlier, but its presence in *The Great Shark Hunt* shows his growing fondness for the piece, which represents a crucial development in his literary style, the blending of his private and public voices. Part 3 also includes other important early newspaper articles, including "What Lured Hemingway to Ketchum?" and "The 'Hashbury' Is the Capital of the Hippies."

In terms of subject matter part 4 is less unified, but it does contain the anthology's most recent articles. It begins with the title essay, "The Great Shark Hunt," a story about Thompson's trip to Cozumel for a deep-sea fishing competition patterned on *Fear and Loathing in Las Vegas*. Two pieces about President Carter follow: "Jimmy Carter and the Great Leap of Faith" and "Address by Jimmy Carter on Labor Day." After the Kentucky piece in part 3, these two appreciative accounts of the Georgia governor-turned-president reinforce Thompson's pride in his Southern heritage.

Unlike Wolfe's *Kandy-Kolored Tangerine-Flake Streamline Baby* or Talese's *Fame and Obscurity*, *The Great Shark Hunt* is not just a collection of previously published newspaper and magazine articles. It also contains chunks from Thompson's three previous books. Readers familiar with his work may find too much overlap, but the excerpts and articles together survey his body of work, turning *The Great Shark Hunt* from a collection into a reader. In terms of antecedents, it resembles the Viking Portables, which typically combine shorter pieces with excerpts from book-length works. With *The Great Shark Hunt* Thompson created his own portable reader. At least this six-hundred-page anthology would be portable once the trade paperback appeared.

The reviews of *The Great Shark Hunt* were mixed. Like Snider, other reviewers failed to recognize Thompson's complex organizational scheme, but some saw value in the volume. Though highly critical, Gene Lyons did recognize Thompson's folk roots: "Just about the only way of taking him seriously is as an updated Western humorist, a teller of tall tales and outrageous whoppers, *Rolling Stone*'s own Mike Fink."[9]

Over the next fifteen years Thompson published only one monograph, *The Curse of Lono*. Illustrated by Ralph Steadman, this Hawaiian adventure was also patterned on *Fear and Loathing in Las Vegas* and designed to recapture its magic. It did not exactly work that way. *The Curse of Lono* is mildly amusing, but Thompson's text is barely longer than one *Rolling Stone* article, padded with boxes and sidebars and long quotations. He never finished the book himself. Editor Alan Rinzler came to Woody Creek to oversee its completion unsuccessfully. One night when Thompson was passed out like a patient on an operating table Rinzler gathered all the manuscript material he could find, returned to New York, and assembled the book himself.[10]

The Great Shark Hunt sold well. In addition to the royalties from this anthology and his three earlier books Thompson had another income stream, which had begun five years earlier. *Fear and Loathing on the Campaign Trail*, Lauren Jones remarked, brought Thompson into the limelight and onto the lecture circuit. Jones's remarks occur in her report of his afternoon lecture on February 12, 1974, at Hill Auditorium on the University of Michigan campus. This public appearance was one of Thompson's first lectures or, to use Jones's term, anti-lectures. He received $1,500 for his appearance. In the future Thompson would travel to other campuses to address his most ardent fans: college students.[11]

His Michigan lecture shows that Thompson quickly established a pattern for his personal appearances. He showed up an hour late and drunk and continued drinking on stage. Instead of preparing a formal lecture—too much work—he would answer questions from the audience. Speaking at Duke University later that year, he entered Page Auditorium late as usual and drunker than usual. In the version he told Plimpton on the plane to Zaire, Thompson is the hero of the story, but the truth differs considerably, as Harriet Sugar reveals in her report for the *Daily Tar Heel*.[12]

Duke program advisor Linda Simmons characterized Thompson as inebriated, incapacitated, incoherent, and inaudible. He abused the audience, threw his glass of bourbon halfway across the stage, kicked the podium hard enough to split its veneer, almost fell into the orchestra pit, and fondled the shaft of the microphone like Onan on a holiday. After forty minutes and with the approval of the student organizing committee, Simmons walked on stage and escorted

Thompson to the nearest exit. The following day she wrote his lecture agent to refuse payment of the $1,500 fee.¹³

Stories of Thompson's lecture hall antics could be multiplied almost endlessly, but the result would be a numbing sameness. One more example will suffice. In 1984 Thompson spoke to a capacity crowd in the grand ballroom of the Memorial Union at the University of Iowa. Reporting the event, Ann Mittman said his performance was "all that Doonesbury cartoonist Garry Trudeau could have asked for."¹⁴ Mittman had in mind Uncle Duke, the character Trudeau had introduced to his comic strip ten years earlier. A balding, drug-taking, hallucinating character who wears aviator shades and writes for *Rolling Stone*, Uncle Duke is an obvious stand-in for Thompson and his self-caricature Raoul Duke.

Trudeau seems guilty of stealing Thompson's intellectual property, but Thompson never sued him—for good reason. Trudeau was his de facto press agent. *Doonesbury* disseminated his image in the newspapers on a daily basis and kept the lecture offers coming. While tolerating Trudeau, Thompson never stopped ranting about the theft of his personal image.

Thompson's appearance fee had gone up to $4,250, but his performance style—drunken mumblings in answer to audience questions—had not changed in ten years. Mittman reported, "He rambled, and his schizophrenic style touched one minute on Geraldine Ferraro's campaign as the nation's first woman candidate for vice president and the next minute on the best marijuana between here and Colombia."¹⁵

To one member of the Iowa audience Thompson brought Colombia to mind for a different reason. Seated toward the back of the ballroom was David Hamilton, Thompson's old friend from Barranquilla. They had not seen one another since they met two decades earlier, but Hamilton, who had followed Thompson's career from Iowa City, understood his influence: "To many students I had known, and to some colleagues, Thompson had been a guide through the sixties and seventies." The year before, in fact, Hamilton had directed a master's thesis about Thompson. Working toward an MA in nonfiction writing, Daniel R. Baldwin used his thesis to explore Thompson's portrayal of the American Dream.¹⁶

In his Iowa talk Thompson touched upon the subject of writing, which he called "a luxury 'in some dark, deep way.'" He did not elaborate, and Mittman could not really tell what he meant. She did quote something else Thompson said about writing, which closes her report: "All my life I have been trying to figure out how to do a story and have somebody else write it."¹⁷

Hamilton, having spent twenty years teaching students how to write, had always emphasized the hard work and ceaseless revision it entails. Now here comes Thompson, a role model for many would-be writers in the audience, who tells them he was trying to write by doing as little work as possible. Seeing no need to renew their acquaintance, Hamilton left the ballroom without saying hello.

Thompson's speaking engagements were lucrative enough that he no longer needed to write for a living. In 1985, however, he received an offer he could not resist. David Bergin, editor of the *San Francisco Examiner*, invited him to write a weekly column for $1,500 per column. Having previously criticized *Examiner* columnist Charles Denton, Thompson now became the paper's newest columnist.

Aware of Thompson's flakiness, publisher Will Hearst wanted to make sure he would honor his weekly commitment, so he assigned another reporter, David McCumber, to manage him: a full-time position. Maria Khan also helped him deliver his columns on time. Thompson had met Khan, a journalism student, when he spoke at Arizona State University. She became his assistant and then his girlfriend, a pattern he would often repeat as he used up one young assistant after another. Khan was better than most. Warren Hinckle called her "Hunter's real life Girl Friday with Rosalind Russell's sense of style and humor."[18]

From September 1985 to March 1987 Thompson contributed a column to the *Examiner* almost weekly. He would gather many of his columns as *Generation of Swine: Tales of Shame and Degradation in the '80s*. This anthology forms the second volume of Gonzo Papers. Few newspapers had republished his *Examiner* columns as they appeared, so Thompson enthusiasts outside of San Francisco had read little of his writing since *The Curse of Lono*.

Reviewing *Generation of Swine* for the *Chicago Tribune*, Gary Dretzka remarked, "For the last 2 1/2 years, we Thompson fans in the hinterlands have only been able to guess at what he has done with his weekly forum." Upon reading *Generation of Swine*, Dretzka realized they had not missed much. He concluded, "Hunting for pearls among the dozens of columns in *Generation of Swine*, requires the kind of patience only those already endeared to Thompson are likely to possess."[19]

Thompson arranged his columns in *Generation of Swine* largely, but not totally, in chronological order. His earliest column, dated September 23, 1985, is the sixth item in the anthology, after which he proceeds chronologically. But Thompson plucked the first five items from their place in the chronology and thus gave them greater priority. "Saturday Night in the City," the first item in *Generation of Swine*, originally appeared on December 9, 1985.

"Saturday Night in the City" begins, "I dropped Maria off in front of the tattoo parlor just before midnight."[20] His opening reference to Maria is characteristic. Thompson immerses readers in his world, expecting us to know the relevant players. San Francisco's tattoo culture is the ostensible subject of this column. With his deadline looming—a gonzo motif wearing thin—he decides to get Maria tattooed at the last minute and chooses a large tattoo of a black panther. He reprinted the image in *Generation of Swine*. It resembles something from the realm of heraldry: "A panther rampant sable, with sinister paw extended." The episode is reminiscent of another San Francisco story, the moment in *Vertigo* when Jimmy Stewart, trying to convince Kim Novak to change her appearance for him and dye her hair blond, says, "It can't matter to you."

Hinckle enjoyed "Saturday Night in the City," calling it "a piece of wonderful madness." Curious about the episode's veracity, he asked Khan for details. Wanting to get a tattoo, she suggested the idea to Thompson. He replied, "This is really gonzo journalism, getting a hideous needle and ink stuck in you for the story."[21]

Thompson's remark shows why he selected this column to open *Generation of Swine*. Much as he had included the pieces that defined gonzo journalism in the first part of *The Great Shark Hunt*, he opens the second volume of Gonzo Papers with "Saturday Night in the City," which establishes the gonzo journalist's prerogative. In light of the true story Thompson's written version of events becomes more disturbing. As he tells it, Maria has no say in the matter. He decides to get her tattooed, and he chooses which tattoo. The one he selects is so large and hideous that it will grossly disfigure her for life. Like a sheet of blank paper scrolled into the typewriter, Maria's body is his to inscribe however he wishes.

Although the opening piece in *Generation of Swine* tells the story of a San Francisco adventure, Thompson's official job title for the *Examiner* was "media critic." He installed a large satellite dish at Owl Farm, which let him watch a wide array of programming. Most of his columns provide random observations on the latest TV headlines. "There was a lot of violence in the news last week," one begins. "There was action all over the globe last week," begins another.[22] Rarely does he sustain his opening topic for an entire column. Often he switches to other subjects, using slight variations of the laziest transition in the writers' playbook: "Meanwhile back at the ranch . . ."

Thompson's imagery is tattered, his creativity exhausted. Unwilling or unable to coin new similes, he falls back on old ones. Football commentator John Madden talks like a voluble Amtrak passenger who "rides the rails from town to town like some kind of Wandering Jew." In one column Thompson characterizes the TV business as "a long plastic hallway where thieves and pimps run free and good men die like dogs, for no good reason." Here he repeats the phrase from Hemingway's "Notes on the Next War" that he had used in his review of *The Red Lances*. Seeing the political downfall of both Oliver North and Gary Hart as figurative deaths in a later *Examiner* column, Thompson repeats himself again. He says, "They died like dogs, for no good reason at all—or at least no real reason except craziness."[23]

Since the columns are arranged in chronological order after the opening cluster, we readers naturally apply our knowledge of the mid-eighties as we read. Approaching late January 1986, we anticipate the biggest news story of the period, the *Challenger* disaster. How will the gonzo journalist treat this tragedy? He devotes less than a sentence to it, burying the story in an article about dog fighting, implicitly echoing Hemingway's words again.

Although a disappointment, *Generation of Swine* still contributed to Thompson's popular reputation. Twayne, the publisher of a series of brief critical biographies of individual American authors, approached William McKeen, a journalism professor at the University of Florida, and invited him to write *Hunter S. Thompson*, which would be the first secondary book about Thompson upon its release in 1991. Within the next two years two additional biographies would appear or three, counting the fictionalized quasi-biography released in 1993.[24]

After accepting the project, McKeen sought his subject's help. Thompson agreed to cooperate—provided it would require no work on his part. At the time he had two employees, David McCumber and Catherine Sabonis-Chafee. Terry Sabonis-Chafee, Thompson's current girlfriend, refused to assume the dual role of girlfriend and girl Friday, so she split the position, recruiting her kid sister to be Thompson's next girl Friday. A journalism student, "Cat," as she was nicknamed, joined McCumber in the unenviable task of motivating Thompson to write a new book.

In 2008 McKeen would expand his Twayne biography into *Outlaw Journalist: The Life and Times of Hunter S. Thompson*, which is outstanding for the number of interviews he conducted while researching the book. Cat told McKeen that the questions he had asked in 1989 helped motivate Thompson to compile another anthology, *Songs of the Doomed: More Notes on the Death of the American Dream*, which Summit Books issued in 1990 as the third volume of Gonzo Papers.

Neither of the first two volumes of Gonzo Papers had contained new material connecting the individual articles, mainly because Thompson could not be bothered to write anything more. *Songs of the Doomed*, on the other hand, does contain new material placing the old articles and excerpts in their biographical context. Thompson did not write the material, but he told stories to Cat, and she wrote them up as McCumber scoured Thompson's files for appropriate items to anthologize.²⁵

With *Songs of the Doomed*, in other words, Thompson had achieved the goal he articulated in Iowa: to do a story and have somebody else write it. The biographers assured him that people were interested in reading about his life, so he used the new book to give them some autobiography. *Songs of the Doomed* scooped would-be biographers, supplying fictional or, at least, wildly exaggerated stories of his life, which the biographers took for truth and repeated. The biographies validated and perpetuated the personal myths Thompson invented. Even McKeen, the best of the biographers, fell into his trap and repeated stories from *Songs of the Doomed* that Thompson invented while speaking with Cat. The new material is often entertaining, but no biographer should accept the truth of any of the book's anecdotes without corroboration.

Fact-checking Hunter S. Thompson is a biographer's nightmare. Attempts to corroborate his personal stories can compound errors. When Jann Wenner and Corey Seymour compiled their oral biography, they interviewed his old friends. Gene McGarr, for one, had plenty of personal anecdotes about their time in New York, but before speaking with them, he reread *Songs of the Doomed* to refresh his memory—or fire his imagination, as the case may be. Instead of relying solely on his own anecdotes, McGarr sometimes repeated what he read in *Songs of the Doomed*.²⁶

The previous material Thompson included in the third volume of Gonzo Papers is a mix of unpublished work and old favorites, arranged in chronological order decade by decade. He included a few unpublished items, but some of the previously published material was threadbare. Predictably, he included the two finest passages from his two finest books: "Midnight on the Coast Highway" and "High-Water Mark," an excerpt from the Linkletter/Melville chapter in *Fear and Loathing in Las Vegas*.

Reviews were largely negative. Finding too much repetition between *Songs of the Doomed* and Thompson's earlier writing, Andro Linklater, not to be confused with Art Linkletter, predicted that readers would "succumb with screams of fear and hatred to the umpteenth re-telling of his attempt to become sheriff of Aspen." Reviewing *Songs of the Doomed* for the *Boston Globe*, Chris Reidy called it "the literary equivalent of a landfill site, with Thompson emptying his notebooks and data-dumping the backlogs of his file cabinets." In short, *Songs of the Doomed* was a "spectacular bonfire of inanities."²⁷

Reidy's clever characterization continues the ongoing comparison between Thompson and Wolfe. After pursuing New Journalism through his 1979 triumph, *The Right Stuff*, Wolfe had switched to fiction. Despite his efforts to elevate New Journalism above the novel, Wolfe finally conceded and started writing fiction. *The Bonfire of the Vanities* was his first novel. Published serially in *Rolling Stone* in 1984 and 1985, it appeared separately in 1987 to great acclaim. Sadly, *Songs of the Doomed* revealed that Thompson lacked the ability, the motivation, and the work ethic to write a new and original book with the scope of either *The Right Stuff* or *The Bonfire of the Vanities*.

One more volume would close the Gonzo Papers. Published in 1994, *Better than Sex: Confessions of a Political Junkie* tells the story of the 1992 presidential campaign and Bill Clinton's first year in office. Whereas Thompson had followed the 1972 campaign back and forth across the continent to write *Fear and Loathing on the Campaign Trail*, he followed the 1992 campaign from Woody Creek by watching TV. *Better than Sex* combines the columns he wrote during the campaign with a variety of other materials: isolated quotations from history, handwritten and barely legible faxes, newspaper clippings, memos, snapshots, clip art, pictures of campaign buttons, and other detritus from the campaign. He devoted five pages to his run for sheriff, making *Better than Sex* the umpteenth and one retelling of the story. An intermittent campaign timeline gives the miscellaneous items some semblance of order, but overall this anthology is a mess. It looks as if Grandma Ray's Goops had edited it.

Not only was Thompson barely writing anything, he was barely reading anything, or so it seems from the scanty references in *Better than Sex*, which are the same ones he had been circulating for decades. The front matter includes a seven-line excerpt from "The Raven." He had already used the poem's famous catchphrase several times. Going to New Hampshire for its presidential primary in *Fear and Loathing on the Campaign Trail*, Thompson writes, "When we got to the Exeter Inn I half expected to see a filthy bearded raven perched over the entrance, croaking 'Nevermore.'" Having called McGovern the "Willy Loman of the Left" after the tragic protagonist of Arthur Miller's *Death of a Salesman*, Thompson now applies the same comparison to Clinton: "Mr. Bill is our Willy Loman." And the title of chapter 4, "The Horror, The Horror," repeats the line from *Heart of Darkness* that Thompson had tacked onto the end of *Hell's Angels*.[28]

In his review for *Irish Times*, Harry Browne says that *Better than Sex* should be titled *Apologies of a Journalistic Burnout Who Blowtorched His Cred by Endorsing Clinton*. Browne explains, "Unfortunately, the apologies, like the book itself, are hopelessly confused. No, not disorienting and stream of consciousness, like parts of Thompson's brilliant early forays, *Fear and Loathing in Las Vegas*, *Hell's Angels* and *Fear and Loathing on the Campaign Trail '72*, but just confused."[29]

A century ago Laura Riding and Robert Graves cowrote *A Pamphlet against Anthologies*. Their focus is multiauthor anthologies of English poetry, but the argument they advance suits Thompson's Gonzo Papers. Anthologies, they argue, often keep alive literary works that should be consigned to oblivion.[30] *The Great Shark Hunt* reprints several excellent pieces, but the next three volumes of Gonzo Papers contain many items that are scarcely worth rereading or remembering, items that should be consigned to oblivion.

Although Thompson had discovered as a teenager that he could write better than his friends, no longer could he make that claim, especially with friends like Tom Wolfe, William Kennedy, and James Salter. In the fifteen-year period during which Thompson published the four anthologies that comprise the Gonzo Papers, Wolfe was not the only writer friend doing excellent work. William Kennedy had published his Pulitzer Prize–winning novel *Ironweed* and seven more books to boot. James Salter had written *Solo Faces*, his fifth novel; the screenplay for *Threshold*, an award-winning Canadian film; and *Dusk and Other Stories*, a collection of short fiction for which he received the PEN/Faulkner Award. Read against the contemporary work of Thompson's writer friends, the Gonzo Papers seem pretty sorry.

CHAPTER 8

Letter Writer

Despite their mediocrity, the Gonzo Papers sold well. Besides generating royalties, they created additional opportunities for lucrative personal appearances. The 1980 release of *Where the Buffalo Roam*, a film starring Bill Murray in an uncanny portrayal of Thompson, fostered further acclaim and additional income. It also cemented Thompson's connection to Hollywood. He could see how to monetize his celebrity, optioning ideas to movie producers, ideas he had no intention of developing.

Friends watched helplessly as Thompson squandered his talent. Terry Sabonis-Chafee found his lackadaisical attitude frustrating: "He always had that lazy-ass way out. If he could traffic in his own name instead of actually doing something, he would." Fame—"that ignominy which drains and cheapens the spirit," as Edward Dahlberg defined it—had become more important to Thompson than his craft.[1] Whenever he called himself a writer in the nineties, it seemed like a sham. Could he perpetuate his reputation as a writer without writing? How?

Thompson had an answer, which was based on a plan he had formulated in his boyhood. To use Mic Moroney's spot-on split infinitive, Thompson had managed throughout his life "to anal-retentively carbon copy" thousands of letters and file them away for the future.[2] By the mid-nineties the correspondence stored at Owl Farm amounted to approximately twenty thousand letters. Thompson coped with his frequent inability to write, paradoxically, by writing. When he could not concentrate on an article or a book, he wrote letters. Paul Krassner explained Thompson's situation: "Compared with completing assignments, it was easier writing three or four letters every night, including those that assured editors that he was busy working on pieces he hadn't even started."[3]

As Thompson understood the situation, his letter writing complemented his dream of being a great writer. A collected edition of letters is a mark of any great writer. Keeping carbons, he looked forward to a published edition of his correspondence. Once he established his literary reputation, his letters would be ready to edit. Sometimes he toyed with publishing them before he established his place in literary history. Upon rereading a few letters to his old Air Force buddy Larry Callen, Thompson wrote him again on June 7, 1959. Then living in his Cuddebackville cabin and wrestling like Pampero Firpo with *Prince Jellyfish*, he told Callen, "Perhaps I'll try to publish my collected letters before, instead of after, I make history."[4]

Given his struggle to write during the nineties, Thompson put into action the plan to publish his letters. He hoped to find a hardworking professor to edit the letters and thus give the collection a scholarly aura. Thompson did not want someone who was too well established, preferring one he could bend to his will. He found his ideal editor in Douglas Brinkley, an opportunistic young professor from Hofstra University. In 1993 Brinkley led a group of students on a bus tour across the United States, stopping at famous locations associated with many writers in American literature, including Woody Creek, Colorado.[5]

Brinkley asked Thompson beforehand if he would speak to his students. Thompson agreed, telling him to stop by the Woody Creek Tavern, the watering hole George Stranahan had opened the previous decade. Thompson's meeting with Brinkley marked the start of their working relationship. Together they conceived the project of editing a set of selected letters in three volumes. Although Brinkley had no training or experience in documentary editing, he did possess a quality Thompson lacked: the ability to get things done. Titled *The Proud Highway: Saga of a Desperate Southern Gentleman, 1955–1967*, the first volume of letters appeared in May 1997, two months before Thompson turned sixty.

Proud Highway did not fool Mic Moroney, who saw the volume for what it was: a way for Thompson to avoid writing new material. Having closely followed his career, Moroney knew Thompson's literary output had become "increasingly incoherent." With little more to say Thompson fell back on what he had written decades earlier, when his mind was sharp and his focus was clear. Upon the release of *Proud Highway*, Moroney observed that Thompson's "main operation nowadays seems reduced to the secretarial task of recycling old achievements," finding *Proud Highway* a "shameless 660-page toecrusher."[6]

Moroney's page count does not include the book's front matter, but readers should not skip Brinkley's nine-page "Editor's Note," an eye-opener, if not a toecrusher. This carefully crafted preface offers an unintentionally revealing overview of the project. Although speaking in an objective voice, Brinkley, an unabashed partisan, planned from the start to depict Thompson as a modern-day hero. The surviving letters, Brinkley explains, go back to 1947, when Thompson was ten. He also mentions the daily letters Thompson wrote his mother from jail in 1955. Choosing his words carefully, Brinkley says that Thompson was incarcerated at the "Jefferson County Jail for a robbery he didn't commit."[7] These familiar words echo the opening credits of *The A-Team*: "In 1972 a crack commando unit was sent to prison by a military court for a crime they didn't commit." As Brinkley portrays him, Thompson, like the A-Team, has been wronged by those in power, and he now defends all the little guys overwhelmed by forces beyond their control.

Brinkley bolsters his heroic portrait with reference to an important scholarly source. Quoting *The American Adam*, R. W. B. Lewis's study of American literature and the national character, Brinkley calls Thompson "an individual standing alone, self-reliant and self-propelling, ready to confront whatever awaited him with the aid of his own unique and inherent resources."[8] Standing alone and self-reliant? One can almost hear Jim Silberman choking on his Waldorf salad at the sound of these words. Not since *Fear and Loathing in Las Vegas* had Thompson written anything on his own. To write an article or compile a book, he needed editors and assistants prodding and pushing him every step of the way. Otherwise, he accomplished nothing.

The editor's note says little about how Brinkley selected the letters for *Proud Highway*. He admits it was a daunting task: he cut fifteen letters for every one he kept. He does say he excluded correspondence of a youthful or personal nature, but otherwise Brinkley does not define his selection criteria. The letters of the ten-year-old Thompson, which could have been kind of fun, are absent. So are the letters he wrote his mother from jail.

Reviewing *Proud Highway* for *TLS*, Peter Blake conjectured that Thompson had a hand in the selection process. He was right. When the book was in press, Thompson told David McCumber, "I never expected to be looking over my life, page by page. It's like an animal eating its own intestines." Blake recognized the collection's underlying and unstated purpose: the letters were chosen to preserve and perpetuate Thompson's legendary reputation. The absence of his youthful letters from prison is one indication of this implicit purpose. Contrite letters home to mother do not make good raw material to construct the gonzo journalist's origin story.[9]

Letters excluded from *Proud Highway* help reveal Brinkley's selection process. Although he included many to Paul Semonin, Brinkley omitted a letter Thompson wrote him the second week of February 1955, which an auction house has since acquired and published. A year ahead of his friend, Semonin was a freshman at Yale University when Thompson was a high school senior. The letter begins, "I fear I must apologize for not writing sooner but I'm afraid that procrastination is one of my many vices." As an adult, Thompson rarely apologized. When he was late paying rent to Stranahan, for example, he would send a brief note with the check. Stranahan explained, "I think it was his way of apologizing, though he'd never actually apologize or write, 'I'm sorry.' Never." Thompson did not want to include a letter revealing what he perceived as a weakness in his younger self.[10]

Thompson's staunchest defenders commonly attribute his later inability to write to substance abuse, seeing drugs and alcohol merely as the gonzo journalist's occupational hazards. But Thompson had been a procrastinator all his life, and he knew it. This letter, which antedates the earliest letter in *Proud Highway*, undercuts Brinkley's thesis about Thompson's self-reliant and self-propelling nature.

Other aspects of this letter to Semonin undermine Thompson's status as a cult figure, a rebel who does what he wants when he wants regardless of what anyone else thinks. Thompson says, "The straight and narrow is the best (if not the most enticing) path to follow for the time being": hardly what Thompson fans want to hear their hero say! In this letter he sounds like a fairly conventional high school senior. He plans to straighten up and get ready for college: "I am applying for Sewanee and have a pretty good chance of making it."

Sewanee, that is, the University of the South, is a prestigious liberal arts college in Tennessee associated with the Episcopal Church. Thompson's desire to attend the school, like his dream to attend Vanderbilt, reinforces his Southern roots. In the fifties Sewanee had a strong creative writing program, but the university was quite conservative. Its students wore academic gowns to class. The image of the future Dark Prince of Gonzo sitting in a classroom at a private religious university wearing an academic gown was not something Brinkley wished to plant in his reader's mind, not for a second.

Following many scholarly editors, Brinkley wrote brief headnotes to introduce each letter. He designed them to provide historical and biographical context and drive the story forward. But Brinkley did little original research to write these headnotes. While editing *Proud Highway*, he spoke with Thompson on the telephone five or six times a week, letting the author of the letters be his fact-checker. The headnotes give the illusion of scholarship, but they, too, manifest the same kind of mythologizing that Thompson demonstrates in *Songs of the Doomed*. Brinkley's headnotes repeat Thompson's lies about himself.

Take for example the headnote to a 1957 letter Thompson wrote from Eglin Air Force Base: "Disregarding Air Force regulations, Thompson took the civilian job as sports editor of the *Playground News* in Fort Walton Beach, writing under the pseudonym Thorne Stockton. While the move boosted his journalism career, it put him in hot water with his superior officers." This headnote is pure fiction. The Air Force did not ban its journalists from freelancing; they simply had to obtain permission to do so. Other Air Force staff writers also moonlighted on *Playground News*. Brinkley's headnote perpetuates the legend of Airman Thompson as a bad boy who defies regulations.[11]

A headnote to a 1957 letter to Virginia Thompson cites *Songs of the Doomed* as a scholarly reference: "Upon arriving in Jersey Shore, Thompson dutifully wrote home full of concern about the obvious dullness of the Pennsylvania mining town. In later years he would write about his harrowing Jersey Shore experiences in *Songs of the Doomed*."[12] This headnote adds credence to Thompson's fanciful stories in the earlier book, giving Thompson's personal mythology the aura of gospel truth.

Brinkley's willingness to accept Thompson's word as fact and his lack of original research sometimes gets him in trouble. His most egregious error occurs in the headnote to an October 19, 1966 letter supposedly written to Charles Kuralt: "Kuralt had mailed Thompson a new essay book: *The Best of the National Observer*, which included more articles by Thompson than by any other journalist."[13] This one-sentence headnote contains at least two errors. The book was not titled *The Best of the National Observer*, nor was Charles Kuralt the one who mailed Thompson the book. The real title is *The Observer's World: People, Places, and Events from the Pages of The National Observer*.

Thompson's salutation—"Dear Charley"—does not refer to Charles Kuralt, Charley Farley, or even Charger Charley the Child Molester. It refers to Charles Preston, the man who edited *The Observer's World* and the one who sent Thompson the book. Without knowledge of the editor's name or the book's title, readers must strain to make sense of the letter. The title offended Thompson, who also disliked Preston's use of footnotes printed in "snipervision type" to identify who wrote which articles. Thompson tells Preston, "Not one of those seven pieces in the book originated in anybody's mind but my own; nor were any written with the help of expense money. What I mean is I figure some of that was my world, too, and my ego doesn't fit real well into footnotes."[14]

The first letter in *Proud Highway* is one Thompson wrote to childhood friend Gerald Tyrrell in 1956 while stationed at Eglin Air Force Base. Before the letter, the volume reprints three pieces Thompson had contributed to *Spectator*: "Open Letter to the Youth of Our Nation," "Security," and "The Night-Watch," a Whitmanesque poem. Included in lieu of any letters Thompson wrote in high school, these items reveal how early he had formulated his life's philosophy and thus serve as touchstones for the ensuing letters, allowing readers to see how Thompson carried out the challenge he set for his contemporaries.

In the letter to Tyrrell, Thompson expresses his characteristic nostalgia for the past. Recalling the Saturday night gatherings of the Athenaeum Literary Association, he says, "I sit at my desk and pound out this missive which will bridge the gap from me to the mythical world of gay laughter and tinkling glasses." Having known Tyrrell since boyhood, Thompson was comfortable joking in a manner both could enjoy. He continues: "I got quite a kick out of your social plight in the fair city of my birth; as I remember her, Sarah McNeil is about as pleasing to the average eye as a wart-hog with Bright's disease."[15] This beautifully crafted sentence offers a nice contrast of styles, illustrating the disjunctive technique characteristic of many early Thompson letters. The elevated diction in the first independent clause gives way to the graphic simile of the second. The derogatory, albeit humorous simile reveals how comfortable Thompson was writing to an old friend and shows his youthful mastery of figurative language.

Thompson had no end of fun regarding the plight of his friend Ralph Peterson. After they had trained together at the Air Force radio school, Thompson was sent to Florida; Peterson got posted to northern Alaska. In one letter Thompson supplies a detailed paragraph comparing Florida's balmy climate with Alaska's bitter cold. The next paragraph begins: "That raucous noise you just heard was probably my screech of laughter, floating through the northern pines and across the frozen wastelands, and into the smelly confines of your shack."[16] Thompson combines the senses of sound and smell—raucous screech, stinky shack—with the airy feel of movement across a huge distance.

In the same letter he boasts to Peterson about his new role as journalist, comparing himself with renowned gossip columnist Walter Winchell. It is exciting to watch Thompson find his calling: "From now on, when I appear somewhere with a pencil in my hand and a gleam in my eye, people will quiver in their shoes and sweat freely. This is the finest thing that could have happened. I now have thousands of readers, and the official sanction of the Base Commander. Move over Winchell . . . HST has emerged from obscurity to jab at the world for awhile. Jesus, what fun!"[17]

Thompson belongs to a literary tradition that goes back to ancient Rome, in which Pliny the Younger cultivated the art of writing letters. A comment by one of Pliny's editors applies to Thompson: "A fine letter does not consist in saying fine things, but in expressing ordinary ones in an uncommon manner." Thompson may not have read Pliny, but he did know the appreciative essay

Somerset Maugham wrote for the London *Sunday Times*. Calling Pliny's *Letters* "a most enjoyable bedside book," Maugham observes, "The more you read his letters the more you feel at home with him."[18]

Proud Highway affirms Thompson's connection to Pliny. In letter after letter he expresses the everyday incidents of his life in an uncommon manner. Thompson excelled as a letter writer by shaping his manner to suit individual correspondents. Having known Tyrell for so long, he could speak with considerable intimacy. The knowledge of radio technology Thompson shared with Peterson gave him technical terms he could draw upon for figures of speech. Thompson wrote one way for old buddies, another way for girlfriends, and still other ways for relatives and bill collectors.

Whereas Thompson emphasizes the fun and excitement of journalism in the letter to Peterson, he portrays his newfound career in a more sedate manner while writing to Aunt Elizabeth. He tells her what she wants to hear, painting a picture of himself as a dedicated and hardworking journalist: "The job is nerve-wracking and the hours are terrible, but I love the work. For the first time, I have found something which will keep me busy and which is also enjoyable. Thus, I have been able to keep out of mischief and finally settle myself on an even keel for once." He assures her that his wild times were behind him but does confess a longing for "the Rabelaisian parties of yesteryear."[19] Discussing wild parties with Aunt Elizabeth, Thompson elevates them with a literary reference, indicating the love of books he shared with her, but also distancing himself from the decadence. Contemporary letters to old friends reveal that his wilder days were most definitely not behind him.

Sometimes Thompson used his letters to test out literary strategies he was so far unwilling to put in his published work. Writing to Rutledge Lilly, another old friend from the Athenaeum Literary Association, Thompson was already experimenting with the humorous catalog. Questioning Lilly's comment that their friend Curtis Moore had become "unrecognizably" drunk, Thompson says:

> One item, I think, deserves extra comment, and that's the one about Curtis becoming "unrecognizably" drunk. Now I've seen drunks and drunks—tall drunks, short drunks, blind drunks, crawling drunks, slithering drunks, mumbling drunks, screeching drunks, crying drunks, sick drunks, dead drunks, speeding drunks, addled drunks, pitiful drunks, and just about any other type of drunk there is—but never have I seen a man who was unrecognizably drunk! The only explanation I can see for such a wonder, is that he must have shattered the "intoxication barrier" in an almost superhuman display of degeneration, dissipation, vice and drink.[20]

Thompson was nineteen when he wrote this letter. Reread the passage, this time aloud, to get the full effect. His pacing, combined with his use of alliteration, repetition, and jet-age lingo, is brilliant.

A serious purpose underlies the letter's humor. His critique of Lilly's English usage reflects Thompson's insistence on using the right word for the right moment. When it came to word choice, he was a great believer in Mark Twain's dictum, "The difference between the *almost*-right word and the *right* word is really a large matter—it's the difference between the lightning bug and the lightning." To be unrecognizably anything means being altered beyond identification. In Tennessee Williams's dark comedy *A House Not Meant to Stand*, for example, Cornelius McCorckle has trouble identifying his Mississippi neighbor Jessie Syles, who tells him, "I am practically unrecognizably transfawned by that cosmetic surgery." "Unrecognizably" is a suitable modifier for getting plastic surgery, not for getting plastered. It seemed impossible to Thompson that someone could be drunk beyond recognition.[21]

His letters to girlfriends strike a different note than those to old Louisville friends. They are boastful, racy, and lyrical. In one letter to Susan Haselden, Thompson calls himself the new Fitzgerald. *Proud Highway* includes few letters to Thompson, but apparently Haselden implied in her response that she would be a grandmother by the time he became the new Fitzgerald. Her implication stung him; in rebuttal he defends himself: "Actually, I am already the new Fitzgerald: I just haven't been recognized yet."[22]

Thompson's letters to girlfriends can be quite seductive. Continuing this letter to Haselden, he celebrates her body as he recalls a special moment they shared: "I remembered that we had come out for a pre-dawn swim in the phosphorous-filled water. Whenever you move around in the water, your whole body lights up and flashes all around." Unwilling to sustain this intimate moment, he switches to a scientific explanation before refocusing the attention on himself: "Not your body. It's really the phosphorous in the water, but I like to think it's a weird omen from the crabs—hailing me as the new Messiah."[23]

This letter to Haselden also contains a wild scene that anticipates Thompson's gonzo humor: "Last weekend was a nightmare. I appeared at high noon on a crowded beach, wearing only flippers and a pair of diving goggles. Somewhere in the melee, my trunks had become lost. Urged on by my drunken and malicious companions, I virtually cleared the beach in five minutes."[24] The image of the teenaged Thompson running around adorned in nothing but flippers and goggles is uproarious, but its humor is not the only aspect of this episode that looks forward to gonzo journalism. The episode blurs the line between truth and fiction. Did Thompson really lose his swim trunks? He says so, but it seems unlikely that they could have slipped over his flippers while he was swimming. Of course, the flippers could be a fiction, as well.

Thompson's letters to Kraig Juenger, a new girlfriend and former Miss Illinois, have a more serious tone than those to his high school girlfriends. Though Haselden was a great Kerouac enthusiast, Thompson does not write like him for her. He does for Juenger. In a letter he wrote in July 1958, just ten months after *On the Road* appeared, Thompson longs to meet her in St. Louis, where she was working, and go for a drive:

> I thought I'd like to drive in from Collinsville with your top down and see *The Student Prince* at the Muny Opera again; and then I thought I'd like to drive through Forest Park and out to the Tic Toc Tap for a tall gin-and-tonic and maybe listen to George Shearing or possibly Errol Garner. And then I decided to drive on out past Collinsville to someplace like Trenton where we could stop and sit in one of those endless fields and drink Crystal Apple Wine out of tall thin glasses while the moon sparkled on the grass and the wind made our cigarettes burn a bright orange in the dark. But it would be late by then and you'd be tired, and the dawn wind would be cold as we drove back to Collinsville. We'd keep the top down, though, and watch the sun climb out of the east and know that New York was a thousand miles and a million quiet towns behind it. Somewhere behind the sun the windows of the Empire State Building would be sparkling in the dawn and the East River would be very quiet and very silver.[25]

The convertible, the wind, tall drinks, and jazz piano: Thompson's letter shares much with *On the Road*. More significant, however, is the narrative pace, the use of conjunctions to hold the bits together and keep them flowing. Thompson also shows the capacity to juxtapose similar images of vastly different magnitude, the sparkling moon and the orange tip of a windblown cigarette.

The continental scope of his geographical imagery reinforces the Kerouac connection. In *On the Road* his mouthpiece Sal Paradise says, "And before me was the great raw bulge and bulk of my American continent; somewhere far across, gloomy, crazy New York was throwing up its cloud of dust and brown steam."[26] Thompson's mind ranges from Collinsville, Illinois, to New York and envisions how the Empire State Building appears as it reflects the rising sun.

A form letter Thompson wrote illustrates another aspect of his literary skill. He designed a letter that, with slight variations, could be sent to whomever might try extracting money from him. Sensing that bill collectors would be loath to deal with a lunatic, Thompson assumes the persona of a lunatic. He laments: "Oh God, what's happening all the time? Everybody wants to steal and drink and sex and take everybody's money away from people who don't even sell anything and there's atomic fallout everywhere and war coming on. The whole world is going crazy and I don't even have a job. You've got to stop threatening me! I'm not well—I have a blister on my leg and that damn disease all over my stomach."[27]

Writing to another set of correspondents—established writers—Thompson speaks as a peer, although he had yet to establish himself as a writer. Algren, Donleavy, Faulkner, Mailer, Styron: all received letters from this young wannabe author. While seeking their opinions and advice, he does not speak as a young sycophant. Rather, he expresses appreciation when appropriate, criticism as needed.

When Algren published *Notes from a Sea Diary* in 1965, Thompson wrote to critique the book. Audaciously, he told Algren: "You have got to get over the idea that you have a sense of humor. No, that's not it. It's this gag-line stuff. You're not a comedy writer." Writing five years before *Fear and Loathing in Las Vegas* established him as one of the great humorists in American literature, Thompson already had a keen understanding of how to write humor. His criticism is on target: Algren could not write jokes. In the opening chapter of *Notes from a Sea Diary* he fires off several facetious one-liners, and they all fall flat.[28]

Thompson wrote Faulkner from his Cuddebackville cabin in 1959, sharing ideas about their profession. "The Writer and the Outer World," a recent article in the *New York Times*, gave him the perfect excuse to write Faulkner. The article was not by Times publisher Arthur Hays Sulzberger, as Brinkley would have us believe, but by Cyrus Lee Sulzberger, his nephew and chief foreign correspondent. In *The Kingdom and the Power* Talese says that Cyrus Sulzberger "typified the trench-coat type of journalist, the sort who not only liked to cover wars and to hobnob with the mighty, but also liked to influence world policy and the men who dictated it."[29] Thompson clipped out Sulzberger's article and enclosed it with his letter.

In his opening paragraph Thompson explains that the article reminded him of something Faulkner had said in his *Paris Review* interview, which Thompson had read and remembered. Thompson's reference shows his familiarity with *Writers at Work*, the first volume of a collection of *Paris Review* interviews. Early in his literary career, he voraciously read the words of authors discussing their craft. In this instance, however, Thompson misremembered his source. It was not *Writers at Work*, but *The Writer Observed*, Harvey Breit's 1956 compilation of interviews he conducted for the *New York Times*. Faulkner had told Breit, "The writer in America isn't part of the culture of this country. He's like a fine dog. People like him around, but he's of no use."[30]

Sulzberger questions the place of writers in the world at large, seeing them separate from current events. "The Writer and the Outer World" mostly consists of an interview with T. S. Eliot, who told Sulzberger, "A writer must prove his qualifications to interject opinions on specific political problems. Jonathan Swift wrote brilliant essays on such matters; but he had indeed proven his qualifications. It's not good enough for the writer just to sign broad statements drawn up by somebody else." After quoting Eliot, Sulzberger explains, "Eliot recognizes that the views of a poet on nuclear defense are likely to be of no more value than the views of a general on sonnet forms."[31]

Continuing his letter to Faulkner, Thompson supplies his view of the writer's role, a view tinged by the frustration he felt with his own lack of success. The writer must maintain his integrity and stay true to his craft, even if it means sacrificing himself: "As far as I can see, the role, the duty, the obligation, and indeed the only choice of the writer in today's 'outer' world is to starve to death as honorably and as defiantly as possible."[32]

In the next paragraph Thompson jokes that Faulkner should send a weekly check to support him, "the only chicken-thieving, novel-writing Southerner in the Catskills who drives an ancient Jaguar, lives in an un-heated cabin, and spends the large part of his weekly unemployment cheque to buy high-test gasoline."[33] With this self-characterization Thompson reinforces his connection to Faulkner, the greatest novel-writing Southerner in the history of American literature.

Taking Thompson's personal story from his magazine and newspaper career through his freelancing days and his unsuccessful efforts to write a novel, *Proud Highway* ends in 1967, the year he published *Hell's Angels*. It thus has the quality of a bildungsroman, the story of a young man who learns the ways of the world, experiences many trials and misfortunes, but ultimately succeeds in his quest to become a writer.

Since *Proud Highway* continues Thompson's story beyond the publication of *Hell's Angels* to the end of 1967, it also sows the seeds of his self-destruction. With the popular and critical success of *Hell's Angels*, Thompson received many offers to contribute to national magazines, most of which he accepted but never wrote. Nearing its end, *Proud Highway* broaches the long-running story of Thompson's blown assignments, the subject of the volume's last two letters.

Unwilling to end *Proud Highway* on this sour note, Thompson had Brinkley add an epilogue. Once again Thompson reused "Midnight on the Coast Highway." Having first written this set piece for *Hell's Angels*, he had reprinted it in *The Great Shark Hunt* and excerpted it in *Songs of the Doomed*. As the epilogue to *Proud Highway*, it has little to do with the preceding letters but reiterates a key concept from *Hell's Angels*, The Edge: "But the edge is still Out There. Or maybe it's In. The association of motorcycles with LSD is no accident of publicity. They are both a means to an end, to the place of definition."³⁴

With "Midnight on the Coast Highway" Thompson ends *Proud Highway* the way he had intended to end *Hell's Angels* before tacking on the last-minute postscript about getting stomped. In other words, the epilogue to *Proud Highway* acknowledges the power of "Midnight on the Coast Highway" as a conclusion, implicitly conveying Thompson's regret that he had not ended *Hell's Angels* with this beautiful set piece, this high white note, as he had planned.

Peter Blake disliked the epilogue to *Proud Highway*. In the volume's penultimate letter, Thompson tells Wolfe about the assignments he has blown while on the verge of blowing another one: "I'm about to dump another article and devote the rest of this wrong year to straightening out my personal papers."³⁵ Blake sees the epilogue as another contribution to the Thompson legend: "It is surely in service of the legend that he doesn't end with the secretarial note to Tom Wolfe about 'straightening out my personal papers,' but closes with the melodramatic finale from *Hell's Angels*." Blake sees the epilogue as camouflage. Reminding readers of the writer he used to be, Thompson masks the sorry figure he had become. The epilogue, Blake concludes, "seems crudely designed to show us that, rather than the sad alcoholic who occasionally emerges from Aspen, the outlaw, like 'The Edge', is still Out (or In) there."³⁶

Other reviewers contrasted Thompson's early letters with his recent work. In his review of *Proud Highway* for the *Washington Post*, Steven Moore concludes, "This is his best book in years; his recent efforts have been entertaining, but *The Proud Highway* vividly brings back the days when (to echo his diction) Thompson stomped the terra like a champion."³⁷ Moore's positive review contains none of Blake's skepticism, but his conclusion turns melancholy upon reflection. *Proud Highway* is so good because it presents texts that Thompson had written at least thirty years earlier. The letters of the teenaged Thompson display a youthful exuberance reminiscent of pop singer Ritchie Valens. Ensconced in his Woody Creek fortress the year *Proud Highway* appeared, the sixty-year-old Thompson seems more like Emperor Flavius Valens, who watched his empire crumble around him, helpless to thwart its decay.

CHAPTER 9

Novelist

Raised on a farm in the Scottish Highlands beyond the reach of television, Ruaridh Nicoll whiled away the long, dark winter nights of his youth reading *Hell's Angels*, *Fear and Loathing in Las Vegas*, and *Fear and Loathing on the Campaign Trail*. Thompson's writings left Nicoll spellbound, turning him toward a career as both journalist and novelist. Before establishing himself as a writer, Nicoll traveled to America, mainly to drift around and see the USA, partly to meet the writer he so greatly admired. In "The Night I Spent Drinking with Hunter S. Thompson," Nicoll says he went to Woody Creek, Colorado, to meet his hero and thus to break the spell: "I thought if I met him he'd be appalling and in one leap I'd be free."[1]

So he would say a quarter century later. According to what the twenty-three-year-old Nicoll said at the time, his 1993 visit to Woody Creek was less purge than pilgrimage, a quest to meet the "high priest of counterculture journalism." After meeting Thompson, Nicoll wandered into the desert seeking the solitude necessary to make sense of the experience. Holed up in an Arizona motel, he wrote the story of his visit to Owl Farm, which would become "The Duke of Hazard," a career-making feature story for the Dublin *Sunday Tribune*. Nicoll's excellent interview has escaped the attention of Thompson's editors, but it sheds light on his role as a novelist, even though it appeared four years before he released his only published novel, *The Rum Diary*.[2]

Nicoll had not made an appointment to see Thompson. Aware the Woody Creek Tavern was his regular hangout, Nicoll showed up hoping to meet him. Befriending Rachel, the bartender, he played backgammon with her, bearing off piece after piece from the gameboard as he waited for Thompson with patient forbearance. A few nights later Thompson arrived with Nicole Meyer, his current girl Friday. Rachel introduced Nicoll to them, and they began discussing books and politics. They got along so well that Thompson invited him back to Owl Farm.[3]

The three gathered in the kitchen. Thompson took his usual seat: "He sat at the kitchen counter, two old-fashioned electric typewriters in front of him, whisky everywhere, a remote control for the vast television." Once drinks were served, Thompson handed Nicoll a chapter from *Polo Is My Life*, one of his unfinished novels, and demanded he read it aloud. In Nicoll's view the chapter read like a cross between Kurt Vonnegut and Jilly Cooper, a popular British romance novelist.[4]

Narrating the experience, Nicoll sketched a vivid word portrait. As Nicoll read from *Polo Is My Life*, Thompson smoked a bong made from a human skull. True heads are always imagining how to make bongs from the odd hollow objects they encounter, but Nicoll's portrait is more than merely an insight into contemporary drug culture. It reaches back to Renaissance portraitists, who often incorporated human skulls in their paintings as reminders of life's transitory nature. The skull is a memento mori, a reminder of death. Sitters portrayed with skulls reflect their awareness of the brevity and fragility of life on earth. The smoking pipe traditionally illustrated life's ephemerality and fragility, as well.[5] Thompson's bong thus brings together these two symbols of life's fleeting nature, and Nicoll's keen eye captured it for posterity.

Thompson loved hearing his words read aloud, and his kitchen readings had become a regular part of his life and the lives of the myrmidons who gathered at Owl Farm. Nicoll's thick Scottish brogue was a special treat for Thompson, who took out his tape recorder to capture the moment and thus let himself listen to Nicoll read *Polo Is My Life* whenever he wished. Thompson also had him read big chunks from some of his other unpublished work, including *The Rum Diary*, the novel set in and inspired by his time in Puerto Rico. Nicoll learned that Paul Kemp, the book's narrator-protagonist, was based on Thompson, as was Addison Fritz Yeamon, another major character. Furthermore, Chenault, Yeamon's girlfriend, was based on Sandy Thompson.[6]

"I shouldn't be talking to you," Thompson said as dawn broke. Speaking these words, he caressed the barrel of the shotgun he held in his lap. He then turned to Meyer, stating, "He's been here for days checking me out. Maybe we ought to shoot him in the head."

Nicoll ended "The Duke of Hazard" with this statement, which gives Thompson the last word. In "The Night I Spent Drinking with Hunter S. Thompson," Nicoll retold the story and repeated Thompson's statement but gave himself the last word: "I knew then, as I know now, that I got the HST show. If he was bored and the fan wasn't too obnoxious, he'd put on an entertainment—it kept him from having to write. Whatever. I left the mountains with my admiration undimmed."[7]

"The Duke of Hazard" reveals where Thompson stood as a novelist in 1993. When he embarked on his literary career thirty-five years earlier, he was set on becoming a great American novelist. *Prince Jellyfish* had progressed far enough for him to send the manuscript to prospective agents, so he was disappointed with their rejections. *The Rum Diary*, a more ambitious novel, slowly expanded to over a thousand pages in manuscript, which would have made a 600-page book, less than half the length of *Some Came Running* but more than three times the ideal length of a novel, 182 pages, the length of *The Great Gatsby*.

The Rum Diary remained unpublished because Thompson could never bring himself to whip it into shape. He had drafted it during the early sixties, but it remained unfinished in 1968, when he got the idea to sell it to Hollywood, which would let him avoid finishing it as a novel. Describing *The Rum Diary* to a film producer, he called it "a hopelessly naïve and half-conceived book—as it stands now. I know I can make it better, but I might also make it worse—by killing a lot of valid notes that tend to embarrass me now, in my balding wisdom." Bill Kennedy urged him to trim it down to a manageable size. After reading it in manuscript, Kennedy said, "The book was full of digressions and wisdom—his essays on the state of the world, the nation, journalism, Puerto Rico."[8]

His chronic procrastination is only one reason to explain Thompson's reluctance to revise *The Rum Diary*. By 1971, the year he wrote *Fear and Loathing in Las Vegas*, he had outgrown *The Rum Diary*. *Fear and Loathing in Las Vegas* is a genre-busting book challenging the boundaries between journalism and fiction. Placing fantastic elements in a story based on real events, it has a novelistic quality, but it is quite unlike any novel ever written. Once gonzo journalism gave Thompson his niche, he found it practically impossible to return to *The Rum Diary*.

Thompson toyed with different ideas for other book-length fictional works. *Guts Ball* was one. Designed as a dark comedic novel, *Guts Ball* would portray some of Nixon's disgraced henchmen as they stage a sadistic football game aboard a transcontinental flight, forcing terrified passengers to participate. Thompson put so little energy into *Guts Ball* that he never bothered to write out his ideas. He recorded them on an audio cassette and replayed the tape to anyone interested. Not many were.

The Silk Road, a story combining the Cuban refugee crisis with drug smuggling, made a little more headway. Thompson wrote an overview of this projected novel and two brief chapters. One chapter, "Fishhead Boys," portrays the arrival of Gene Skinner and the narrator at the Key West airport. The narrator is much the same as Thompson's persona in his gonzo journalism. Skinner calls him "Doc," as Thompson's close friends called him. Gene Skinner's name pays homage to Gene McGarr, but the character is essentially a replacement for Raoul Duke. The Fishhead Boys are two local thieves who steal their luggage. Doc and Skinner retrieve their stolen bags, capture the thieves, and torture them mercilessly.

A catalog of themes and motifs fills one long paragraph of Thompson's overview. It begins: "The raw elements of the story are (in no special order): sex, violence, greed, treachery, big money, fast boats, blue water, Cuba, CIA politics, Fidel Castro's sense of humor, one murder, several rapes, heavy gambling, massive drug smuggling, naked women, mean dogs, total breakdown of law and order [. . .]."[9] The catalog continues for another two hundred words. It sounds intriguing, but a list does not a novel make.

The rest of his overview shows that Thompson had little plot to bind these raw elements together, so he fell back on his old favorite. The narrator, he says, will speak "from a POV not unlike that of Nick Carraway in *The Great Gatsby*," and Skinner "may in fact be a lineal descendant of Jay Gatsby, in a different time and a very different place." A surviving page of manuscript notes for *The Silk Road* extends the comparison. After wondering whether Skinner is a good guy or a bad guy, Thompson asks himself, "Was Gatsby a good guy or a bad guy?"[10] Thompson had critiqued William Golding for applying the same formula from one book to the next. Using *The Great Gatsby* as his template for *The Silk Road*, Thompson followed a formula that was not even original. It would not be the last time.

"The Murder of Colonel Evans," another chapter from *The Silk Road*, also reflects Thompson's failure of imagination. Doc, Skinner, and Evans are seated in a hotel bar in the Florida Keys watching a news report about Operation Eagle Claw, President Carter's botched attempt to rescue the Iran hostages, which resulted in the death of several American sailors. Evans defends the operation, but Skinner, predictably, says, "*They blew the mission!* They killed each other for no good reason at all."[11]

Thompson took *Polo Is My Life* further than either *Guts Ball* or *The Silk Road*. He mostly worked on it in Washington, DC, where he hired freelance copy editor Shelby Sadler as his research assistant. A Cornell graduate and a discriminating film buff—she found *Dr. Strangelove* brilliant, Andy Warhol's films excruciating—Sadler also had considerable literary knowledge. She was the one who recognized echoes of Coleridge's "Dejection, An Ode" in *The*

Great Gatsby. With a good memory for detail—she was once a contestant on *Jeopardy!*—Sadler left an excellent account of *Polo Is My Life*.[12]

When Thompson met a polo player named Paula Baxt, he was smitten. She was married, but that did not stop him from flirting. He urged Paula to run away with him, but she replied, "I can't go with you Hunter. Polo is my life." Suddenly, Thompson had a title and an approach for a novel. "It all led into class and money and all of that. Paula Baxt was Hunter's Daisy Buchanan," Sadler explained. "Hunter took this all very seriously—he was infatuated with her, and her husband became Tom Buchanan in his mind, and it just went on from there."[13]

Although he had yet to finish, let alone publish, any novels by the time Nicoll visited Owl Farm, Thompson seems to have reached a state of equilibrium with his fiction. "Kubla Khan," one of his favorite poems, provides a key to understanding Thompson's unfinished novels. The poem's full title is "Kubla Khan; or, A Visitation in a Dream: A Fragment." Each of Thompson's novel manuscripts could share the same subtitle. Call one *The Silk Road: A Fragment*, another *Polo Is My Life: A Fragment*.

To publish these novels in a conventional manner Thompson would have had to polish them to a high sheen. He did not need to polish, let alone finish them, to share these novels in manuscript with good friends and devoted acquaintances. Gathering in the Owl Farm kitchen with a small group of people and having them read his manuscript fragments aloud, Thompson demonstrated that he was not a classical typehead, as Chester Anderson claimed. He was not, to repeat Anderson's charge, "trapped in a typographical, mechanical reality of unrelated fragments of no whole."[14] Rather, Thompson used the manuscript fragments of his novels to bring people together in a kind of communal reading experience antedating Gutenberg Man.

Thompson did publish fragments from three novels in *Songs of the Doomed*: two chapters and the overview from *The Silk Road*; a three-chapter, twenty-two-page selection from *Prince Jellyfish*; and a four-chapter, thirty-three-page selection from *The Rum Diary*. These selections allow readers to approximate the kitchen readings, letting them read some of the same fragments that Thompson's guests had read while visiting Owl Farm, fragments that make no pretensions of being complete, polished, unified works.

The fragment of *Prince Jellyfish* in *Songs of the Doomed* is long enough to reveal the work's autobiographical nature. The life of Welburn Kemp, its hero, closely parallels the life of his creator. Thompson was from Louisville; Kemp is from Nashville. Thompson served as sports editor of his air base newspaper; Kemp has served as sports editor of his army base newspaper. Thompson had wanted to attend a prestigious Southern university; Kemp is a graduate of Washington and Lee University in Virginia. Thompson worked as a copyboy for *Time*; Kemp writes unsigned articles for *Business Age*. Like Thompson, Kemp wants to write the Great American Novel.

"Hit Him Again Jack, He's Crazy," the first chapter from *Prince Jellyfish* in *Songs of the Doomed*, relates Kemp's efforts to get a last-minute date for New Year's Eve. He follows a pretty woman on the Manhattan sidewalk to invite her to a New Year's Eve party. Kemp imagines her coyly resisting before finally acquiescing. When she gets home, however, she yells to Jack, apparently her husband, that some crazy guy was pursuing her. With a belt for a bullwhip Jack chases the frightened Kemp through lower Manhattan.

At the party uptown later that evening Kemp meets a young woman, who wonders why he does not have a date. Kemps explains that when he went to pick up his date, a man started chasing him with a whip. Luckily, Kemp says, he knew judo, so he was able to subdue the man. The incident shows Kemp's quick thinking. He takes a real-life incident and turns it into a fanciful story to impress the young woman.

What he thinks to himself departs even further from the truth. Although written in the third person, the narrative presents Kemp's thoughts. To help dramatize the daydream Thompson peppered his text with ellipsis dots: "Kemp saw himself standing off a whole pack of lunatics with whips, cutting them down like weeds with the back of his hand . . . nimble and quick, silent and deadly. . . . 'Attack *me*, will you!' . . . whap! . . . slash! . . . screams of pain . . . now standing above a ring of prostate bodies, wiping the blood off the back of his hand with a handkerchief."[15] Kemp's dream of personal glory follows a pattern James Thurber established in "The Secret Life of Walter Mitty." Thompson, who considered Thurber a great comic writer, especially enjoyed Walter Mitty, Thurber's most famous fictional character and the greatest daydreamer in American literature.[16]

"Interview," the second chapter from *Prince Jellyfish* in *Songs of the Doomed*, tells the story of Kemp's interview with a New York newspaper. Beforehand, he has another Walter Mitty–daydream, imagining himself as the trench-coat type of journalist: "He had a vision of himself as a reporter—trench-coated, sabre-tongued, a fearless champion of truth and justice. He saw himself working late at night, lonely and feverish at a desk in the empty newsroom, pounding out stories that would rock the city at dawn."[17]

The brash tone, brooding indignation, and sense of superiority that Kemp displays at the interview reflect Thompson's own character. William Turner, the managing editor who interviews Kemp, tells him the era of the old-time prima donna journalist is over, but Kemp, like his creator, sees himself in the mold of an old-timer, the reporter who keeps a flask in his hip pocket and a fifth in his desk drawer, who goes anywhere, anytime to get his story, whose fine reporting lets him get away with all sorts of aberrant behavior. When Turner offers him a position as copyboy, Kemp storms out of Turner's office.

"Cherokee Park," the third chapter from *Prince Jellyfish* in *Songs of the Doomed*, has a continuity problem. Kemp was from Nashville, but Cherokee Park is in Louisville. The end of this chapter signals the limits of Thompson's imagination. Its chase scene is entirely too similar to the chase scene in "Hit Him Again Jack, He's Crazy." But one conjoined word pair forms an evocative synecdoche that redeems the chapter. Recalling a time of late nights in Lovers' Lane, Kemp remembers it as an era of "soft lips and six-packs."[18]

The fragment of *The Rum Diary* in *Songs of the Doomed* reflects Thompson's decision to leave the rest of the novel unpublished, but he had a change of heart before the nineties ended and agreed to let Simon and Schuster issue the novel. Lynn Nesbit had known about *The Rum Diary* for a long time, but she also knew that Thompson's dissatisfaction with the work made him hesitant to publish it. She explained why he finally decided to release the novel: "*The Rum Diary* came out when it did because he needed money, absolutely. He never would've published that twenty years before."[19]

It is hard to understand why he needed money. *Proud Highway* had been a bestseller, and his previous books were selling well, especially with the recent release of the film adaptation of *Fear and Loathing in Las Vegas*. Thompson had been wanting to bring his greatest book to the cinema for a long time with no luck. In the late eighties David Lynch expressed an interest in adapting it—until a more compelling project took precedence. When an interviewer asked about the possibility of Lynch adapting the book, Thompson replied, "He wanted to do that, as a matter of fact, then he got onto that *Twin Peaks* thing."[20] Directed by Terry Gilliam and starring Johnny Depp, *Fear and Loathing in Las Vegas* premiered in May 1998. Although the film made plenty of money for him, Thompson somehow still needed more. Given his chronic financial irresponsibility, Thompson's spending had reached an unprecedented level of extravagance.

He had revised *The Rum Diary* off and on for years without getting it the way he wanted. Agreeing to publish the novel in the late nineties meant agreeing to let Simon and Schuster edit the manuscript for him. Given his mental and physical deterioration, Thompson simply could not do the work himself. When *Hell's Angels* was in press, he argued with his editors over practically every word, screaming about the changes they tried to impose on him. Sadly, he now gave the corporate editors at Simon and Schuster carte blanche to fix the manuscript however they saw fit.

When Marianne Macdonald came to Owl Farm to interview Thompson before the release of *The Rum Diary*, she had much the same experience as Nicoll had had five years earlier. She, too, got the HST show. Macdonald found two others at Owl Farm, filmmaker Wayne Ewing and Heidi Opheim, the latest girl Friday in an increasingly long succession. Young, pretty, and practically interchangeable, Thompson's girls Friday, by this point in his life, seem like so many Stepford wives.

When Opheim mentioned a disagreeable journalist who had visited recently, Thompson growled, "We shoulda tied her up in the basement." Macdonald, in response, tried to make herself unobtrusive, but Thompson would not let her off so easily. He demanded that she read a fragment from *The Rum Diary*, then in galleys. For convenience Thompson had punched holes in the galleys and put the sheets in a three-ring binder, so Macdonald read from that. Starting with the first paragraph of chapter 17—another echo of "The Raven"—she began, "I was awakened the next morning by a tapping on my door, a soft yet urgent tapping."

"More emphasis on the words," he interrupted, urging her to slow down and articulate, ironic advice from the mumble-mouthed Thompson.

Macdonald resumed. Before she could finish the paragraph, however, she heard Thompson rapping on the kitchen counter to signal a passage he particularly liked. Macdonald really endeared herself to Thompson once he asked what she thought about *The Rum Diary*. She replied, "I think it is reminiscent less of *Gatsby* than *Heart of Darkness*." Her reply elicited his applause.[21]

Her interview appeared in the London *Observer*, timed to coincide with the release of *The Rum Diary* in the United Kingdom. Upon Thompson's death Macdonald wrote a reminiscence, in which she describes him in an unguarded moment reading the binder containing *The Rum Diary*. The melancholy of nostalgia almost overwhelms him: "Thompson leafed through the galleys like an 80-year-old with her wedding album."[22]

The published version of *The Rum Diary* begins well. A preface titled "San Juan, Winter of 1958" describes Al's Backyard, a local bar where reporters from the *San Juan Daily News* gather before and after work. A bare-bones establishment with only three items on the menu—beer, rum, and hamburgers—Al's Backyard is an oasis, a place they can always return to when life beyond the backyard gets too hectic.

Thompson abandoned the third-person point of view of *Prince Jellyfish* in favor of the first-person. Otherwise, he borrowed much from the earlier manuscript, cannibalizing *Prince Jellyfish* for *The Rum Diary*. Welburn Kemp became Paul Kemp, an homage to Thompson's friend Paul Semonin. Although based on Thompson, Paul Kemp does share a major characteristic with Semonin: he comes from a family that has been prominent in the community for generations. Like Welburn Kemp, Paul Kemp attended a prestigious Southern university—Vanderbilt—but, unlike Welburn, Paul dropped out. Paul also served in the army and worked on the base newspaper where he was stationed.[23]

The biggest difference between Welburn Kemp and Paul Kemp is their age. Welburn is approximately twenty-six, but Paul is almost thirty-two by the end of *The Rum Diary*. Although both characters are based on Thompson, Paul's age distances him from his creator. Thompson was in his early twenties when he started *The Rum Diary*. In other words, Paul Kemp is a projection of what Thompson imagined his life would be like if he pursued a full-time career in journalism, which would take him around the globe from one short-term newspaper position to another.

As it stands, *The Rum Diary* suggests that Thompson had not worked out the kinks in Paul Kemp's character. Boarding his flight from New York to San Juan in the first chapter, Kemp spies a blond woman, pretty and petite, standing in the same line: "She had a fine little body and an impatient way of standing that indicated a mass of stored-up energy."[24] More dynamo than virgin, the young woman would turn out to be Chenault, Yeamon's girlfriend.

Kemp hopes to save her the seat next to him, but an old Puerto Rican man takes it. Kemp grabs the man and tries to toss him into the aisle. His behavior in this hilarious scene is reminiscent of Sebastian Dangerfield's behavior in *The Ginger Man*. As *The Rum Diary* develops, Kemp's actions on the plane turn out to be anomalous. Never again does he show such impulsive, self-centered violence. Rather, Kemp is Nick Carraway redivivus, a contemplative man who carefully describes what he sees and considers what it means. Apparently, Thompson enjoyed the airplane scene so much he could not bring himself to cut it, even though it clashed with Kemp's emerging personality.

Yeamon, the other character in *The Rum Diary* Thompson based on himself, is in his twenties. A frank self-portrait, Yeamon is a young man angry at everything. Kemp recognizes his younger self in him but twinges because Yeamon has the energy and enthusiasm Kemp has lost. A jaded Kemp says, "Listening to him, I realized how long it had been since I'd felt like I had the world by the balls."[25]

Upon its appearance in 1998 *The Rum Diary* met a mixed reception. Commonly, reviewers said it was readable but shallow. The plot was undeveloped, the characters uninteresting: sentiments not dissimilar to what the agents who rejected *The Rum Diary* had said thirty years earlier. Many reviewers complained about the incessant drinking that takes place—although what did they expect from a book called *The Rum Diary*? Some of Thompson's reviewers were downright hostile. The most startling remark occurs in Ruaridh Nicoll's review for the *Glasgow Herald*, startling because of its frankness but also because of Nicoll's long-standing admiration of its author: "*The Rum Diary* is shit."[26]

Nicoll only had four hundred words for his review in the *Glasgow Herald*, so he did not have room to detail what was wrong with the book. Its reactionary nature is one major problem. Thompson relies much too heavily on his literary models, *The Great Gatsby* and *The Sun Also Rises*. Patterned on these two works, *The Rum Diary* has an aesthetic that was seventy years old. Thompson ignored the development of the postmodern novel taking place around him. As he drafted and revised *The Rum Diary* in the sixties, many important postmodern novels appeared: John Barth's *Sotweed Factor*, Donald Barthelme's *Snow-White*, Joseph Heller's *Catch-22*, Ken Kesey's *Sometimes a Great Notion*, Norman Mailer's *American Dream*, and Thomas Pynchon's *V*, but none of these novels inspired *The Rum Diary*.

James Wood observes in the opening paragraph of his review of *The Rum Diary* that its "only value is that it illuminates one of the least interesting, but most dominant, strands in American fiction—the drained legacy of Hemingway." Toward the end of his review Wood brings in a more recent author for comparison, finding Thompson's skepticism to be "an anti-intellectualism masquerading as intellectual pugnacity. This is exactly the mode, forty years after Thompson wrote this book, of a contemporary writer like Bret Easton Ellis."[27]

Wood is onto something, but he ends his review a paragraph later without developing this comparison further. As published, *The Rum Diary* is more *American Psycho* than *American Dream*. Wood complains about its literary impoverishment: "It seems like a victim of sensory deprivation—there are no details beyond the ordinary, no moments of pathos, no exaltation, no aesthetic or visionary aeration, no metaphysical reckoning, no stylistic lavishness or verbal plenty, no moral expansion."[28] Of course, Wood could only judge *The Rum Diary* by the version published in 1998, but in its thousand-page unedited version, the work had contained extraordinary detail, metaphysical reckoning, and stylistic lavishness, which the editors at Simon and Schuster cut.

The Rum Diary reads like an Ellis novel because it was edited in the nineties, when Ellis was at his peak. Previous biographies and critical studies have situated *The Rum Diary* in the sixties when Thompson first drafted it, but it really belongs to the nineties, the decade it was edited and published. *The Rum Diary*, the book on which Hunter had lavished so much time and care as a young man, the book for which Sandy had sacrificed so much to help her husband bring it alive, he handed to his publisher in the nineties to make money.

As originally written, *The Rum Diary* had been filled with moments of reflection and introspection. Some of these passages survive in the *Rum Diary* fragment in *Songs of the Doomed* but were drained from it for the 1998 book version. In one scene, for example, Kemp and Yeamon go out to the beach and throw a coconut back and forth like a football. The pleasant scene provides some relief after an ugly fight between Yeamon and Chenault, but otherwise the book makes nothing of it. The editors at Simon and Schuster deleted a paragraph in which Kemp considers what football means to American culture: "But there is no getting away from football. Americans are cursed with it. The quarterback is God, and to stand back there with the ball—or the nut—resting easily in your hand, your arm cocked and hell breaking loose all around you, is to know the real essence of the mythical American; a foolish game with no foundation in reality, and yet a childish faith that a man can be a good sport and a winner on the same day."[29] Thompson's image of the quarterback as mythical American is quite appealing. The world is rushing toward him bent on his destruction, yet the quarterback maintains his composure, surveys the field before him, and, in a split second, recognizes the best possible way to accomplish his goal.

Three pages later Kemp, Yeamon, and Bob Sala—a character partly based on Bob Bone—go out for drinks and dinner. Kemp devotes five paragraphs to exploding the "myth of Latin virility." The section is so homophobic that it is understandable why the editors at Simon and Schuster cut it, but the omitted section verifies their editorial motivation. They were not trying to preserve a literary artifact from the sixties; they were fashioning a marketable product for the nineties.

In the *Rum Diary* fragment there is much consistency between Kemp exploding the myth of Latin virility and Kemp identifying the quarterback as the mythical American. As Thompson originally wrote *The Rum Diary*, Kemp is a myth buster, a first-person narrator who describes what he sees and analyzes its ultimate significance. To turn Thompson's unwieldy manuscript into a marketable product the corporate editors bled his cultural analysis from the book. No wonder James Wood found *The Rum Diary* "more blank than frank."

Concluding his review, Nicoll said that *The Rum Diary* never should have been published. In light of the major differences between the published version and the manuscript, perhaps it could be said that the novel should not have been published in the form it was. Although the editors at Simon and Schuster were the ones who cut hundreds of pages from the manuscript, Thompson bears the ultimate responsibility: he was the one who sanctioned their editorial work. When Nesbit said he published *The Rum Diary* because he needed money, there was something she implied but did not say: Thompson was too decrepit to write a new bestseller. Besides his cache of correspondence and a file of scraps and clippings and half-finished pieces, *The Rum Diary* was the last literary capital he had left. When Thompson first drafted *The Rum Diary* at Big Sur, he saw it as the Great American Novel or, at least, the "Great Puerto Rican Novel," a work of art that would secure his place in the history of American literature. By the nineties *The Rum Diary* was little more than a literary ATM.

Conclusion

Pliny the Younger used one of his letters to tell the story of Gaius Julius Bassus, a first-century Roman senator charged with corruption. Pliny knew the story well; he was the one who defended Bassus against the charges before the senate. The trial reminded Roman citizens and fellow senators of Bassus's previous escapades. This revival of interest in him encouraged the senators to forgive any recent transgressions and exonerate him of all charges. When Bassus left the senate chamber, a concourse of Romans met him with great joy and acclaim.

The situation Thompson faced on the eve of the twenty-first century parallels the case of Bassus in the first. The release of *Proud Highway* in 1997 triggered a revival of interest in his work and prompted readers to forgive the disappointing Gonzo Papers. The Thompson revival continued with the 1998 publication of *Fear and Loathing in Las Vegas* in the Modern Library, the vaunted series of great books from around the world that Random House has been publishing since the twenties. In 1999 Random House distinguished Thompson further with its release of *Hell's Angels* in the same series. He could now boast that he ranked with some of the greatest authors in modern literature.

Published in 2000, *Fear and Loathing in America: The Brutal Odyssey of an Outlaw Journalist, 1968–1976*, Thompson's second volume of letters, was well situated to capitalize on the revival. Reviewing the first volume, Mic Moroney had predicted the second would be more interesting, given that it would cover the period of *Fear and Loathing in Las Vegas* and *Fear and Loathing on the Campaign Trail*.[1] As a work of scholarship, *Fear and Loathing in America* is superior to *Proud Highway*, mainly because Brinkley recruited

Shelby Sadler to research and write the footnotes and many of the headnotes, but as the second volume of Thompson's life in letters, the book is tedious.

Brinkley was less discriminating in his selection of letters for *Fear and Loathing in America* than he had been with the earlier volume. Whereas he had omitted fifteen letters for every one in *Proud Highway*, he omitted five letters for every one in the new volume. Even with a tinier font, *Fear and Loathing in America* is nearly a hundred pages longer, making it more of a toecrusher than *Proud Highway*. Although Moroney expected the second volume would be more interesting because it would shed light on the period of Thompson's second and third books, it takes an inordinately long time getting there. Not until halfway through the volume does Thompson reach *Fear and Loathing in Las Vegas*, and even then he says little about it.

Fear and Loathing in America says more about the books Thompson did not write than those he did. Numerous letters convey his frustration with "The Death of the American Dream," enough to fill a good-sized book in themselves. The letters in *Fear and Loathing in America* retell the story of Thompson's 1970 campaign for sheriff of Pitkin County, this time in its fullest detail yet. (That raucous noise you hear is probably Andro Linklater's scream of fear and hatred at being subjected to this story yet again.) The critical term Sadler applies to Warhol's movies suits *Fear and Loathing in America*: excruciating.

The single biggest difference between *Proud Highway* and *Fear and Loathing in America*, the reason why the first volume of correspondence works and the second does not, concerns Thompson's place in his literary career. Taking him from his entry into journalism at Eglin Air Force Base through the publication of *Hell's Angels*, *Proud Highway* is the story of a young writer finding his way in the world. Having achieved success with his first book and thus recognized his literary and commercial worth, Thompson becomes a prima donna in *Fear and Loathing in America*. Unable to generate story ideas on his own, he insists that devising new ideas is his editor's job. He is forever demanding money, expecting publishers to reimburse his expenses no matter how extravagant, paranoid that they are ripping him off. In letter after letter Thompson seems convinced that he is right and everyone else is wrong.

Occasionally, a little gem gleams from its tarnished setting. Take the letter Thompson wrote Bob Bone on May 17, 1968. It begins with a tiresome paragraph about how Thompson was cleverly coaxing some extra expense money from the *Los Angeles Times* to write an article the newspaper would never publish. The letter improves with the second paragraph, which responds to a letter from Bone, then living in Mallorca. Thompson was astonished by Bone's risky, yet successful career decisions. He observes, "Only a lunatic, for

CONCLUSION 127

instance, would quit an up-mobile job in NY and run off to Brazil for a gig with the Rio Chamber of Commerce . . . and then expect to come back to NY and pick up a job with *Life* . . . and then flee again for a fantasy-style job in/on Mallorca." Bone was living the life the teenaged Thompson challenged others to live, daring to risk his security for adventure and excitement. Thompson tells Bone he should write a book on the subject, calling it "How to Beat the NY Big-Salary-Death-in-Life Syndrome."[2]

Bone would move to Hawaii and author a series of travel books known as the Maverick Guides. For his guide to Hawaii, he used the definition of "maverick" as his epigraph: "one who moves in a different direction than the rest of the herd—often a nonconformist."[3] Bone saw his old friend for the last time in December 2001, when Thompson came to Hawaii to cover the Honolulu Marathon for ESPN.com.

The previous year John Walsh, who had worked with Thompson at *Rolling Stone* and was now with ESPN, invited him to write a weekly online column. Aware Thompson was in a precipitous decline, Walsh also knew his name still attracted readers. Not until Thompson accepted the responsibility of writing the column did Walsh realize the task may have been beyond him. Thompson had trouble stringing his thoughts together. His attention span was practically nil, and he had difficulty focusing. Putting a thousand coherent words together had become virtually impossible. Walsh and his staff would give him tips, clues, and story ideas, but they seldom registered. Thompson would start in one direction before switching to an alternate and unrelated topic. His columns were so short, so disjointed, so insignificant that editors struggled to piece them together into something usable.[4]

When he reached Hawaii in 2001, Thompson looked terrible. Bone's account of his physical state parallels Walsh's account of his mental state. After he and Bone took their seats at a Waikiki restaurant one night, Thompson started rocking back and forth in his chair. His bizarre movements seemed unconscious to Bone, who asked his old friend if he realized what he was doing. The question did not register.[5]

Between the release of *Fear and Loathing in America* in 2000 and his suicide on February 20, 2005, Thompson eked out two more books with the help of his last personal assistant, Anita Bejmuk, who began working for him in 1999, moved into Owl Farm in 2000, and married him in 2003. Considering his mental and physical deterioration during the last years of his life, one gets the impression that Anita Thompson, who was thirty-five years younger than her new husband, assumed the role of a caregiver in an assisted living facility, less girl Friday and more Nurse Ratched.

Kingdom of Fear: Loathsome Secrets of a Star-Crossed Child in the Final Days of the American Century appeared in 2003. Thompson told interviewers that it was a new work, but he assembled *Kingdom of Fear* much the same way as *Songs of the Doomed*. *Kingdom of Fear* is what Horace called *disjecta membra poetae*, a set of scattered literary fragments. Thompson scraped the sump, gathering whatever leftover scraps and clippings and half-finished pieces he had at Owl Farm and connecting them with largely fictional, but seemingly autobiographical episodes. He could not write this new material himself. Rather, he related these anecdotes orally during his kitchen readings, and Anita recorded, transcribed, and edited them.

Early in *Kingdom of Fear* Thompson says that when he was nine years old FBI agents came to his house to investigate the destruction of a US mailbox. Upon the book's release, few readers questioned this episode, although Thompson's FBI file, now a matter of public record, has nothing about it. One author opens his critical study of Thompson's work by recounting the supposed FBI episode without questioning its veracity. Not until David Wills released *High White Notes* in 2021 did anyone ask whether the incident really happened. Wills suggested that Thompson invented the story, observing that the US Postal Inspection Service would have investigated the vandalism of a mailbox, not the FBI. Like those in *Songs of the Doomed*, none of the anecdotes in *Kingdom of Fear* should be taken at face value without corroborating evidence.[6]

Thompson continued writing his ESPN column into 2003, but it never improved. Angry rants about last Sunday's football game are dated as soon as next Sunday rolls around. In 2004 Thompson collected his ESPN columns as *Hey Rube: Blood Sport, the Bush Doctrine, and the Downward Spiral of Dumbness: Modern History from the Sports Desk*. In the aggregate the columns seem even worse than they do individually. *Hey Rube* is Thompson's *Senilia*. Besides exposing redundancies in language, literary references, and imagery, the collection reinforces the belligerent tone that runs through his columns. Thompson seems to hate everyone. Call him Timon of Aspen.

Walsh gave Thompson the freedom to write about other topics beyond sports, but even these alternate topics cannot save *Hey Rube*. The piece for September 29, 2003 is an obituary for George Plimpton. Thompson says, "There are so many wild and beautiful stories I could tell you about being with George, having savage and unnatural adventures all over the world, that I am feeling dumb and paralyzed when I try to write them down."[7] This sentence shows Thompson's fear coming true: he had become a parody of himself. The conjoined word pair is a defining stylistic feature of gonzo journalism. Putting three pairs together in one sentence, Thompson imitated himself—with one key difference. These word pairs resemble his best writing in form alone. They lack the power and panache of the conjoined word pairs he wrote thirty years earlier.

As an account of George Plimpton, the article is a cop-out: Thompson was too lazy or too unstable to write out some anecdotes for posterity, not even to honor an old friend, not even to pay tribute to the founder of the *Paris Review* and a pioneer of New Journalism. Perhaps ESPN.com was not the right outlet for a lengthy appreciation of George Plimpton, but practically any national magazine would have taken such a piece and paid handsomely for it. Thompson could not write it.

Far from being a swan song, *Hey Rube* is yet another reminder that its author's best writing was behind him, had been for decades. Readers generally agree that his first three books are his best three books. Historians of journalism prefer *Fear and Loathing on the Campaign Trail*, which marks a major shift in the way presidential campaigns are reported. Thompson puts the reporter out front, making the story of the news gathering process foremost, exposing the fallacy of objective reportage, and daring to say what other reporters only fantasized about saying.

Literary historians prefer *Hell's Angels* or *Fear and Loathing in Las Vegas*. *Fear and Loathing on the Campaign Trail* is not nearly as well-crafted as the two previous books. Contemporary reviewers considered *Hell's Angels* a sociological exposé, but sociological exposés seldom have staying power. *Hell's Angels* endures, not because of its sociology but because of its literary quality. The book's fine writing still makes it a delight to read. Never out of print, *Hell's Angels* can be found everywhere from the campus library at the Artic University of Norway to the take-a-book, leave-a-book shelf at the Launceston Youth Hostel in Tasmania.

Fear and Loathing in Las Vegas is an American classic. William Crawford Woods, whose *New York Times* review contributed much to its recognition, foresaw its presence in the classroom, observing that the book is "a trendy English teacher's dream, a text for the type who teaches Emily Dickinson and Paul Simon from the same mimeograph sheet." With *Fear and Loathing in Las Vegas*, Woods continued, Thompson has "written himself into the history of American literature in what I suspect will be a permanent way."[8]

Joe Klein, who considered Thompson the best of the New Journalists, said that he was "one of the few writers extant who can rest assured that people will be reading his work 200 years from now." Klein made this remark just seven years after *Fear and Loathing in Las Vegas* appeared, and it does seem to overestimate Thomson's significance to literary history—but perhaps not. Writing the month Thompson died, Declan Lynch called him "one of the great American prose writers of the twentieth century."[9]

Over fifty years have now passed since *Fear and Loathing in Las Vegas* appeared, but with every passing year it has gained new readers, who have added new episodes to the history of the book.[10] In 1984 one man reporting for jury duty walked into the Lucas County Courthouse in Toledo, Ohio, with a copy of the Popular Library paperback edition of *Fear and Loathing in Las Vegas* tucked into the pocket of his tweed jacket. After reading the book while awaiting jury selection, the man was chosen to serve on a jury in a drunk-driving case!

In *Savage Journey*, a recent study of Thompson's life and work, Peter Richardson writes that it is an error to categorize *Fear and Loathing in Las Vegas* as journalism or nonfiction, but he refrains from calling it a novel, which would also be an error in categorization. Interviewers often asked Thompson whether *Fear and Loathing in Las Vegas* is fiction or nonfiction. When one asked him to categorize the book, Thompson replied, "I would classify it, in Truman Capote's words, as a 'nonfiction novel' in that almost all of it was true and did happen. I warped a few things, but it was a pretty accurate picture." Asked a similar question later, Thompson was more hostile, telling the interviewer that fact and fiction are artificial categories: "I'm a writer. Fiction and Nonfiction are best-seller terms created by the best-seller list."[11]

The ambiguity of truth in *Fear and Loathing in Las Vegas* is one of the book's most appealing and sophisticated aspects. Thompson puts readers in an epistemological quandary. We read a book based on true events, which becomes so outrageous that we must keep saying to ourselves, "Is this true? No, surely it is not true. Is it? How can it be?" Thompson may have ignored postmodern fiction when he wrote *The Rum Diary*, but *Fear and Loathing in Las Vegas* suits the postmodern aesthetic, forcing readers to question the whole concept of truth, to scrutinize how the tone, genre, and format of written works shape our perception of reality.

Wolfe concluded his fine tribute to Thompson by calling him the twentieth century's "greatest comic writer in the English language."[12] Wolfe's superlative is astonishing, but it is also quite shrewd. Identifying Thompson's humor as his greatest attribute, he avoided pinning him down to any particular literary genre. There are humorous novels, humorous travel books, humorous essays, and, in Thompson's case, humorous sociological exposés and humorous political reportage. Some humorists have crossed boundaries from one genre to another. After all, the author of *Huckleberry Finn* also wrote *Innocents Abroad*. Others stick to a single genre. Tim Moore, one of Britain's

CONCLUSION

finest contemporary humorists, limits himself to travel writing. Thompson used humor to blur the boundaries between genres. His humor manifests his edgework. It, too, is a form of boundary negotiation as it challenges the line between fact and fiction.

The example of Tim Moore may offer a good way to understand Thompson more fully. After Moore established a reputation as a travel writer, an interviewer asked if he had any plans to write a novel. Implicit within her question is the assumption that the novel is the consummate literary form and that any good writer must aspire to write one. Moore told her that he would love to write fiction but could not create plot and character out of thin air: "I'm not able to think of things unless I've seen them with my own eyes."[13]

"A man's got to know his limitations," Dirty Harry says. Perhaps Moore knows his better than Thompson ever knew his limitations. Like Moore, Thompson had trouble writing about anything unless he had seen it with his own eyes. Although he had a great imagination, he, too, could not write something out of thin air. He did not need much. Remember Doctor Brainwaves. In that case Thompson took a conversation about a Bolivian con man and turned it into a personal encounter with a Brazilian psychiatrist who teaches him how to read Nixon's mind. In the case of *Fear and Loathing in Las Vegas*, Thompson really did visit Las Vegas to cover the Mint 400 and the district attorneys' drug conference. Having done so, he could use these two experiences as starting points, which triggered his imagination and let it run wild, enabling him to create all sorts of humorous variations on reality.

Thompson's need for a starting point in reality can explain his failures as well as his successes. Once he got a satellite dish installed at Owl Farm, he thought he could write about whatever he watched on television, but, needless to say, TV is no substitute for reality. As many pieces in *Generation of Swine*, *Better than Sex*, and *Hey Rube* indicate, TV could not spark Thompson's imagination the way direct experience could. Thompson's speaking engagements let him travel extensively, but once he established his literary reputation, he abandoned the adventuresome travel that had taken him the length of South America and the width of North America. Now he would fly to his destination, take a limousine to a luxury hotel, and gorge himself on room service until his handlers came to collect him. In short, he stopped having the kind of travel experiences that are good for the imagination, not to mention the soul.

The need for an external spark to fire his imagination can also explain Thompson's failure as a novelist. There is a reason why every novel he ever attempted is a pale imitation of *The Great Gatsby*. He thought F. Scott Fitzgerald's greatest novel was also the greatest novel in American literature, so he continually used it as the basis for the novels he attempted. It never worked.

The Great Gatsby was Thompson's white whale. As he struggled to write in his waning years, his mind kept going back to Fitzgerald's masterpiece.

Speaking with Thompson on the telephone one day, Shelby Sadler told him that her home in Rockville, Maryland, was walking distance from St. Mary's Church Historic Cemetery, where Scott and Zelda Fitzgerald were buried. Astonished, Thompson made plans to visit the cemetery when he was in town.[14] During his next trip to Washington he and Sadler met at her home, and together they started toward the cemetery. For Sadler it was usually a fifteen-minute walk, but it took longer this time, partly because of Thompson's chronic back pain, but also because they stopped at a florist to buy a white rose to place upon the grave.

One headstone serves for both Scott and Zelda, who are buried in the same grave. Their headstone provides the basic information that most headstones provide: full names, birthdates, and death dates. What distinguishes their burial plot is the long granite ledger that rests atop their grave. The ledger is mostly blank, but onto the bottom third is inscribed the last sentence from *The Great Gatsby*: "So we beat on, boats against the current, borne back ceaselessly into the past."

Thompson had not expected to read this, his favorite sentence in American literature, on Fitzgerald's grave. He gently placed the white rose on the ledger across these words, after which he craned his neck and looked skyward. They lingered for a moment before turning around and walking back to Sadler's home. Thompson was silent the whole way.

NOTES

Chapter 1: An Introduction to Hunter S. Thompson

1. Gelett Burgess, *Goops and How to Be Them* (New York: Frederick A. Stokes, 1900), n.p.; Anita Thompson, ed. *Ancient Gonzo Wisdom: Interviews with Hunter S. Thompson* (Cambridge, MA: Da Capo Press, 2009), 204.

2. Jann Wenner and Corey Seymour, eds., *Gonzo: The Life of Hunter S. Thompson, An Oral Biography* (New York: Little, Brown, 2007), 16; Byron Crawford, "Neighbor from Childhood Recalls Hunter S. Thompson," *Courier-Journal*, February 20, 2008, B1.

3. William McKeen, *Outlaw Journalist: The Life and Times of Hunter S. Thompson* (New York: Norton, 2008), 11–13.

4. Paul Semonin, quoted in McKeen, *Outlaw Journalist*, 16; Hunter S. Thompson to Paul Semonin, undated letter postmarked February 11, 1955, Catalog, April 2019, Nate D. Sanders Auctions: Fine Autographs and Memorabilia, natedsanders.com; Floyd Smith, quoted in Peter O. Whitmer, *When the Going Gets Weird: The Twisted Life and Times of Hunter S. Thompson: A Very Unauthorized Biography* (New York: Hyperion, 1993), 47.

5. Anita Thompson, *Ancient Gonzo Wisdom*, 260.

6. "Tearful Youth Is Jailed Amid Barrage of Pleas," *Courier-Journal*, June 16, 1955, 21.

7. Hunter S. Thompson to Carol Overdorf, January 15, 1958, *The Proud Highway: Saga of a Desperate Southern Gentleman, 1955–1967*, ed. Douglas Brinkley (New York: Villard, 1997), 98–99.

8. Quoted in Joseph Cox, "Shore Lines," *Express*, May 17, 1967, 3.

9. "Paul Overdorf, *Herald* Editor," *Express*, January 6, 1960, 6; "Joseph Cox, 74, Columnist, Dies," *Express*, January 6, 1972, 1.

10. Joseph Cox, "Shore Lines," *Express*, May 17, 1967, 3.

11. Thompson to Susan Haselden, April 13 and November 12, 1958, *Proud Highway*, 115, 140; Harold Bloom, *The Anxiety of Influence: A Theory of Poetry* (New York: Oxford University Press, 1973); William Kennedy, "A Box of Books," *Harper's*, April 2006, 76.

12. Hunter S. Thompson, *The Great Shark Hunt: Strange Tales from a Strange Time* (New York: Summit Books, 1979), 123.

13. Thompson to Larry Callen, July 4, 1958, *Proud Highway*, 128–129; W. Somerset Maugham, "Books of the Year," *Sunday Times*, December 25, 1955, 4.

14. Whitmer, *When the Going Gets Weird*, 93; Beverly Orndorff, "Faulkner Looks Back on Happy Year at University of Virginia," *Times-Dispatch*, May 24, 1958, 4; Thompson to Larry Callen, July 4, 1958, *Proud Highway*, 128.

15. Thompson to Larry Callen, July 14, 1958, *Proud Highway*, 132; Hunter S. Thompson to Eugene W. McGarr, January 29, 1970, *Fear and Loathing in America: The Brutal Odyssey of an Outlaw Journalist, 1968–1976*, ed. Douglas Brinkley and Shelby Sadler (New York: Simon and Schuster, 2000), 277.

16. E. Jean Carroll, *Hunter: The Strange and Savage Life of Hunter S. Thompson* (New York: Dutton, 1993), 73–74.

17. William H. A. Carr, "Off B'way," *New York Post*, August 24, 1960, 42; John Tytell, *The Living Theatre: Art, Exile, and Outrage* (New York: Grove Press, 1995), 153; Jack Kerouac to Allen Ginsberg, March 24, 1959, *Selected Letters, 1957–1969*, ed. Ann Charters (New York: Penguin, 1999), 219–20.

18. Thompson to William J. Kennedy, July 21, 1961, *Proud Highway*, 279.

19. Robert W. Bone, *Fire Bone! A Maverick Guide to a Life in Journalism* (Walnut Creek, CA: Peripety Press, 2017), 106–9.

20. Quoted in Bone, *Fire Bone!* 110.

21. "Al Romm, Who Set Hard-Hitting Tone for NY's *Times Herald-Record*, Dies," *Palm Beach Post*, January 4, 2000, 17; Al Romm, quoted in Whitmer, *When the Going Gets Weird*, 104.

22. Kevin J. Hayes, *Stephen Crane* (Tavistock, Northumberland: Northcote House, 2004), 70; Thompson to Jim Silberman, October 17, 1973, *Fear and Loathing in America*, 549.

23. Wenner and Seymour, *Gonzo*, 42–43; Thompson to William Kennedy, July 16, 1960, *Proud Highway*, 218.

24. Eric C. Shoaf, *Gonzology: A Hunter Thompson Bibliography* (Charlotte, NC: Cielo, 2018), 86.

25. Gonzalo Velázquez, *Annuario bibliográfico puertorriqueño: Indice alfabético de libros, folletos, revistas y periódicos publicados en puerto rico durante, 1959–1960* (San Juan: Departamento de Instrucción Pública, 1966), 352; Thompson to Virginia Thompson, January 14, 1960, *Proud Highway*, 203.

26. Thompson to Sandy Conklin, January 26, 1960, *Proud Highway*, 207.

27. Velázquez, *Annuario bibliográfico puertorriqueño*, 352.

28. Bone, *Fire Bone!* 123–24.

29. Thompson to Jim Silberman, January 13, 1970, *Fear and Loathing in America*, 260.

30. Leo E. Litwak, "A Trip to Esalen Institute—Joy Is the Prize," *New York Times Magazine*, December 31, 1967, 28.

31. Thompson to William Kennedy, October 21, 1961, *Proud Highway*, 291.

32. Thompson to Clifford Ridley, April 6, 1963, *Proud Highway*, 369; Hunter S. Thompson, "Baja California Has Honky Tonks, Solitude," *Chicago Daily Tribune*, October 8, 1961, D10.

33. Hunter S. Thompson, "Big Sur: The Tropic of Henry Miller," *Rogue*, October 1961, 35.

34. Thompson, "Big Sur," 36.

35. Thompson to Lionel Olay, October 25, 1963, *Proud Highway*, 407.

36. Hunter S. Thompson, "Whither the Old Copper Capital of the West? To Boom or Bust?" *National Observer*, June 1, 1964, 13; "Mining, Diversified Opportunities Spur Industrial Growth in Butte, Montana," *Journeymen and Apprentices of the Plumbing and Pipe Fitting Industry Journal* 78, no. 2 (February 1963): 8–19.

37. Thompson, "Whither the Old Copper Capital," 13.

38. Joseph Cox, "Shore Lines," *Express*, June 10, 1964, 12; "Tap Room Reporter 'Analyzes Butte,'" *Montana Standard-Post*, June 7, 1964, 6.

39 88 Cong. Rec. 13,419 (1964).

40. "Then It Was Missoula's Turn," *Montana Standard-Post*, June 19, 1964, 4; Hunter S. Thompson, *Hell's Angels: A Strange and Terrible Saga* (New York: Random House, 1967), 203.

41. Richard M. Dorson, *America in Legend: Folklore from the Colonial Period to the Present* (New York: Pantheon, 1973), 253.

42. Charles Denton, "Did We Make Them What They Are Today?" *San Francisco Examiner*, December 3, 1964, 35.

43. Charles Denton, "Some Answers to a Mother's Questions," *San Francisco Examiner*, December 10, 1964, 41.

44. Charles Denton, "And Then You Wrote—On UC Rebels and LOLs," *San Francisco Examiner*, December 15, 1964, 27.

45. Robert W. Bone, "Bob Bone Remembers Hunter," *Travel*, February 23, 2005, travel-travelword.blogspot.com.

46. Denton, "Did We Make Them?" 35.

Chapter 2: Foreign Correspondent

1. Hunter S. Thompson, "Nobody Is Neutral under Aruba's Hot Sun," *National Observer*, July 16, 1962, 14.

2. Hunter S. Thompson, "'Leery Optimism' at Home for Kennedy Visitor," *National Observer*, June 24, 1962, 11.

3. Hunter S. Thompson, "Munoz Skilfully Keeps Foes Off-Balance," *Courier-Journal*, May 29, 1960, 28.

4. Thompson, "Leery Optimism," 11.

5. Thompson, "Nobody Is Neutral," 14.

6. Hunter S. Thompson, "Democracy Dies in Peru, But Few Seem to Mourn Its Passing," *National Observer*, August 27, 1962, 16.

7. Thompson, "Democracy Dies in Peru, But Few Seem to Mourn Its Passing," *Richmond Times-Dispatch*, September 12, 1962, 14.

8. Hunter S. Thompson, "Latin Close-Up: Why Ecuador Is Seeking US Aid," *National Observer*, July 30, 1962, 1.

9. Hunter S. Thompson, "Operation Triangular: Bolivia's Fate Rides with It," *National Observer*, October 15, 1962, 13; Hunter S. Thompson, "A Never-Never Land

High above the Sea," *National Observer*, April 15, 1963, 11; Thomas C. Field, *From Development to Dictatorship: Bolivia and the Alliance for Progress in the Kennedy Era* (Ithaca, NY: Cornell University Press, 2014), ix.

10. Hunter S. Thompson, "Uruguay Goes to Polls, with Economy Sagging," *National Observer*, November 19, 1962, 14.

11. Thompson, "Nobody Is Neutral," 14.

12. Thompson, "Nobody Is Neutral," 14; Hunter S. Thompson, "Chatty Letters During a Journey from Aruba to Rio," *National Observer*, December 31, 1962, 14.

13. Hunter S. Thompson, "How Democracy Is Nudged Ahead in Ecuador," *National Observer*, September 17, 1962, 13.

14. Thompson, "How Democracy Is Nudged," 13.

15 87 Cong. Rec. 15,424–25; 19,842–43 (1962).

16. Thompson to Daryl Harrington, December 17, 1962, *Proud Highway*, 360.

17. Brian Kevin, *The Footloose American: Following the Hunter S. Thompson Trail across South America* (New York: Broadway Books, 2014), 314.

18. Thompson, "Chatty Letters," 14; Hunter S. Thompson, "A Footloose American in a Smugglers' Den," *National Observer*, August 6, 1962, 13; Eric Newby, ed., *A Book of Travellers' Tales* (London: Collins, 1985), 493.

19. Thompson, "Footloose American," 13.

20. Thompson, "Footloose American," 13.

21. Thompson, "Footloose American," 13.

22. Hunter S. Thompson, *Fear and Loathing in Las Vegas: A Savage Journey to the Heart of the American Dream* (New York: Random House, 1971), 178.

23. David Hamilton, "In an Innertube, on the Amazon," *Michigan Quarterly Review* 29, no. 3 (Summer 1990): 372, 382.

24. Thompson to Paul Semonin, May 26, 1962, *Proud Highway*, 339.

25. Hunter S. Thompson, "Beer Boat Blues," *Courier-Journal*, November 11, 1962, 163.

26. Thompson to Paul Semonin, May 26, 1962, *Proud Highway*, 337–40.

27. Thompson to Paul Semonin, June 6, 1962, *Proud Highway*, 340.

28. Thompson to Paul Semonin, August 4, 1962, *Proud Highway*, 349–50.

29. Thompson, "Chatty Letters," 14.

30. Thompson, "Chatty Letters," 14.

31. Thompson, "Chatty Letters," 14.

32. Thompson to Larry Callen, July 14, 1958, *Proud Highway*, 132; William Kennedy, "A Box of Books," *Harper's Magazine*, April 2006, 76.

33. Harold C. Gardiner, "The Recognition of Shock," *America*, May 20, 1961, 316.

34. Gardiner, "Recognition of Shock," 317.

35. Thompson, "Chatty Letters," 14; William McKeen, *Hunter S. Thompson* (Boston: Twayne, 1991), 19.

36. Robert W. Bone, *Fire Bone! A Maverick Guide to a Life in Journalism* (Walnut Creek, CA: Peripety Press, 2017), 150.

37. Kevin, *Footloose American*, 338, 333.

38. Hunter S. Thompson, "Brazilian Soldiers Stage a Raid in Revenge," *National*

Observer, February 11, 1963, 13; Hunter S. Thompson, *The Great Shark Hunt: Strange Tales from a Strange Time* (New York: Summit Books, 1979), 362–65.

39. Thompson, *Great Shark Hunt*, 362.

40. Thompson, *Great Shark Hunt*, 364.

41. Hunter S. Thompson, "Why Anti-Gringo Winds Often Blow South of the Border," *National Observer*, August 19, 1963, 18.

42. Jann Wenner and Corey Seymour, eds., *Gonzo: The Life of Hunter S. Thompson, An Oral Biography* (New York: Little, Brown, 2007), 61; Hunter S. Thompson, "Recession, Political Upheaval Take the Fun out of Life in Argentina," *National Observer*, December 10, 1962, 2; Hunter S. Thompson, *Hell's Angels: A Strange and Terrible Saga* (New York: Random House, 1967), 175.

43. Thompson, "Anti-Gringo Winds," 18.

44. Hamilton, "In an Innertube," 389–90.

45. Thompson to Clifford Ridley, September 9, 1963, *Proud Highway*, 398; Thompson, "Anti-Gringo Winds," 18.

46. Thompson to Clifford Ridley, April 6, 1963, *Proud Highway*, 371; "Did We Make Them?" 35.

Chapter 3: Literary Critic

1. Hunter S. Thompson to Paul Semonin, *The Proud Highway: Saga of a Desperate Southern Gentleman, 1955–1967*, ed. Douglas Brinkley (New York: Villard, 1997), April 18, 1965, 508.

2. Hunter S. Thompson, "Dr. Pflaum Looks at the Latins, But His View Is Tired and Foggy," *National Observer*, March 9, 1964, 19.

3. Hunter S. Thompson, "One of the Darkest Documents Ever Put Down Is *The Red Lances*," *National Observer*, October 7, 1963, 19; Ernest Hemingway, *By-Line*, ed. William White (Harmondsworth: Penguin, 1970), 203.

4. Thompson, "One of the Darkest Documents," 19.

5. Hunter S. Thompson, "The 'Faulkner of Latin America': First Look at an Old, Old Book," *National Observer*, January 27, 1964, 17; Robert G. Mead, Jr., "Asturias' *El señor presidente*, and US Critics," *Hispania* 47, no. 2 (May 1964): 410–12.

6. Hunter S. Thompson, "Brazilian's Fable of a Phony Carries the Touch of Mark Twain," *National Observer*, April 20, 1964, 17.

7. Bruce Weber, "L. Rust Hills, 83, Fiction Editor at *Esquire*," *New York Times*, August 15, 2008, B5; Terry Southern, *Now Dig This: The Unspeakable Writings of Terry Southern, 1950–1995*, ed. Nile Southern and Josh Alan Friedman (New York: Grove, 2001), 5; Thompson to Rust Hills, June 20, 1959, *Proud Highway*, 171–72.

8. Gay Talese, "Looking for Hemingway," *Esquire*, July 1963, 44.

9. Hunter S. Thompson, "Where Are the Writing Talents of Yesteryear?" *National Observer*, August 5, 1963, 17.

10. Thompson to William J. Kennedy, August 15, 1963, *Proud Highway*, 387.

11. Rust Hills, "The Structure of the American Literary Establishment," *Esquire*, July 1963, 43.

12. Quoted in Joan Shelley Rubin, "Repossessing the Cozzens-Macdonald Imbroglio:

Middlebrow Authorship, Critical Authority, and Autonomous Readers in Postwar America," *Modern Intellectual History* 7, no. 3 (2010): 576.

13. Burton Raffel, "Letter to the Editor," *New York Times*, October 13, 1963, BR50; Mark Harris, "Hot Lunch Center," *New York Times*, August 4, 1963, BR4.

14. Thompson to Elizabeth McKee, September 12, 1959, *Proud Highway*, 187.

15. Thompson to Frank Campbell, March 7, 1961, *Proud Highway*, 257-58.

16. Thompson to Sterling Lord, June 26, 1961, *Proud Highway*, 257-58, 264.

17. Jann Wenner and Corey Seymour, eds., *Gonzo: The Life of Hunter S. Thompson, An Oral Biography* (New York: Little, Brown, 2007), 83.

18. Thompson to Candida Donadio, February 15, 1962, and to William J. Kennedy, March 14, 1962, *Proud Highway*, 319, 328.

19. Thompson, "Where Are the Writing Talents," 17.

20. Nelson Algren, *Notes from a Sea Diary: Hemingway All the Way* (New York: Putnam, 1965), 11; Thompson, "Where Are the Writing Talents," 17.

21. Thompson, "Where Are the Writing Talents," 17.

22. Norman Mailer, "Norman Mailer Versus Nine Writers," *Esquire*, July 1963, 64-65.

23. Thompson, "Where Are the Writing Talents," 17.

24. James Baldwin, "As Much Truth as One Can Bear," *New York Times*, January 14, 1962, BR11.

25. Thompson to Semonin, November 15, 1964, *Proud Highway*, 469; Wenner and Seymour, *Gonzo*, 45.

26. Hunter S. Thompson, *Hell's Angels: A Strange and Terrible Saga* (New York: Random House, 1967), 87.

27. Thompson to Candida Donadio, February 15, 1962, *Proud Highway*, 320.

28. Thompson, "Where Are the Writing Talents," 17.

29. Anita Thompson, ed., *Ancient Gonzo Wisdom: Interviews with Hunter S. Thompson* (Cambridge, MA: Da Capo Press), 102.

30. Henry Allen, "For Hunter Thompson, Outrage Is the Only Way Out," *Washington Post*, July 23, 1972, BW4; Thompson, "Where Are the Writing Talents," 17.

31. Hunter S. Thompson, "Donleavy Proves His Lunatic Humor Is Original," *National Observer*, November 11, 1963, 17.

32. Thompson to Abner Sundell, June 25, 1964, *Proud Highway*, 458.

33. Hunter S. Thompson, "Golding Tries *Lord of the Flies* Formula Again, But It Falls Short," *National Observer*, April 27, 1964, 16.

34. Hunter S. Thompson, "The Crow, a Novelist, and a Hunt: Man in Search of His Primitive Self," *National Observer*, December 2, 1963, 17.

35. Thompson to William J. Kennedy, November 22, 1963, *Proud Highway*, 420.

36. Philippians, 2:12; Juan de Valdés, *Divine Considerations Treating of Those Things which Are Most Profitable, Most Necessary, and Most Perfect in Our Christian Profession* (Cambridge: E.D., 1646), 299.

37. Robert Southey, *The Minor Poems* (London: Longman, 1815), 2:123; Robert Southey, *Essays, Moral and Political* (London: John Murray, 1832), 2:172; William Golding, *Lord of the Flies* (1954; reprinted, New York: Capricorn, 1959), 114.

38. Thompson to William J. Kennedy, November 22, 1963, *Proud Highway*, 420–21.

39. Thompson to William Faulkner, March 30, 1959, *Proud Highway*, 164; Malcolm Cowley, ed., *Writers at Work: The Paris Review Interviews* (New York: Penguin, 1958), 125.

40. Mario Puzo, "Sinatra Started to Shout Abuse, Swearing He'd Beat the Hell out of Me," *Mail on Sunday*, February 22, 2009, 40; Thompson to William J. Kennedy, June 24, 1964, *Proud Highway*, 456.

41. Hunter S. Thompson, "When the Beatniks Were Social Lions," *National Observer*, April 20, 1964, 1, 14; Thompson to Eugene W. McGarr, April 9, 1964, and to Paul Semonin, April 28, 1964, *Proud Highway*, 450–52.

42. Hunter S. Thompson, "What Lured Hemingway to Ketchum?" *National Observer*, May 25, 1964, 1, 13; Ernest Hemingway, *Death in the Afternoon* (New York: Scribner, 1932), 278.

43. Thompson, "What Lured Hemingway," 13.

44. Ernest Hemingway, ed., *Men at War: The Best War Stories of All Time* (New York: Crown, 1942), xv.

45. Thompson to Lionel Olay, October 25, 1963, *Proud Highway*, 406.

Chapter 4: New Journalist

1. Tom Wolfe, "The New Journalism," in Tom Wolfe and E. W. Johnson, eds., *New Journalism with an Anthology* (New York: Harper and Row, 1973), 10, 14, 23; John Seelye, "The Shotgun behind the Lens," *New Republic*, August 11, 1973, 22.

2. Kevin J. Hayes, *A Journey through American Literature* (New York: Oxford University Press, 2012), 152; Terry Southern, *Now Dig This: The Unspeakable Writings of Terry Southern, 1950–1995*, ed. Nile Southern and Josh Alan Friedman (New York: Grove, 2001), 5.

3. Thompson to Peter Collier, October 11, 1967, and Tom Wolfe to Thompson, November 23, 1967, *The Proud Highway: Saga of a Desperate Southern Gentleman, 1955–1967*, ed. Douglas Brinkley (New York: Villard, 1977), 644, 650; Wolfe, "New Journalism," 23; Peter S. Prescott, "Two Kinds of Books," *Women's Wear Daily*, October 28, 1966, 24.

4. Peter S. Prescott, "Fiction Is Flagging," *Women's Wear Daily*, February 10, 1967, 32.

5. Hayes, *Journey through American Literature*, 152.

6. Harilaos Stecopoulos, "An Editor's Arc: A Conversation with David Hamilton," *Los Angeles Review of Books*, May 17, 2020, lareviewofbooks.org.

7. Prescott, "Fiction Is Flagging," 32.

8. Kurt Vonnegut, "A Political Disease," *Harper's*, July 1973, 94; Joe Klein, "The New! Old! New!! Journalism!!!," *Mother Jones*, December 1979, 62.

9. Thompson to Paul Semonin, June 9, 1965; to Sara Blackburn, May 17, 1965; and to Angus Cameron, June 10, 1965; *Proud Highway*, 522, 516, 524.

10. Thompson to Angus Cameron, June 28, 1965, *Proud Highway*, 529.

11. Thompson to Angus Cameron, June 28, 1965, *Proud Highway*, 529.

12. Seelye, "Shotgun," 23–24.

13. Hunter S. Thompson to Paul Semonin, July 6, 1965, quoted in *Fine Books and Manuscripts, Including Americana* (New York: Sotheby's, 2018), lot 303.

14. Hunter S. Thompson, *Songs of the Doomed: More Notes on the Death of the American Dream* (New York: Summit Books, 1990), 109.

15. Hunter S. Thompson, *Hell's Angels: A Strange and Terrible Saga* (New York: Random House, 1967), 3.

16. Kevin T. McEneaney, *Hunter S. Thompson: Fear, Loathing, and the Birth of Gonzo* (Lanham, MD: Rowman and Littlefield, 2016), the most extreme example of this practice, seems to assume that Thompson read every author he mentions in his work.

17. McKeen, *Outlaw Journalist*, 109.

18. Robert Christgau, "Life Styles: The Boxing Fan," *Esquire*, May 1967, 120–23; Hunter S. Thompson, "Life Styles: The Cyclist," *Esquire*, January 1967, 57.

19. Joseph Cox, "Shore Lines," *Express*, December 15, 1966, 7.

20. Joseph Cox, "Shore Lines," *Express*, May 17, 1967, 3; Robert W. Bone, *Fire Bone! A Maverick Guide to a Life in Journalism* (Walnut Creek, CA: Peripety Press, 2017), 188; Charles Kuralt to Thompson, June 1, 1967, *Proud Highway*, 615.

21. Giles Playfair, "Middle-Aged Rebels," *New Society*, November 9, 1967, 676; Jeremy Brien, "Fireballs," Bristol *Evening Post*, October 26, 1967, 7.

22. Julian Mitchell, "California's Rotten Angels," *Times Saturday Review*, October 28, 1967, 21.

23. Prescott, "Fiction Is Flagging," 32; Peter Worsley, "The Violent Society," *Guardian*, November 24, 1967, 13.

24. Chester Anderson, "Heaven and Hell on Wheels," *Los Angeles Free Press*, June 9, 1967, 9–10; Marshall McLuhan, *Understanding Media: The Extensions of Man* (1964; New York: New American Library, 1966), 159–60.

25. Leo E. Litwak, "On the Wild Side," *New York Times Book Review*, January 29, 1967, 6, 44.

26. Richard M. Dorson, *America in Legend: Folklore from the Colonial Period to the Present* (New York: Pantheon, 1973), 255–57.

27. Thompson to Peter Collier, November 14, 1967, *Proud Highway*, 649.

28. Jean-Luc Godard, *Pierrot le fou*, trans. Peter Whitehead (New York: Simon and Schuster, 1969), 74; Albert J. Guerard, ed., *Stories of the Double* (Philadelphia: Lippincott, 1967), 9; Studs Terkel, "A Full-Time Social Vendetta," *Chicago Tribune*, March 5, 1967, L3.

29. Thompson, *Hell's Angels*, 7.

30. William Kennedy, "A Box of Books," *Harper's*, April 2006, 76; George Sylvester Viereck and Paul Eldridge, *My First Two Thousand Years* (New York: Fawcett, 1956), 39.

31. Thompson, *Hell's Angels*, 50.

32. Thompson, *Hell's Angels*, 92.

33. Thompson, *Hell's Angels*, 128–29.

34. Thompson, *Hell's Angels*, 54.

35. Thompson, *Hell's Angels*, 161, 163; Ralph Ellison, *Invisible Man* (1952; New York: Vintage, 1995), 33.

36. Thompson, *Hell's Angels*, 247.

37. Hunter S. Thompson to Tom Wolfe, October 26, 1968, *Fear and Loathing in America: The Brutal Odyssey of an Outlaw Journalist, 1968–1976*, ed. Douglas Brinkley and Shelby Sadler (New York: Simon and Schuster, 2000), 143.

38. Thompson to Paul Semonin, November 6, 1963, *Proud Highway*, 410; Hunter S. Thompson, "The Silk Road," in Steve Crist and Laila Nabulsi, eds., *Gonzo* (Los Angeles: Ammo Books, 2007), 187; Joe Klein, "Forever Weird," *New York Times Book Review*, November 18, 2007, 15.

39. Kennedy, "Box of Books," 76.

40. Thompson, *Hell's Angels*, 181.

41. Thompson, *Hell's Angels*, 48.

42. Worsley, "Violent Society," 13.

43. Hunter S. Thompson, *Songs of the Doomed: More Notes on the Death of the American Dream* (New York: Summit Books, 1990), 110–11; Richard M. Elman, "Hell's Angels," *New Republic*, February 25, 1967, 34; Gerald Nicosia, "What a Long, Strange Trip It's Been," *Washington Post*, November 18, 1990, P1.

44. Thompson, *Hell's Angels*, 274.

45. Stephen Lyng, "Edgework and the Risk-Taking Experience," in *The Sociology of Risk-Taking*, ed. Stephen Lyng (New York: Routledge, 2005), 3–4.

46. Joseph Conrad, *Heart of Darkness and The Secret Sharer* (New York: New American Library, 1950), 61, 149.

47. Albert J. Guerard, introduction to Joseph Conrad, *Heart of Darkness and The Secret Sharer*, 8–9, 15.

48. Thompson to Chuck Alverson, November 28, 1966, *Proud Highway*, 589.

49. Wenner and Seymour, *Gonzo*, 84; Thompson, *Hell's Angels*, 278.

Chapter 5: Gonzo Journalist

1. Hunter S. Thompson, "The 'Hashbury' Is the Capital of the Hippies," *New York Times*, May 14, 1967, SM14; David S. Wills, *High White Notes: The Rise and Fall of Gonzo Journalism* (St. Andrews, Scotland: Beatdom Books, 2021), 182.

2. Thompson, "Hashbury," 29, 122.

3. Joseph Cox, "Shore Lines," *Express*, May 17, 1967, 3.

4. Joan Didion, "Slouching Towards Bethlehem," *Saturday Evening Post*, September 23, 1967, 89.

5. Linda Blandford, "Beyond the Homosexuality, *Cruising* Is a Cry for Comfort and Understanding," *Guardian*, March 7, 1980, 10; Hunter S. Thompson to Gerald Walker, January 15, 1968, *Fear and Loathing in America: The Brutal Odyssey of an Outlaw Journalist, 1968–1976*, ed. Douglas Brinkley and Shelby Sadler (New York: Simon and Schuster, 2000), 20; Hunter S. Thompson, *Fear and Loathing in Las Vegas: A Savage Journey to the Heart of the American Dream* (New York: Random House, 1971), 76.

6. Bill Cardoso, "The Origin of Gonzo," in Warren Hinckle, ed., *Who Killed Hunter S. Thompson? The Picaresque Story of the Birth of Gonzo, Illustrated* (San Francisco: Last Gasp, 2017), 253; Hunter S. Thompson to Lynn Nesbit, December 16, 1968, *Fear and Loathing in America*, 147.

7. Cardoso, "Origin of Gonzo," 254.

8. Cardoso, "Origin of Gonzo, 254; Thompson to Jim Silberman, January 13, 1970, *Fear and Loathing in America*, 266.

9. Hunter S. Thompson, *The Great Shark Hunt: Strange Tales from a Strange Time* (New York: Summit Books, 1979), 179.

10. Thompson, *Great Shark Hunt*, 85.

11. Thompson, *Great Shark Hunt*, 95.

12. James Salter, *Light Years* (New York: Random House, 1975), 161.

13. Hunter S. Thompson, *Songs of the Doomed: More Notes on the Death of the American Dream* (New York: Summit Books, 1990), 136; Timothy Denevi, *Freak Kingdom: Hunter S. Thompson's Manic Ten-Year Crusade against American Fascism* (New York: Public Affairs, 2018), 335.

14. Bill Cardoso, *The Maltese Sangweech and Other Heroes* (New York: Athenaeum, 1984), 137.

15. Thompson to Warren Hinckle, April 28, 1970, *Fear and Loathing in America*, 293.

16. Ralph Steadman, *The Joke's Over: Bruised Memories: Gonzo, Hunter S. Thompson, and Me* (Orlando, FL: Harcourt, 2006), 9.

17. Jerome Klinkowitz, *Keeping Literary Company: Working with Writers Since the Sixties* (Albany: State University of New York Press, 1999), 39; Kurt Vonnegut, *Slaughterhouse-Five: or, The Children's Crusade, A Duty-Dance with Death* (New York: Dell, 1969), 172.

18. Hinckle, *Who Killed Hunter S. Thompson?* 91.

19. Hinckle, *Who Killed Hunter S. Thompson?* 91; Thompson to Sidney Zion, February 5, 1971, *Fear and Loathing in America*, 358.

20. Cardoso, "Origin of Gonzo," 254; Ralph Steadman, quoted in Douglas Martin, "Bill Cardoso, 68, Editor Who Coined 'Gonzo,'" *New York Times*, March 16, 2006, A25.

21. Hinckle, *Who Killed Hunter S. Thompson?* 8; Phil Baker, "A New Face in the Snakepit," *TLS*, November 6, 1998, 24; Fred Bruning, "To the Mint with Gonzo," *Newsday*, June 25, 1972, 19.

22. Thompson, "The Kentucky Derby Is Decadent and Depraved," in Hinckle, *Who Killed Hunter S. Thompson?* 222.

23. Harold Beaver, *The Great American Masquerade* (London: Vision, 1985), 153; Rosemarie Zagarri, ed., *David Humphreys' 'Life of General Washington' with George Washington's 'Remarks'"* (Athens: University of Georgia Press, 1991), 18; Mark Twain, *Adventures of Huckleberry Finn*, ed. Walter Blair and Victor Fischer (Berkeley: University of California Press, 1985), 153.

24. Thompson, "Kentucky Derby," 215, 223.

25. Tom Wolfe, quoted in Thompson to Jim Silberman, November 25, 1970, *Fear and Loathing in America*, 337; Tom Wolfe, headnote to Thompson, "The Kentucky Derby Is Decadent and Depraved," in Tom Wolfe and E. W. Johnson, eds., *New Journalism with an Anthology* (New York: Harper and Row, 1973), 172.

26. Wenner and Seymour, *Gonzo*, 99; Thompson to Jim Silberman, January 13, 1970, *Fear and Loathing in America*, 263.

27. Alex Traub, "George Stranahan, Benefactor of Physicists and Beer Lovers, Dies at 89," *New York Times*, June 21, 2021, B6; Wenner and Seymour, *Gonzo*, 137.

28. Thompson to Jim Silberman, March 3, 1968, and to Selma Shapiro, April 24, 1968, *Fear and Loathing in America*, 45, 59.

29. Thompson to Ralph Ginzburg, November 18, 1968, *Fear and Loathing in America*, 145.

30. Thompson to Hughes Rudd, October 18, 1968, *Fear and Loathing in America*, 140.

31. *William Byrd's Histories of the Dividing Line betwixt Virginia and North Carolina*, ed. William K. Boyd (New York: Dover, 1967).

32. Thompson to Jim Silberman, February 11, 1969, *Fear and Loathing in America*, 164.

33. Thompson to Jim Silberman, August 30, 1969, *Fear and Loathing in America*, 205.

34. Thompson to Steve Geller, December 10, 1969, and to Jim Silberman, January 13, 1970, *Fear and Loathing in America*, 227, 264.

35. Thompson, *Great Shark Hunt*, 199.

36. Thompson, *Fear and Loathing in Las Vegas*, 3.

37. Robert Burns, "Written with a Pencil," *Poetical Works* (Chicago: Henneberry, 1901), 101.

38. Samuel Johnson, quoted in Allen Tate, *The Man of Letters in the Modern World: Selected Essays, 1928–1955* (New York: Meridian, 1955), 14; Roberto Loiederman, "The Darker Side of a Night with Hunter S. Thompson," *Los Angeles Times*, February 27, 2005, R12.

39. Kevin J. Hayes, *A Journey through American Literature* (New York: Oxford University Press, 2012), 13.

40. Thompson, *Fear and Loathing in Las Vegas*, 188; Sally Vincent, "The Ballad of Ralph and Hunter," *Independent*, September 30, 2008, 20; Steadman, *Joke's Over*, 205; Declan Lynch, "We Really Should Be Asking, Why Doesn't Everyone Do It This Way?" Dublin *Sunday Independent*, February 27, 2005, 14.

41. Patrick Hynan, "Into the Bloated Cadaver, The Exact Shape of 50 States," Toronto *Globe and Mail*, July 15, 1972, 29.

42. Kevin J. Hayes, *The Cambridge Introduction to Herman Melville* (New York: Cambridge University Press, 2007), 121–22; Ken Kesey, *One Flew over the Cuckoo's Nest* (New York: Viking, 1962), 81.

43. *Crime in America—Illicit and Dangerous Drugs: Hearings on H. R. 17, Day 2, Before the Select Comm. on Crime*, 91st Cong. 148 (1969), (statement of Art Linkletter).

44. Peter O. Whitmer, *When the Going Gets Weird: The Twisted Life and Times of Hunter S. Thompson: A Very Unauthorized Biography* (New York: Hyperion, 1993), 5.

45. Captain John Smith, *The Generall Historie of Virginia, New England and the Summer Isles* (Glasgow: James MacLehose, 1907), 1:205.

46. Thompson, *Fear and Loathing in Las Vegas*, 68.

47. Bryan Marquand, "Bill Cardoso, Journalist Helped Define Hunter Thompson Image," *Boston Globe*, March 15, 2006, A20; Hunter S. Thompson, *Fear and Loathing*

on the Campaign Trail '72 (San Francisco: Straight Arrow Books, 1973), 83; Cardoso, "Origin of Gonzo," 255.

48. Paul Krassner, "The Gonif of Gonzo," *Los Angeles Times*, June 29, 1997, BR8.

49. Mort Sheinman, "Fear and Loathing in Las Vegas," *Women's Wear Daily*, June 23, 1972, 36; George R. Gay, "A Savage Journey in Gonzo Style," *San Francisco Examiner*, July 2, 1972, 30, 34; "This Month's Top Paperbacks," *Bookseller*, October 7, 1972, 1999.

Chapter 6: Campaign Trailblazer

1. Paul Krassner, "Blowing Deadlines with Hunter," in Warren Hinckle, ed., *Who Killed Hunter S. Thompson? The Picaresque Story of the Birth of Gonzo, Illustrated* (San Francisco: Last Gasp, 2017), 278.

2. Jann Wenner and Corey Seymour, eds., *Gonzo: The Life of Hunter S. Thompson, An Oral Biography* (New York: Little, Brown, 2007), 158.

3. Nancy Frizzelle, "A Sur Thing: The Coast," *Women's Wear Daily*, October 5, 1972, 3.

4. Hunter S. Thompson, *Fear and Loathing on the Campaign Trail '72* (San Francisco: Straight Arrow Books, 1973), 48.

5. Steven d'Arazien, "Wild Man's View of the Campaign," *Nation*, August 13, 1973, 120.

6. Kurt Vonnegut, "A Political Disease," *Harper's*, July 1973, 94.

7. Denise Demong, "Thompson: Getting High on Politics," *Women's Wear Daily*, June 23, 1972, 36.

8. William Greider, "Amok-Raking Journalist," *Washington Post*, May 13, 1973, BW8.

9. Thompson, *Fear and Loathing on the Campaign Trail*, 81, 72.

10. Thompson, *Fear and Loathing on the Campaign Trail*, 28.

11. Thompson, *Fear and Loathing on the Campaign Trail*, 29.

12. Thompson, *Fear and Loathing on the Campaign Trail*, 36.

13. Thompson, *Fear and Loathing on the Campaign Trail*, 63–65.

14. Ralph Whitehead, Jr., "The Gonzo Morality," *Columbia Journalism Review* 8, no. 3 (September-October 1979): 72.

15. Thompson, *Fear and Loathing on the Campaign Trail*, 356–57.

16. Hinckle, *Who Killed Hunter S. Thompson?* 73.

17. Thompson, *Fear and Loathing on the Campaign Trail*, 151–52.

18. Thompson, *Fear and Loathing on the Campaign Trail*, 152.

19. Kandy Stroud, "Ed's Whistlestops: Toots and Touts," *Women's Wear Daily*, February 22, 1972, 37.

20. Thompson, *Fear and Loathing on the Campaign Trail*, 222.

21. Thompson, *Fear and Loathing on the Campaign Trail*, 121.

22. Thompson, *Fear and Loathing on the Campaign Trail*, 240–41.

23. Thompson, *Fear and Loathing on the Campaign Trail*, 242.

24. Thompson, *Fear and Loathing on the Campaign Trail*, 242–43.

25. Thompson, *Fear and Loathing on the Campaign Trail*, 344; Hunter S. Thompson, "A Never-Never Land High above the Sea," *National Observer*, April 15, 1963, 11.
26. Thompson, *Fear and Loathing on the Campaign Trail*, 344.
27. Thompson, *Fear and Loathing on the Campaign Trail*, 344–45.
28. David Jordan, "Speeding Down the Road to Babylon," *Manhattan Mercury*, May 27, 1973, 26.
29. Thompson, *Fear and Loathing on the Campaign Trail*, 124.
30. Thompson, *Fear and Loathing on the Campaign Trail*, 147.
31. Anatole Broyard, "Maunder in the Cafeteria," *New York Times*, January 9, 1973, 37.
32. Thompson, *Fear and Loathing on the Campaign Trail*, 187.

Chapter 7: Anthologist

1. Joe Klein, "Forever Weird," *New York Times Book Review*, November 8, 2007, 15.
2. Annie Leibovitz, *Annie Leibovitz at Work*, ed. Sharon DeLano (New York Random House, 2008), 29.
3. Laura Palmer, "Mystery Is the Precinct Where I Found Peace," in *War Torn: Stories of War from the Women Reporters Who Covered Vietnam*, ed. Denby Fawcett (New York: Random House, 2002), 254, 266.
4. Laura Palmer, "Saigon: Living in the Bull's-Eye; Drowning in a Sea of Sadness," *Rolling Stone*, June 5, 1975, 26–33.
5. Klein, "Forever Weird," 15; Palmer, "Mystery Is the Precinct," 266.
6. Jann Wenner and Corey Seymour, eds., *Gonzo: The Life of Hunter S. Thompson, An Oral Biography* (New York: Little, Brown, 2007), 220.
7. Norman Snider, "The Great Shark Hunt," *Globe and Mail*, September 8, 1979, 51.
8. Harold Beaver, *The Great American Masquerade* (London: Vision, 1985), 152.
9. Gene Lyons, "How Stoned Were You?" *Nation*, October 13, 1979, 342.
10. Wenner and Seymour, *Gonzo*, 235.
11. Lauren Jones, "Hunter Thompson: Gonzo Unleashed," *Ann Arbor Sun*, March 8, 1974, 4.
12. George Plimpton, *Shadow Box* (New York: Putnam, 1977), 252; Harriet Sugar, "Thompson Unprepared for Speech," *Daily Tar Heel*, October 24, 1974, 4.
13. Harriet Sugar, "Duke Refuses to Pay Thompson," *Daily Tar Heel*, October 28, 1974, 1.
14. Ann Mittman, "'Gonzo Journalist' Performs as Expected in U of I Session," *Cedar Rapids Gazette*, November 29, 1984, 10A.
15. Mittman, "Gonzo Journalist," 10A.
16. David Hamilton, "In an Innertube, on the Amazon," *Michigan Quarterly Review* 29, no. 3 (Summer 1990): 391; Daniel R. Baldwin, "Thompson Hunting: A Search for Hunter S. Thompson: A Quest for the American Dream" (master's thesis, University of Iowa, 1983).

17. Mittman, "Gonzo Journalist," 10A.
18. Hinckle, *Who Killed Hunter S. Thompson?* 178.
19. Gary Dretzka, "'Swine' Is Lean on Dr. Gonzo Pearls," *Chicago Tribune*, July 19, 1988, E3.
20. Hunter S. Thompson, *Generation of Swine: Tales of Shame and Degradation in the '80s* (New York: Summit Books, 1988), 13.
21. Hinckle, *Who Killed Hunter S. Thompson?* 174, 179.
22. Thompson, *Generation of Swine*, 68, 108.
23. Thompson, *Generation of Swine*, 39, 43, 239.
24. William McKeen, *Hunter S. Thompson* (Boston: Twayne, 1991); Paul Perry, *Fear and Loathing: The Strange and Terrible Saga of Hunter S. Thompson* (New York: Thunder's Mouth Press, 1992); Peter O. Whitmer, *When the Going Gets Weird: The Twisted Life and Times of Hunter S. Thompson: A Very Unauthorized Biography* (New York: Hyperion, 1993); E. Jean Carroll, *The Strange and Savage Life of Hunter S. Thompson* (New York: Dutton, 1993).
25. McKeen, *Outlaw Journalist: The Life and Times of Hunter S. Thompson* (New York: Norton, 2008), 301–2.
26. Wenner and Seymour, *Gonzo*, 25–26.
27. Andro Linklater, "Ravings of a Drug-Crazed Wykehamist," *Spectator*, October 12, 1991, 32; Chris Reidy, "Thompson's Brazen Bonfire of Inanities," *Boston Globe*, November 23, 1990, 124.
28. Thompson, *Fear and Loathing on the Campaign Trail*, 71, 81; Hunter S. Thompson, *Better than Sex: Confessions of a Political Junkie* (New York: Random House, 1994), 229, 45.
29. Harry Browne, "Hunter Blowtorches His Cred," *Irish Times*, February 28, 1995, 10.
30. Laura Riding and Robert Graves, *A Pamphlet against Anthologies* (Garden City, NY: Doubleday, Doran, 1928).

Chapter 8: Letter Writer

1. Jann Wenner and Corey Seymour, eds., *Gonzo: The Life of Hunter S. Thompson, An Oral Biography* (New York: Little, Brown, 2007), 292; Edward Dahlberg, *Alms for Oblivion* (Minneapolis: University of Minnesota Press, 1964), 49.
2. Mic Moroney, "The Raging Buzzard Circles the Past," *Irish Times*, October 4, 1997, 66.
3. Paul Krassner, "The Gonif of Gonzo," *Los Angeles Times*, June 29, 1997, BR8.
4. Hunter S. Thompson to Larry Callen, June 7, 1959, *The Proud Highway: Saga of a Desperate Southern Gentleman, 1955–1967* (New York: Villard, 1997), 168.
5. Douglas Brinkley, "Contentment Was Not Enough," *Rolling Stone*, March 24, 2005, 36–37.
6. Moroney, "Raging Buzzard," 66.
7. Douglas Brinkley, "Editor' Note," *Proud Highway*, xxii.
8. R. W. B. Lewis, *The American Adam: Innocence, Tragedy and Tradition in the Nineteenth Century* (Chicago: Phoenix Books, 1955), 5; Brinkley, "Editor's Note," xxiii.

9. Peter Blake, "On the High Gonzo Trail," *TLS*, October 31, 1997, 29; David McCumber, "The Mad Adventure Continues as the Doctor of Gonzo Journalism Celebrates the 25th Anniversary of *Fear and Loathing in Las Vegas*," *Los Angeles Times*, December 9, 1996, E1.

10. Hunter S. Thompson to Paul Semonin, undated letter, postmarked February 11, 1955, Catalog, April 2019, Nate D. Sanders Auctions: Fine Autographs and Memorabilia, natedsanders.com; Wenner and Seymour, *Gonzo*, 94.

11. Douglas Brinkley, headnote for Thompson to Porter Bibb III, February 6, 1957, *Proud Highway*, 43; William McKeen, *Outlaw Journalist: The Life and Times of Hunter S. Thompson* (New York: Norton, 2008), 31.

12. Douglas Brinkley, headnote for Thompson to Virginia Thompson, November 29, 1957, *Proud Highway*, 76.

13. Douglas Brinkley, headnote for Thompson to Charles Kuralt [i.e., Charles Preston], October 19, 1966, *Proud Highway*, 587.

14. Thompson to Charles Kuralt [i.e., Charles Preston], October 19, 1966, *Proud Highway*, 587–588.

15. Thompson to Gerald Tyrrell, September 22, 1956, *Proud Highway*, 11, 13.

16. Thompson to Ralph Peterson, October 25, 1956, *Proud Highway*, 20.

17. Thompsonn to Ralph Peterson, October 25, 1956, *Proud Highway*, 21.

18. William Melmoth, ed. and trans., *The Letters of Pliny the Consul* (London: R. Dodsley, 1747), 1:97; Thompson to Larry Callen, July 4, 1958, *Proud Highway*, 129; W. Somerset Maugham, "Books of the Year," *Sunday Times*, December 25, 1955, 4.

19. Thompson to Elizabeth Ray, October 18, 1956, *Proud Highway*, 16.

20. Thompson to Rutledge Lilly, December 12, 1956, *Proud Highway*, 34.

21. Wenner and Seymour, *Gonzo*, 347; Hugh Rawson and Margaret Miner, eds., *The Oxford Dictionary of American Quotations* (New York: Oxford University Press, 2006), 362; Tennessee Williams, *A House Not Meant to Stand*, ed. Thomas Keith (New York: New Directions, 2008), 9.

22. Thompson to Susan Haselden, July 13, 1957, *Proud Highway*, 57.

23. Thompson to Susan Haselden, July 13, 1957, *Proud Highway*, 58.

24. Thompson to Susan Haselden, July 13, 1957, *Proud Highway*, 59.

25. Thompson to Kraig Juenger, July 4, 1958, *Proud Highway*, 131.

26. Jack Kerouac, *On the Road* (1957; New York: Penguin, 1991), 79.

27. Thompson, "Debt Letter," April 2, 1958, *Proud Highway*, 115.

28. Thompson to Nelson Algren, February 10, 1966, *Proud Highway*, 558.

29. Gay Talese, *The Kingdom and the Power: Behind the Scenes at the New York Times, the Institution that Influences the World* (New York: Random House, 1969), 204.

30. Harvey Breit, *The Writer Observed* (Cleveland, OH: World, 1956), 283.

31. C. L. Sulzberger, "The Writer and the Outer World," *New York Times*, March 30, 1959, 30.

32. Thompson to William Faulkner, March 30, 1959, *Proud Highway*, 164.

33. Thompson to William Faulkner, March 30, 1959, *Proud Highway*, 164.

34. Thompson, "Midnight on the Coast Highway," *Proud Highway*, 661.
35. Thompson to Tom Wolfe, November 28, 1967, *Proud Highway*, 652–53.
36. Blake, "On the High Gonzo Trail," 29.
37. Steven Moore, "Going for the Gonzo," *Washington Post*, May 25, 1997, 15.

Chapter 9: Novelist

1. Ruaridh Nicoll, "The Night I Spent Drinking with Hunter S. Thompson," *Guardian*, March 27, 2016, 47.
2. Ruaridh Nicoll, "The Duke of Hazard," *Sunday Tribune*, March 14, 1993, B1; Ruaridh Nicoll, "Scotland: All by Myself, I Wanna Be . . . ," *Observer*, January 8, 2006, 10.
3. Nicoll, "Duke of Hazard," B1.
4. Nicoll, "Duke of Hazard," B1.
5. Hans J. Van Miegroet, "Vanitas," in *The Dictionary of Art*, ed. Jane Turner (New York: Grove, 1996), 31:882.
6. Nicoll, "Duke of Hazard," B1; Ruaridh Nicoll, "A Rum Way to Be Remembered," *Glasgow Herald*, November 5, 1998, 22.
7. Nicoll, "Night I Spent Drinking," 47.
8. Hunter S. Thompson to Lawrence Truman, October 3, 1968, *Fear and Loathing in America: The Brutal Odyssey of an Outlaw Journalist, 1968–1976*, ed. Douglas Brinkley and Shelby Sadler (New York: Simon and Schuster, 2000), 134; Jann Wenner and Corey Seymour, eds., *Gonzo: The Life of Hunter S. Thompson, An Oral Biography* (New York: Little, Brown, 2007), 63.
9. Hunter S. Thompson, *Songs of the Doomed: More Notes on the Death of the American Dream* (New York: Summit Books, 1990), 217.
10. Thompson, *Songs of the Doomed*, 218; Hunter S. Thompson, "The Silk Road," in Steve Crist and Laila Nabulsi, *Gonzo* (Los Angeles: Ammo Books, 2007), 187.
11. Thompson, *Songs of the Doomed*, 223.
12. Shelby Sadler, notes to Hunter S. Thompson, *Fear and Loathing in America: The Brutal Odyssey of an Outlaw Journalist, 1968–1976*, ed. Douglas Brinkley and Shelby Sadler (New York: Simon and Schuster, 2000), 92, 300; Wenner and Seymour, *Gonzo*, 274.
13. Wenner and Seymour, *Gonzo*, 273.
14. Chester Anderson, "Heaven and Hell on Wheels," *Los Angeles Free Press*, June 9, 1967, 9.
15. Thompson, *Songs of the Doomed*, 49.
16. Hunter S. Thompson to Clifford Ridley, September 9, 1963, *The Proud Highway: Saga of a Desperate Southern Gentleman, 1955–1967*, ed. Douglas Brinkley (New York: Villard, 1997), 396; Thompson to Lawrence Truman, October 3, 1968, *Fear and Loathing in America*, 133.
17. Thompson, *Songs of the Doomed*, 51.
18. Thompson, *Songs of the Doomed*, 60.
19. Wenner and Seymour, *Gonzo*, 331.

20. Anita Thompson, ed., *Ancient Gonzo Wisdom: Interviews with Hunter S. Thompson* (Cambridge, MA: Da Capo Press, 2009), 175.

21. Marianne Macdonald, "Fear and Weird Clothing," *Observer*, October 11, 1998, 7.

22. Marianne Macdonald, "Fear, Loathing, Guns: At Home with King Gonzo," *London Times*, February 22, 2005, sec. T2, 4.

23. Hunter S. Thompson, *The Rum Diary: The Long Lost Novel* (New York: Simon and Schuster, 1998), 59.

24. Thompson, *Rum Diary*, 8.

25. Thompson, *Rum Diary*, 23.

26. Nicoll, "Rum Way," 22.

27. James Wood, "More Blank than Frank," *Guardian*, November 21, 1998, B10.

28. Wood, "More Blank than Frank," B10.

29. Thompson, *Songs of the Doomed*, 79.

Conclusion

1. Mic Moroney, "The Raging Buzzard Circles the Past," *Irish Times*, October 4, 1997, 66.

2. Hunter S. Thompson to Bob Bone, May 17, 1968, *Fear and Loathing in America: The Brutal Odyssey of an Outlaw Journalist, 1968–1976*, ed. Douglas Brinkley and Shelby Sadler (New York: Simon and Schuster, 2000), 76.

3. Robert W. Bone, *The Maverick Guide to Hawaii*, 7th ed. (Gretna, LA: Pelican, 1983), ii.

4. Jann Wenner and Corey Seymour, eds., *Gonzo: The Life of Hunter S. Thompson, An Oral Biography* (New York: Little, Brown, 2007), 383–84.

5. Robert W. Bone, *Fire Bone! A Maverick Guide to a Life in Journalism* (Walnut Creek, CA: Peripety Press, 2017), 342.

6. Hunter S. Thompson, *Kingdom of Fear: Loathsome Secrets of a Star-Crossed Child in the Final Days of the American Century* (New York: Simon and Schuster, 2003), 5–6; William Stephenson, *Gonzo Republic: Hunter S. Thompson's America* (London: Continuum, 2012), 1; David S. Wills, *High White Notes: The Rise and Fall of Gonzo Journalism* (St. Andrews, Scotland: Beatdom Books, 2021), 468.

7. Hunter S. Thompson, *Hey Rube: Blood Sport, the Bush Doctrine, and the Downward Spiral of Dumbness: Modern History from the Sports Desk* (New York: Simon and Schuster, 2004), 240.

8. Crawford Woods, "Fear and Loathing in Las Vegas," *New York Times*, July 23, 1972, BR17.

9. Joe Klein, "The New! Old! New!! Journalism!!!," *Mother Jones*, December 1979, 66; Declan Lynch, "We Really Should Be Asking, Why Doesn't Everyone Do It This Way?" Dublin *Sunday Independent*, February 27, 2005, 14.

10. Kevin J. Hayes, "Savage Journey," *Dalhousie Review* 102, no. 3 (Autumn 2022): 438, the source of the following anecdote.

11. Peter Richardson, *Savage Journey: Hunter S. Thompson and the Weird Road to*

Gonzo (Berkeley: University of California Press, 2022), 4; Anita Thompson, *Ancient Gonzo Wisdom*, 176, 314.

12. Tom Wolfe, "The 20th Century's Greatest Comic Writer in English," *Wall Street Journal*, February 22, 2005, D10.

13. Stephanie Merritt, "It's Better to Travel Hopelessly," *Observer*, February 18, 2001, D17.

14. Wenner and Seymour, *Gonzo*, 274.

BIBLIOGRAPHY

Books by Hunter S. Thompson

Better than Sex: Confessions of a Political Junkie. New York: Random House, 1994.
The Curse of Lono. New York: Bantam Books, 1983.
Fear and Loathing in America: The Brutal Odyssey of an Outlaw Journalist, 1968–1976. Edited by Douglas Brinkley and Shelby Sadler. New York: Simon and Schuster, 2000.
Fear and Loathing in Las Vegas: A Savage Journey to the Heart of the American Dream. New York: Random House, 1971.
Fear and Loathing on the Campaign Trail '72. San Francisco: Straight Arrow Books, 1973.
Generation of Swine: Tales of Shame and Degradation in the '80s. New York: Summit Books, 1988.
The Great Shark Hunt: Strange Tales from a Strange Time. New York: Summit Books, 1979.
Hell's Angels: A Strange and Terrible Saga. New York: Random House, 1967.
Hey Rube: Blood Sport, the Bush Doctrine, and the Downward Spiral of Dumbness: Modern History from the Sports Desk. New York: Simon and Schuster, 2004.
Kingdom of Fear: Loathsome Secrets of a Star-Crossed Child in the Final Days of the American Century. New York: Simon and Schuster, 2003.
The Proud Highway: Saga of a Desperate Southern Gentleman, 1955–1967. Edited by Douglas Brinkley. New York: Villard, 1997.
The Rum Diary: The Long Lost Novel. New York: Simon and Schuster, 1998.
Screw-Jack. New York: Simon and Schuster, 2000.
Songs of the Doomed: More Notes on the Death of the American Dream. New York: Summit Books, 1990.

Books about Hunter S. Thompson

Bone, Robert W. *Fire Bone! A Maverick Guide to a Life in Journalism.* Walnut Creek, CA: Peripety Press, 2017.
Carroll, E. Jean. *Hunter: The Strange and Savage Life of Hunter S. Thompson.* New York: Dutton, 1993.
Cleverly, Michael, and Bob Braudis. *The Kitchen Readings: Untold Stories of Hunter S. Thompson.* New York: Harper Perennial, 2008.
Crist, Steve, and Laila Nabulsi, eds. *Gonzo.* Los Angeles: Ammo Books, 2007.

Denevi, Timothy. *Freak Kingdom: Hunter S. Thompson's Manic Ten-Year Crusade against American Fascism*. New York: Public Affairs, 2018.

Harrell, Margaret A., and Ron Whitehead. *The Hell's Angels Letters: Hunter S. Thompson, Margaret Harrell and the Making of an American Classic*. San Francisco: Norfolk Press, 2020.

Hinckle, Warren, ed. *Who Killed Hunter S. Thompson? The Picaresque Story of the Birth of Gonzo, Illustrated*. San Francisco: Last Gasp, 2017.

Kevin, Brian. *The Footloose American: Following the Hunter S. Thompson Trail across South America*. New York: Broadway Books, 2014.

McEneaney, Kevin T. *Hunter S. Thompson: Fear, Loathing, and the Birth of Gonzo*. Lanham, MD: Rowman and Littlefield, 2016.

McKeen, William. *Hunter S. Thompson*. Boston: Twayne, 1991.

McKeen, William. *Outlaw Journalist: The Life and Times of Hunter S. Thompson*. New York: Norton, 2008.

Perry, Paul. *Fear and Loathing: The Strange and Terrible Saga of Hunter S. Thompson*. New York: Thunder's Mouth Press, 1992.

Richardson, Peter. *Savage Journey: Hunter S. Thompson and the Weird Road to Gonzo*. Berkeley: University of California Press, 2022.

Shoaf, Eric C. *Gonzology: A Hunter Thompson Bibliography*. Charlotte, NC: Cielo, 2018.

Steadman, Ralph. *The Joke's Over: Bruised Memories: Gonzo, Hunter S. Thompson, and Me*. Orlando, FL: Harcourt, 2006.

Stephenson, William. *Gonzo Republic: Hunter S. Thompson's America*. London: Continuum, 2012.

Thompson, Anita, ed. *Ancient Gonzo Wisdom: Interviews with Hunter S. Thompson*. Cambridge, MA: Da Capo Press, 2009.

Thompson, Juan F. *Stories I Tell Myself: Growing p with Hunter S. Thompson*. New York: Alfred A. Knopf, 2016.

Torrey, Beef, and Kevin Simonson, eds. *Conversations with Hunter S. Thompson*. Jackson: University Press of Mississippi, 2008.

Wenner, Jann, and Corey Seymour, eds. *Gonzo: The Life of Hunter S. Thompson, An Oral Biography*. New York: Little, Brown, 2007.

Whitmer, Peter O. *When the Going Gets Weird: The Twisted Life and Times of Hunter S. Thompson: A Very Unauthorized Biography*. New York: Hyperion, 1993.

Wills, David S. *High White Notes: The Rise and Fall of Gonzo Journalism*. St. Andrews, Scotland: Beatdom Books, 2021.

Wolfe, Tom, and E. W. Johnson, eds. *The New Journalism with an Anthology*. New York: Harper and Row, 1973.

INDEX

A-Team, 103
Acosta, Oscar, 68
"Address by Jimmy Carter on Labor
   Day" (Thompson), 92
Advertisements for Myself (Mailer), 67
Algren, Nelson, 34–35
   Man with the Golden Arm, 37
   Notes from a Sea Diary, 35, 47, 110
   Walk on the Wild Side, 37
Ali, Muhammad, 1, 62, 89
"Almost Working Artist" (Thompson),
   31
Amado, Jorge
   Gabriela, Clove and Cinnamon, 31, 37
   Home Is the Sailor, 31, 37
America, 24
American Adam (Lewis), 103
American Dream (Mailer), 122
"American Pie" (McLean), 70
American Psycho (Ellis), 122
Amigoe di Curacao, 18
Amis, Kingsley
   Lucky Jim, 5
Anderson, Chester, 49, 117
Anderson, Sherwood
   Portable Sherwood Anderson, 24
   Winesburg, Ohio, 3
Arena of Decision (Pflaum), 29
Armstrong, Neil, 66
Around the World in Eighty Days
   (Verne), 74
Asturias, Miguel Angel
   Señor presidente, 30–31
Autobiography of Alice B. Toklas (Stein),
   31

"Baja California" (Thompson), 9
Baker, Phil, 63, 79
Baldwin, Daniel R., 94
Baldwin, James, 36
"Balloon Hoax" (Poe), 79
Bang the Drum Slowly (Harris), 33
Bannon, Rachel, 113
Barger, Sonny, 34
Barrie, J. M.
   Peter Pan, 17
Barth, John
   Sotweed Factor, 122
Barthelme, Donald, 33
   Snow-White, 122
Bassus, Gaius Julius, 125
"Battle of Aspen" (Thompson), 67–68
Baxt, Paula, 117
Bear (Faulkner), 7, 47
Because I Was Flesh (Dahlberg), 71
"Beer Boat Blues" (Thompson), 20, 22
Bejumuk, Anita, 127–28
Benedek, László
   Wild One, 48
Beowulf (Raffel), 33
"Berenice" (Poe), 34
Bergen, Edgar, 8
Bergin, David, 95
Better than Sex (Thompson), 99, 131
Bible, 39
"Big Sur" (Thompson), 9
Black, Carol, 6
Blake, Peter, 103, 112
Bogart, Humphrey, 16
Bone, Bob, 6–8, 13, 25, 48, 123,
   126–27

INDEX

Bonfire of the Vanities (Wolfe), 99
Bookseller, 73
Boston Globe, 59, 98
Boston Globe Magazine, 59
Bourjaily, Vance, 38–39
  Unnatural Enemy, 38
Brazil Herald, 26
Brazilian Business, 25
"Brazilian Soldiers Stage a Raid" (Thompson), 26
"Brazilian's Fable of a Phony" (Thompson), 31
"Brazilshooting" (Thompson), 26
Breathless (Godard), 32
Breit, Harvey
  Writer Observed, 110
Brinkley, Douglas, 102–5, 110–11, 125–26
  "Editor's Note," 102
Brown, James, 32–33, 45
Browne, Harry, 99
Broyard, Anatole, 86
Bruning, Fred, 63
Burgess, Gelett
  Goops and How to Be Them, 1
Burke's Peerage, 32
Burns, Robert
  "Written with a Pencil," 69
Burroughs, William, 71
Byrd, William
  History of the Dividing Line, 66
  Secret History of the Line, 66
Byrds
  "My Back Page," 58
  "One Hundred Years from Now," 59

Caddyshack (Ramis), 3
Callen, Larry, 3, 102
Cameron, Angus, 45
Capote, Truman, 34–35, 130
  In Cold Blood, 35
Cardoso, Bill, 59–60, 62–63, 72, 89
Carter, Jimmy, 92, 116
Cassady, Neal, 86
Castro, Fidel, 116
Catch-22 (Heller), 34, 122
Catcher in the Rye (Salinger), 45, 47

Céline, Louis-Ferdinand, 64
Cervantes, Saavedra Miguel de
  Don Quixote, 70
Chancellor, John, 77
Chaplin, Charlie, 16
"Chatty Letters" (Thompson), 23, 25, 92
Cheever, John, 33
Chicago Tribune, 9, 95
Christgau, Robert
  "Life Styles: The Boxing Fan," 48
Clinton, Bill, 99
Cocteau, Jean
  Orpheus, 48–49
Coleridge, Samuel, 50
  "Dejection, An Ode," 116
  "Kubla Khan," 3, 117
  Rime of the Ancient Mariner, 50
Collier, Peter, 49
Command Courier, 3
Confidence-Man (Melville), 71
Congressional Record, 19
Conklin, Sandy, 8, 11, 25, 47, 61, 65, 74, 90, 114, 122
Conrad, Joseph
  Heart of Darkness, 22, 47, 53–56, 99, 120
  Lord Jim, 53
  Rescue, 53
  Secret Sharer, 53–56
Cooper, James Fenimore, 69
Cooper, Jilly, 114
Corso, Gregory, 5–6
"Cotton Candy Heart" (Thompson), 31
Courier-Journal (Louisville), 8, 22
Cousteau, Jacques, 62
Cox, Joseph
  "Shore Lines," 4, 11, 48, 58
Cozzens, James Gould, 33
Crane, Stephen, 5
  Maggie, 7
  Monster, 7
  Red Badge of Courage, 42
Cronenberg, David
  Dead Ringers, 91
Crouse, Timothy, 74
"Crow, a Novelist, and a Hunt" (Thompson), 38

INDEX

Cruising (Walker), 57–58
Curse of Lono (Thompson), 93, 95

Dahlberg, Edward, 71–72, 101
   Because I Was Flesh, 71
Daily Tar Heel, 93
Daley, Richard J., 61, 65
Dante Alighieri
   Inferno, 70
d'Arazien, Steven, 76
Dead Ringers (Cronenberg), 91
Death in the Afternoon (Hemingway), 40
Death of a Salesman (Miller), 99
"Dejection, An Ode" (Coleridge), 116
"Democracy Dies in Peru" (Thompson), 16–17
Denton, Charles, 12–13, 95
Depp, Johnny, 119
"Descent into the Maelström" (Poe), 21
Dharma Bums (Kerouac), 4
Dickinson, Emily, 129
Didion, Joan
   "Slouching Towards Bethlehem," 58
Dietrich, Marlene, 50–51
Divine Considerations (Valdés), 39
"Dr. Pflaum Looks at the Latins" (Thompson), 29–30
Doctor Sax (Kerouac), 5
Dr. Strangelove (Kubrick), 116
Domitian, 92
Don Quixote (Cervantes), 70
Donadio, Candida, 34, 36–37, 40
Donleavy, J. P., 110
   Ginger Man, 37, 47, 58, 121
   Singular Man, 37–38
"Donleavy Proves His Lunatic Humor" (Thompson), 38
Doonesbury (Trudeau), 94
Dorson, Richard, 12, 49
Dos Passos, John, 3
Dostoevsky, Fyodor
   Gambler, 7
Dragnet (Webb), 44
Dretzka, Gary, 95
"Duke of Hazard" (Nicoll), 113–15

Dusk and Other Stories (Salter), 100
Dylan, Bob, 44
   "My Back Pages," 58

Editor and Publisher, 3, 7
"Editor's Note" (Brinkley), 102
Edwards, Joe, 67
Eldridge, Paul Eldridge
   My First Two Thousand Years, 50
Electric Kool-Aid Acid Test (Wolfe), 53
Eliot, T. S., 111
Ellis, Bret Easton
   American Psycho, 122
Ellison, Ralph
   Invisible Man, 52
Elman, Richard, 54
Esquire, 31–33, 35, 42, 47–48
Evans, Robert J., 3–4, 48, 80, 116
Evening Post (Bristol), 48, 58
Ewing, Wayne, 120
Express (Lock Haven), 4

Fame and Obscurity (Talese), 40, 92
Farley, Charles L., 4, 8, 105
Faulkner, William, 3, 5, 7, 30, 36, 40, 100, 110–11
   Bear, 7, 47
   Soldier's Pay, 30, 33
   Sound and the Fury, 5
   "Faulkner of Latin America" (Thompson), 30
Fear and Loathing in America (Thompson), 125–27
Fear and Loathing in Las Vegas (Gilliam), 119
Fear and Loathing in Las Vegas (Thompson), 13, 19, 21, 44, 59, 66, 68–73, 75, 91–93, 98–99, 103, 110, 113, 115, 119, 125–26, 129–31
Fear and Loathing on the Campaign Trail (Thompson), 13, 75–87, 91, 93, 99, 113, 125, 129
Ferraro, Geraldine, 94
50th State Bowler, 8
Fight (Mailer), 62
Fink, Mike 93
Firpo, Pampero, 102

Fisher, Ham
  Joe Palooka, 50
Fitzgerald, F. Scott, 3, 7, 24, 46, 52, 65, 108
  Great Gatsby, 11, 13, 30, 36–37, 47, 115–17, 122, 131–32
  Portable F. Scott Fitzgerald, 24
  This Side of Paradise, 33
Fitzgerald, Zelda, 132
"Footloose American in a Smugglers' Den" (Thompson), 20–23, 26, 92
Foreman, George, 62, 89
Franco, Francisco, 60
Franklin, Benjamin
  "Speech of Miss Polly Baker," 79

Gabriela, Clove and Cinnamon (Amado), 31, 37
Gambler (Dostoevsky), 7
Gardiner, Harold C.
  "Recognition of Shock," 24
Garner, Errol, 109
Garnett, Edward, 53
Generation of Swine (Thompson) 95–97, 131
Gilliam, Terry
  Fear and Loathing in Las Vegas, 119
Ginger Man (Donleavy), 37, 47, 58, 121
Ginsberg, Allen, 6
Glasgow Herald, 122
Gleason, Ralph J., 68
Godard, Jean-Luc, 50
  Breathless, 32
Goddard, Don, 62–63
Goddard, Natali, 62
Godfather (Puzo), 40
Golding, William, 116
  Lord of the Flies, 38–39
  Spire, 38
"Golding Tries Lord of the Flies Formula Again" (Thompson), 38
Goops and How to Be Them (Burgess), 1
Grant, Cary, 18
Graves, Robert
  Pamphlet against Anthologies, 100
Great Gatsby (Fitzgerald), 11, 13, 30, 36–37, 47, 115–17, 122, 131–32

Great Shark Hunt (Thompson), 26–7, 90–93, 96, 100, 111
Green Hills of Africa (Hemingway), 40
Greene, Graham, 27
Greider, William, 76
Guerard, Albert J., 33, 53, 55
  Stories of the Double, 50
Guts Ball (Thompson), 115–16

Halifax, George Savile, *marquis de*, 47
Hamilton, David, 22, 27–28, 43, 94–95
Harper's, 76
Harris, Mark
  Bang the Drum Slowly, 33
Hart, Gary, 97
Haselden, Susan 4, 108–9
"Hashbury Is the Capital of the Hippies" (Thompson), 57–58, 92
Hawks, Howard
  His Girl Friday, 18
"Hawthorne and His Mosses" (Melville), 24, 71
Hearst, Will, 95
Heart of Darkness (Conrad), 22, 47, 53–56, 99, 120
Hefner, Hugh, 60
Hell's Angels (Thompson), 4, 12–13, 20, 27, 34, 36, 45–58, 65, 68–70, 73, 99, 111–13, 119, 125–26, 129
Heller, Joseph, 84
  Catch-22, 34, 122
Hemingway, Ernest 3, 7, 30–32, 35–36, 40–41, 45–46, 65, 92, 97, 122
  Death in the Afternoon, 40
  Green Hills of Africa, 40
  Men at War, 40
  "Notes on the Next War," 30, 97
  Sun Also Rises, 3, 37, 47, 122
  Torrents of Spring, 33
Hendrix, Jimi, 67
Henning, Joanie, 1
"High-Water Mark" (Thompson), 98
High White Notes (Wills), 53, 128
Hills, Rust, 31, 35, 71
  "Structure of the American Literary Establishment," 32–35, 38
Hinckle, Warren, 60–63, 78–79, 95–96
His Girl Friday (Hawks), 18

INDEX

Hispania, 30
History of the Dividing Line (Byrd), 66
Hitchcock, Alfred
   Vertigo, 96
Hitler, Adolf, 16
Hoffman, Abbie
   Steal This Book, 73
Home Book of Quotations (Stevenson), 47
Home Is the Sailor (Amado), 31, 37
Homer
   Iliad, 82
   Odyssey, 70
Horatius Flaccus, Quintus, 128
"Horse Swap" (Longstreet), 62
House Not Meant to Stand (Williams), 108
"How Democracy Is Nudged Ahead in Ecuador" (Thompson), 18–19
Huckleberry Finn (Twain), 31, 47, 49, 63, 69, 130
Hughes, Harold, 76
Humphrey, Hubert, 81
Huston, John
   Red Badge of Courage, 42
Hynan, Patrick, 70

Iliad (Homer), 82
"Imp of the Perverse" (Poe), 70
In Cold Blood (Capote), 35
Inferno (Dante), 70
Innocents Abroad (Twain), 130
Invisible Man (Ellison), 52
Iowa Review, 27
Irish Times, 99
Ironweed (Kennedy), 100

"Jacket Copy of *Fear and Loathing in Las Vegas*" (Thompson), 91
Jefferson, Thomas, 47
Jefferson Airplane, 44, 67
Jeopardy!, 117
Jersey Shore Herald, 3–4
"Jimmy Carter and the Great Leap of Faith" (Thompson), 92
"Joe Louis" (Talese), 40
Joe Palooka (Fisher), 50
Johannson, Ingemar, 37
Johnson, Lyndon B., 80–81
Johnson, Samuel, 69
Jones, James
   Some Came Running, 24, 35, 115
Jones, Lauren, 93
Jonny Quest, 69
Joplin, Janis, 44
Juenger, Kraig, 109
Jull, Louis, 3
Juvenalis, Decimus Junius, 92

Kandy-Kolored Tangerine Flake Streamline Baby (Wolfe), 42, 45
Kansas City Star, 35
Kennedy, Jackie, 21, 84
Kennedy, John F., 8, 10–11, 15–16, 39, 67
Kennedy, William J., 7, 9, 32, 36, 39–40, 115
   Ironweed, 100
"Kentucky Derby Is Decadent and Depraved" (Thompson), 63–64, 66, 69, 78, 86, 91
Kerouac, Jack, 4–6, 33, 54, 71, 77, 86, 109
   Dharma Bums, 4
   Doctor Sax, 5
   Maggie Cassidy, 5
   On the Road, 4, 54, 65, 67, 77, 109
   Subterraneans, 4
   Visions of Cody, 86
Kesey, Ken, 33, 52–53, 71–72
   One Flew over the Cuckoo's Nest, 37, 71
   Sometimes a Great Notion, 37, 122
Khan, Maria, 95–96
Khrushchev, Nikita, 84
Killy, Jean-Claude, 60–61, 64, 66, 68, 91
King Lear (Shakespeare), 81
Kingdom and the Power (Talese), 49, 110
Kingdom of Fear (Thompson), 128
Klein, Joe, 44, 88, 90, 129
Kooning, Willem de, 6
Kramer, Philip, 7–8
Krassner, Paul, 35, 73–74, 101
"Kubla Khan" (Coleridge), 3, 117
Kubrick, Stanley
   Dr. Strangelove, 116

Kuralt, Charles 25, 48, 105
  "On the Road," 77
Kurosawa, Akira
  Rashomon, 6

Latin America (Roberts), 29
"Latin Close-Up" (Thompson), 17
Lawrence, D. H.
  Portable D. H. Lawrence, 24
Leary, Timothy, 72
"Leery Optimism at Home" (Thompson), 15–16
Leibovitz, Annie, 89
Leopold, Nathan, 12
Lewis, R. W. B.
  American Adam, 103
Leyda, Jay
  Portable Melville, 24
Lie Down in Darkness (Styron), 32–33, 37
Liebling, A. J., 33
  Press, 47
"Life Styles: The Boxing Fan" (Christgau), 48
"Life Styles: The Cyclist" (Thompson), 48
Light Years (Salter), 61
Lilly, Rutledge, 107–8
Linklater, Andro, 98, 126
Linkletter, Art, 71–72, 91, 98
Linkletter, Diane, 72, 91
Linson, Art
  Where the Buffalo Roam, 101
Liston, Sonny, 82–83
Litwak, Leo, 9, 33, 49
Loeb, Richard, 12
London, Jack, 11
  "Nam-Bok the Unveracious," 21
Longstreet, Augustus Baldwin
  "Horse Swap," 62
"Looking for Hemingway" (Talese), 31–32
Lord Jim (Conrad), 53
Lord, Sterling, 33–34
Lord Jim (Conrad), 53
Lord of the Flies (Golding), 38–39
Los Angeles Times, 68, 83, 126
"Louisvillian in Voodoo Country" (Thompson), 8

Luce, Henry, 5, 24
Lucky Jim (Amis), 5
Lynch, David
  Twin Peaks, 119
Lynch, Declan, 70, 130
Lynch, Thomas C., 46
Lyng, Stephen, 55
Lyons, Gene, 92

M (Sack), 49
McCumber, David, 95, 97–98, 103
Macdonald, Marianne, 120
McGarr, Eugene, 5–6, 40, 98, 116
McGee, Gale W., 19
McGovern, George, 76–77, 81, 83–96, 91, 99
McKee, Elizabeth, 33
McKeen, William, 25, 98
  Outlaw Journalist, 97, 125
McLean, Don
  "American Pie," 70
McLuhan, Marshall
  Understanding Media, 49
McNeil, Sarah, 106
McWilliams, Carey, 45
Madden, John, 96
Maggie (Crane), 7
Maggie Cassidy (Kerouac), 5
Magic Christian (Southern), 31, 47
Mailer, Norman, 35–37, 39, 41, 62, 89, 110
  Advertisements for Myself, 67
  American Dream, 122
  Fight, 62
  Naked and the Dead, 35
  "Norman Mailer Versus Nine Writers," 32, 35
Man of Letters in the Modern World (Tate), 69–70
Man with the Golden Arm (Algren), 37
Mankiewicz, Frank, 81–82
Mansfield, Mike, 11
Mason, Charley, 40
Maugham, Somerset, 5, 16, 107
Melville, Herman, 20, 24, 37, 64, 71–72, 90–91, 98
  Confidence-Man, 71
  "Hawthorne and His Mosses," 24, 71

INDEX

Moby-Dick, 69, 71
Portable Melville, 24
Typee, 20
"Memoirs of a Wretched Weekend" (Thompson), 59–60, 66, 91
Men at War (Hemingway), 40
Mencken, H. L., 3, 49
Meyer, Nicole, 113–14
Middletown Daily Record, 6
"Midnight on the Coast Highway" (Thompson), 54–56, 98, 112
Miller, Arthur
  Death of a Salesman, 99
Miller, Henry, 9–10, 71
  Tropic of Cancer, 10
Mitchell, Julian, 48–49
Mittman, Ann, 94
Moby-Dick (Melville), 69, 71
Monster (Crane), 7
Montana Standard-Post, 11
Moore, Curtis, 107
Moore, Steven, 112
Moore, Tim, 130–31
Moroney, Mic, 101–2, 125–26
"Motorcycle Gangs" (Thompson), 45
"Munoz Skilfully Keeps Foes Off-Balance" (Thompson), 16
Muñoz Marin, Luis, 16
"Murders in the Rue Morgue" (Poe), 70
Murphy, Dennis, 9
Murphy, Michael, 9
Murphy, Vinnie, 9–10
Murray, Bill, 101
Muskie, Edmund, 76, 79–80, 82, 84
"My Back Pages" (Dylan), 58
My First Two Thousand Years (Viereck and Eldridge), 50

Naked and the Dead (Mailer), 35
"Nam-Bok the Unveracious" (London), 21
Narrative of Arthur Gordon Pym (Poe), 43
Nation, 45–46, 76
National Enquirer, 49
National Observer, 10–12, 15–29, 38, 40, 45, 57, 105
Nellis, Joseph, 71

Nesbit, Lynn, 59, 119, 124
"Never-Never Land High Above the Sea" (Thompson), 17
New York Herald-Tribune, 32
New York Post, 6
New York Times, 6, 30, 40, 110, 129
New York Times Book Review, 32
New York Times Sunday Magazine, 57
Newby, Eric, 20
  Short Walk in the Hindu Kush, 20
Newsweek 15, 46
Nicoll, Ruaridh, 117, 120, 122–23
  "Duke of Hazard," 113–15
  "The Night I Spent Drinking with Hunter S. Thompson," 113–14
"Night-Watch" (Thompson), 105
Nixon, Richard, 8, 59–60, 67, 75, 78, 83–84, 86, 89, 91–2, 115, 131
"Nobody Is Neutral under Aruba's Hot Sun" (Thompson), 15–6, 18, 26
"Norman Mailer Versus Nine Writers" (Mailer), 32, 35
North, Oliver, 97
Notes from a Sea Diary (Algren), 35, 47, 110
"Notes on the Next War" (Hemingway), 30, 97
Novak, Kim, 96

O'Brien, Larry, 80–81
O'Hara, Frank, 5–6
Observer (London), 15, 120
Observer's World (Preston), 105
Odyssey (Homer), 70
Olay, Lionel, 9, 33, 41
On the Road (Kerouac), 4, 54, 65, 67, 77, 109
"On the Road" (Kuralt), 77
One Flew over the Cuckoo's Nest (Kesey), 37, 71
"One Hundred Years from Now" (Byrds), 59
"One of the Darkest Documents" (Thompson), 30
"Open Letter to the Youth of Our Nation" (Thompson), 2, 105
"Operation Triangular" (Thompson), 17
Opheim, Heidi, 120

Orpheus (Cocteau), 48–49
Outlaw Journalist (McKeen), 97, 125
Overdorf, Carol, 4
Overdorf, Paul I., 4

Palmer, Laura, 89–90
Pamphlet against Anthologies (Graves and Riding), 100
Paper Lion (Plimpton), 43
Paris Review, 31–32, 40, 110, 129
Partisan Review, 32, 60
Patterson, Floyd, 82–83
Perkins, Max, 65
Peter Pan (Barrie), 17
Peterson, Ralph, 106–7
"Philosophy of Composition" (Poe), 91
Picture (Ross), 42
Pflaum, Irving P.
  Arena of Decision, 29–30
Playboy, 47, 60
Playground News, 3, 105
Plimpton, George, 31, 43, 89, 93, 128–29
  Paper Lion, 43
Plinius Caecilius Secundus
  Letters, 106–7, 125
Plutarchus, 70
Poe, Edgar Allan, 42–43
  "Balloon Hoax," 79
  "Berenice," 34
  "Descent into the Maelström," 21
  "Imp of the Perverse," 70
  "Murders in the Rue Morgue," 70
  Narrative of Arthur Gordon Pym, 43
  "Philosophy of Composition," 91
  "Raven," 91, 99, 120
Polo Is My Life (Thompson), 114, 116–17
Portable D. H. Lawrence, 24
Portable F. Scott Fitzgerald, 24
Portable Melville, 24
Portable Sherwood Anderson, 24
Prescott, Peter S., 43–44, 49
Press (Liebling), 47
Preston, Charles
  Observer's World, 105
Prince Jellyfish (Thompson), 7, 33–34, 45, 102, 115, 117–20

Proud Highway (Thompson), 102–12, 119, 125–26
Pump House Gang (Wolfe), 53, 67, 76
Puzo, Mario
  Godfather, 40
Pynchon, Thomas
  V, 122

Rabbit, Run (Updike), 32
Rabelais, François, 107
Radical Chic and Mau-Mauing the Flak Catchers (Wolfe) 64
Raffel, Burton
  Beowulf, 33
Ramis, Harold
  Caddyshack, 3
Ramparts, 49, 60, 68
Rashomon (Kurosawa), 6
"Rat Fink" (Sherman), 44
"Raven" (Poe), 91, 99, 120
Ray, Elizabeth, 107
Ray, Lucille, 1, 10, 99
Reader's Digest, 77
Realist, 35, 74
"Recession, Political Upheaval" (Thompson), 27
"Recognition of Shock" (Gardiner), 24
Red Badge of Courage (Crane), 42
Red Badge of Courage (Huston), 42
Red Lances (Pietri), 30–31, 97
Reidy, Chris, 98
Rescue (Conrad), 53
Reston, James, 6
Rexroth, Kenneth, 35
Richardson, Peter
  Savage Journey, 130
Richmond Times-Dispatch, 5, 17
Riding, Laura
  Pamphlet against Anthologies, 100
Ridley, Clifford 10, 12, 20, 23, 26–29, 31
Right Stuff (Wolfe), 98–99
Rimbaud, Arthur, 54
Rime of the Ancient Mariner (Coleridge), 50
Rinzler, Alan, 93
Roberts, Edwin A.
  Latin America, 29
Rogue, 9–10

INDEX

Rolling Stone, 63, 67–68, 70, 72, 74–75, 77–78, 88–89, 93–94, 99, 127
Romberg, Sigmund
   Student Prince, 109
Romm, Al, 6, 74
Ross, Lillian
   Picture, 42
Rosset, Barney, 34
Roth, Philip, 34
Rudd, Hughes, 66
Rum Diary (Thompson) 8–10, 15, 29, 34, 37, 39, 45, 65, 113–15, 117, 119–24, 130
Russell, Rosalind, 18, 95

Sabonis-Chafee, Catherine, 97–98
Sabonis-Chafee, Terry, 97–98, 101
Sack, John
   M, 49
Sadler, Shelby, 116–17, 126, 132
Salazar, Ruben, 68
Salinger, J. D.
   Catcher in the Rye, 45, 47
Salter, James 33, 61–62
   Dusk and Other Stories, 100
   Light Years, 61
   Solo Faces, 100
   Threshold, 100
San Juan Star, 7
San Francisco Chronicle, 68
San Francisco Examiner, 12, 73, 95–97
Sandburg, Carl, 61
Saturday Evening Post, 58
"Saturday Night in the City" (Thompson), 95–96
Savage Journey (Richardson), 130
Scanlan's Monthly, 60–63, 78
Seberg, Jean, 32
Secret History of the Line (Byrd), 66
"Secret Life of Walter Mitty" (Thurber), 118
Secret Sharer (Conrad), 53–56
"Security" (Thompson), 2, 8, 105
Seelye, John, 42, 46
Semonin, Paul, 2, 8, 22–23, 29, 36, 40, 46, 53, 67, 103–4, 120–21
Señor presidente (Asturias), 30–31
Set This House on Fire (Styron), 35, 37

Sewanee Review, 32, 104
Seymour, Corey, 98
Shaffer, Fred, 18–19
Shakespeare, William
   King Lear, 81
Shearing, George, 109
Sherman, Alan
   "Rat Fink," 44
Sheridan, Peter, 80
Shock of Recognition (Wilson), 24
"Shore Lines" (Cox), 4, 11, 48, 58
Short Walk in the Hindu Kush (Newby), 20
Silberman, Jim, 45, 47, 64–68, 75, 90, 103
Silk Road (Thompson), 115–17
Simmons, Linda, 93
Simon, Paul, 129
Singular Man (Donleavy), 37–38
Slaughterhouse-Five (Vonnegut), 62
"Slouching Towards Bethlehem" (Didion), 58
Smith, Captain John, 10, 72
Snider, Norman, 93
   Dead Ringers, 91
Soldier's Pay (Faulkner), 30, 33
Solo Faces (Salter), 100
Some Came Running (Jones), 24, 35, 115
Sometimes a Great Notion (Kesey), 37, 122
Songs of the Doomed (Thompson), 4, 61, 97–99, 104–5, 111, 117–19, 123, 128
Sotweed Factor (Barth), 122
Sound and the Fury (Faulkner), 5
Southern, Terry, 33–34, 84
   Magic Christian, 31, 47
   "Twirling at Ole Miss," 42
Southey, Robert, 39
Spectator, 2, 105
"Speech of Miss Polly Baker" (Franklin), 79
Spire (Golding), 38
Sportivo, 7–8
Sports Illustrated, 7
Steadman, Ralph, 62–64, 70, 89, 93
Steal This Book (Hoffman), 73
Stein, Gertrude
   Autobiography of Alice B. Toklas, 31

Stephansky, Ben, 17
Stevenson, Burton
  Home Book of Quotations, 47
Stevenson, Robert Louis
  Strange Case of Dr. Jekyll and Mr. Hyde, 50–52
Stewart, Jimmy, 96
Stories of the Double (Guerard), 50
Stranahan, George, 65, 102, 104
Strange Case of Dr. Jekyll and Mr. Hyde (Stevenson), 50–52
"Strange Rumblings in Aztlan" (Thompson), 68
Stroud, Kandy, 80
"Structure of the American Literary Establishment" (Hills), 32–35, 38
Student Prince (Romberg), 109
Styron, William, 32–35, 41, 110
  Lie Down in Darkness, 32–33, 37
  Set This House on Fire, 35, 37
Subterraneans (Kerouac), 4
Sugar, Harriet, 93
Sulzberger, Arthur Hays, 110
Sulzberger, Cyrus Lee, 110–11
  "Writer and the Outer World," 110
Sun Also Rises (Hemingway), 3, 37, 47, 122
Sunday Ramparts, 68
Sunday Times (London), 107
Sunday Tribune (Dublin), 113
Superman, 5
Swift, Jonathan, 111

Talese, Gay, 31, 42–43, 49, 92, 110
  Fame and Obscurity, 40, 92
  "Joe Louis," 40
  Kingdom and the Power, 49, 110
  "Looking for Hemingway," 31–32
Tate, Allen
  Man of Letters in the Modern World, 69–70
"Temptations of Jean-Claude Killy" (Thompson), 60, 66, 68, 91
Terkel, Studs, 50
Terry the Tramp, 46, 50–52, 55
This Side of Paradise (Fitzgerald), 33
Thompson, Anita, 127–28
Thompson, Hunter S.

"Address by Jimmy Carter on Labor Day," 92
"Almost Working Artist," 31
"Baja California," 9
"Battle of Aspen," 67–68
"Beer Boat Blues," 20, 22
Better than Sex, 99, 131
"Big Sur," 9
"Brazilian Soldiers Stage a Raid," 26
"Brazilian's Fable of a Phony," 31
"Brazilshooting," 26
"Chatty Letters," 23, 25, 92
"Cotton Candy Heart," 31
"Crow, a Novelist, and a Hunt," 38
Curse of Lono, 93, 95
"Dr. Pflaum Looks at the Latins," 29–30
"Death of the American Dream," 64–69, 75, 97, 126
"Democracy Dies in Peru," 16–17
"Donleavy Proves His Lunatic Humor," 38
"Faulkner of Latin America," 30
Fear and Loathing in America, 125–27
Fear and Loathing in Las Vegas, 13, 19, 21, 44, 59, 66, 68–73, 75, 78, 85, 91–93, 98–99, 103, 110, 113, 115, 119, 125–26, 129–31
Fear and Loathing on the Campaign Trail, 13, 75–87, 91, 93, 99, 113, 125, 129
"Footloose American in a Smugglers' Den," 20–23, 26, 92
Generation of Swine, 95–97, 131
"Golding Tries Lord of the Flies Formula Again," 38
Great Shark Hunt, 26–27, 90–93, 96, 100, 111
Guts Ball, 115–16
"Hashbury Is the Capital of the Hippies," 57–58, 92
Hell's Angels, 4, 12–13, 20, 27, 34, 36, 45–58, 65, 68–70, 73, 99, 111–13, 119, 125–26, 129
Hey Rube, 128–29, 131
"High-Water Mark," 98
"How Democracy Is Nudged Ahead in Ecuador," 18–19

INDEX

"Jacket Copy of *Fear and Loathing in Las Vegas,*" 91
"Jimmy Carter and the Great Leap of Faith," 92
"Kentucky Derby Is Decadent and Depraved," 63–64, 66, 69, 78, 86, 91
Kingdom of Fear, 128
"Latin Close-Up," 17
"Leery Optimism," 15–16
"Life Styles: The Cyclist," 48
"Louisvillian in Voodoo Country," 8
"Memoirs of a Wretched Weekend," 59–60, 66, 91
"Midnight on the Coast Highway," 54–56, 98, 112
"Motorcycle Gangs," 45
"Munoz Skilfully Keeps Foes Off-Balance," 16
"Never-Never Land High Above the Sea," 17
"Night-Watch," 105
"Nobody Is Neutral under Aruba's Hot Sun," 15–16, 18, 26
"One of the Darkest Documents," 30
"Open Letter to the Youth of Our Nation," 2, 105
"Operation Triangular," 17
Polo Is My Life, 114, 116–17
Prince Jellyfish, 7, 33–34, 45, 102, 115, 117–20
Proud Highway, 102–12, 119, 125–26
"Recession, Political Upheaval," 27
Rum Diary, 8–10, 15, 29, 34, 37, 39, 45, 65, 113–15, 117, 119–24, 130
"Saturday Night in the City," 95–96
"Security," 2, 8, 105
Silk Road, 115–17
Songs of the Doomed, 4, 61, 97–99, 104–5, 111, 117–19, 123, 128
"Strange Rumblings in Aztlan," 68
"Temptations of Jean-Claude Killy," 60, 66, 68, 91
"Traveler Hears Mountain Music Where It's Sung," 10, 92
"Uruguay Goes to Polls," 17
"What Lured Hemingway to Ketchum?" 40, 92
"When the Beatniks Were Social Lions," 40
"Where Are the Writing Talents of Yesteryear?" 32, 34, 37
"Whither the Old Copper Capital of the West?" 11
"Why Anti-Gringo Winds Often Blow South of the Border," 26–28
Thompson, Jack Robert, 1–2
Thompson, Juan Fitzgerald, 11, 47
Thompson, Sandy, 8, 11, 25, 47, 61, 65, 74, 90, 114, 122
Thompson, Virginia Ray, 1–3, 103, 105
Threshold (Salter), 100
Thurber, James
 "Secret Life of Walter Mitty," 118
Time, 5–6, 15, 24, 46, 89, 118
Times (London), 5, 48
"Traveler Hears Mountain Music Where It's Sung" (Thompson), 10, 92
Torrents of Spring (Hemingway), 33
Tracy, John Terence, 46, 50–52, 55
Tropic of Cancer (Miller), 10
Trudeau, Garry
 Doonesbury, 94
Twain, Mark, 31, 36, 49, 108
 Huckleberry Finn, 31, 47, 49, 63, 69, 130
 Innocents Abroad, 130
Twin Peaks (Lynch), 119
"Twirling at Ole Miss" (Southern), 42
Typee (Melville), 20
Tyrrell, Gerald, 105–6

Understanding Media (McLuhan), 49
Unnatural Enemy (Bourjaily), 38
Updike, John
 Rabbit, Run, 32
"Uruguay Goes to Polls" (Thompson), 17
Uslar Pietri, Arturo
 Red Lances, 30–31, 97

V (Pynchon), 122
Valdés, Juan de
 Divine Considerations, 39
Van Kuijk, Jos, 18
Velázquez, Gonzalo, 7
Valencia, Guillermo León, 15–16, 23

Valens, Flavius, 112
Valens, Ritchie, 112
Verne, Jules
  Around the World in Eighty Days, 74
Vertigo (Hitchcock), 96
Viereck, George Sylvester
  My First Two Thousand Years, 50
Villon, François, 47
Visions of Cody (Kerouac), 86
Vonnegut, Kurt, 44, 76, 114
  Slaughterhouse-Five, 62

Walk on the Wild Side (Algren), 37
Walker, Gerald, 57–59, 83
  Cruising, 57–58
Wall Street Journal, 15
Wallace, George, 81
Walsh, John, 127–28
Warhol, Andy, 116, 126
Washington, George, 63
Washington Post, 37, 76, 112
Webb, Jack
  Dragnet, 44
Wenner, Jann, 68, 74–75, 86, 98
"What Lured Hemingway to Ketchum?" (Thompson), 40, 92
"When the Beatniks Were Social Lions" (Thompson), 40
"Where Are the Writing Talents of Yesteryear?" (Thompson), 32, 34, 37
Where the Buffalo Roam (Linson), 101
"Whither the Old Copper Capital of the West?" (Thompson), 11
Whitman, Walt, 105

"Why Anti-Gringo Winds Often Blow South of the Border" (Thompson), 26–28
Wild One (Benedek), 48
Williams, Tennessee
  House Not Meant to Stand, 108
Williamson, Bill, 26
Wills, David
  High White Notes, 53, 128
Wilson, Edmund
  Shock of Recognition, 24
Winchell, Walter, 106
Winesburg, Ohio (Anderson), 3
Wolfe, Tom, 42–45, 48–49, 53–54, 60, 64, 67, 88, 92, 98–100, 112, 130
  Bonfire of the Vanities, 99
  Electric Kool-Aid Acid Test, 53
  Kandy-Kolored Tangerine Flake Streamline Baby, 42, 45
  New Journalism, 42, 64
  Pump House Gang, 53, 67, 76
  Radical Chic and Mau-Mauing the Flak Catchers, 64
  Right Stuff, 98–99
Women's Wear Daily, 43, 73, 76, 80
Wood, James, 122–23
Woods, William Crawford, 129
"Works in Progress, 1963," 34–35, 37
Worsley, Peter, 49, 54
"Writer and the Outer World" (Sulzberger), 110
Writer Observed (Breit), 110
Writers at Work, 110
"Written with a Pencil" (Burns), 69